THE NATIONAL INSTITUTE OF
ECONOMIC AND SOCIAL RESEARCH

Occasional Papers
XLI

THE GROWTH AND EFFICIENCY
OF PUBLIC SPENDING

THE GROWTH AND EFFICIENCY OF PUBLIC SPENDING

M.S. LEVITT

and

M.A.S. JOYCE

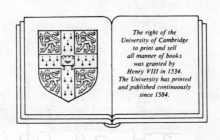

The right of the
University of Cambridge
to print and sell
all manner of books
was granted by
Henry VIII in 1534.
The University has printed
and published continuously
since 1584.

CAMBRIDGE UNIVERSITY PRESS

CAMBRIDGE

NEW YORK   NEW ROCHELLE   MELBOURNE   SYDNEY

Published by the Press Syndicate of the University of Cambridge
The Pitt Building, Trumpington Street, Cambridge CB2 1RP
32 East 57th Street, New York, NY 10022, USA
10 Stamford Road, Oakleigh, Melbourne 3166, Australia

First published 1987

Printed in Great Britain at the University Press, Cambridge

British Library cataloguing in publication data

Levitt, M.S.
The growth and efficiency of public
spending. – (Occasional papers. The
National Institute of Economic and Social
Research; 41).
1. Finance, Public
I. Title   II. Joyce, M.A.S.   III. National
Institute of Economic and Social Research
IV. Series
336   HJ141

Library of Congress cataloguing in publication data

Levitt, M. S., 1938–
The growth and efficiency of public spending.
(Occasional papers / The National Institute of
Economic and Social Research; 41)
1. Great Britain – Appropriations and expenditures.
2. Government spending policy – Great Britain.
I. Joyce, M. A. S.   II. Title.   III. Series: Occasional
papers (National Institute of Economic and Social
Research); 41.
HJ7764.L475   1987   339.5'22'0941   87-11636

ISBN 0 521 34621 5

CONTENTS

TABLES

SYMBOLS IN THE TABLES

...   not available
—   nil or negligible
n.a.   not applicable

CHARTS

PREFACE

This book has as its principal antecedent a previous NIESR study by Wilfred Beckerman and associates, *The British Economy in 1975* (Cambridge University Press, 1964), especially the contributions by Kit Jones and Deborah Paige. The first part of our study focuses on past and future trends in spending, along the lines of the earlier analysis; the results of that work are reported in Part I below.

The majority of our time was spent exploring issues associated with the quantification and analysis of output and relative performance in a variety of government services. The results of those elements of our work form Parts II and III of the book. That is to say, whereas Part I focuses on trends in inputs, the remainder of the book is concerned with outputs, and with their relationship to inputs.

We have benefited at every stage of our work from the encouragement and advice of Andrew Britton, whose idea it was to mount the study in the first place. Several of Levitt's former official colleagues, especially Ian Byatt, Michael Parsonage and Michael Spackman, and our NIESR colleagues have provided valuable advice and guidance; at NIESR we are especially grateful to Keith Cuthbertson, Hassan Feisal, Stephen Hall, Kit Jones, Ann Morgan, Sig Prais, Tony Smith and Chris Trinder for this, and to Joan Dare, Diane Swan and Pam Watts for their regular computational support. In America Donald Fisk and Jerome Mark (Bureau of Labor Statistics), John Leach (General Accounting Office) and Professor John Kendrick (George Washington University) provided valuable assistance with the analyses reported in Chapters 5 and 7.

The data envelope analysis reported in Chapter 12 was undertaken for us by John Cubbin of Queen Mary College, London, using a model developed by himself and John Wriglesworth. We are grateful for his help in producing and analysing the results.

We are particularly indebted to Professor Tony Atkinson, who read the entire book in draft and who offered several constructive suggestions for improving the form and substance of the text.

The work could not have been undertaken at all without the cooperation of officials in many government departments, who provided their time for discussions and helped us to acquire the data analysed below. We especially wish to acknowledge this support from officials in the CSO, DES, DHSS, Home Office, MOD and HM Treasury.

Naturally we are alone responsible for the views expressed below, and for any mistakes which we might have made in analysing the data we have used.

Cheerful secretarial support during the study was provided by Pat Facey. Fran Robinson took us, and our various drafts and tables, in hand to produce the book in a state fit for public view.

We are indebted to HM Treasury and the Economic and Social Research Council for their financial support for this study.

National Institute of Economic   M.S. LEVITT
and Social Research 1987   M.A.S. JOYCE

INTRODUCTION

For several decades the amount spent by government has grown both absolutely in real or cost terms (that is, excluding the effects of general inflation) and as a share of national output. The general upward trend in the amount spent was only interrupted, temporarily, at times of exceptional external strain on the value of the pound, to demonstrate that we were putting our financial house in order to obtain foreign credit. But in recent years it has been the government's aim to reduce the share of government spending in national output, and to make any improvement in the effectiveness of services depend on the achievement of increased efficiency. Such is the background to the study presented in this book. Against that background, we outline past trends in the growth and composition of public spending, consider spending prospects to the mid- and late-1990s, and discuss the measurement and the promotion of efficiency in a number of government services or activities. This introductory chapter sets the background to the study and notes some important related issues.

THE DEBATE OVER THE ROLE OF THE PRICE MECHANISM

A central concern of this book is the efficiency of public services. There are wider questions about the relative efficiency of the public and private sectors, and about what services, in principle, ought to be provided by one sector rather than the other. One argument put forward against public spending and its growth is that market solutions to problems of resource allocation should be favoured on fundamental political grounds, irrespective of whether in practice in particular circumstances a state provided service might be shown to be more efficient in the conventional sense. (For one example of this view see Rowley and Peacock, 1975.) Such a view involves a political preference for a minimalist role for the government so as to curb the growth of state power and to maximise that of private citizens and privately owned institutions. This argument is in fact often associated with the further belief that services run by the state are likely to be less efficient in practice than those subject to market forces. This is because of the weakness of the incentives to control costs in state services, to curb unnecessary demands by consumers, and because bureaucratically administered services are not responsive to consumers' preferences. In terms of the overall efficiency of the economy, the tax burden on the one hand and welfare benefits on the other damage incentives and disturb choices. Those sharing these views, associated with Buchanan and the Friedmans in America, and the Institute of Economic Affairs (IEA) in Britain, oppose industrial and housing subsidies. They recommend that most social security arrangements, the ownership of national assets and the provision of services other than pure public goods (such as the maintenance of the basic legal framework and institutions, the armed forces, and some police functions) should be turned over or returned to the private sector (with some special arrangements for those too poor to cope, especially if this is through no fault of their own). This view had relatively little practical impact on the growth of total British general government spending in the 1960s and much of the 1970s, but its regular expression helped to form the climate of opinion from which recent policies emerged in the middle and later 1970s.

There are also those who favour state provision on fundamental political grounds, irrespective of questions of relative public and private efficiency, whether because of commitment to state ownership and control over resources, ethical objections to the role of profits in services such as health, or a belief in the role of state-run services and transfers as agents of social and political cohesion.

Public spending is also defended by those who emphasise market failure. This view has been somewhat in retreat in recent years, although more so in relation to some areas of spending than others. But it is not without continued influence and popular support. Market failure is a major theme of much of the literature on public finance and welfare economics. It emphasises the gap between the abstract model of the price mechanism, with its competitive firms and well-informed rational consumers, and reality. Markets may fail for many reasons: monopoly and restrictive practices; lack of information, especially among the consumers of education and health services but also producers – hence R & D policy; costs or benefits falling on other than immediate producers or consumers; the impossibility of excluding those who refuse to pay for certain services from benefiting from their provision; institutional impediments to the market-clearing role of prices; the practical difficulties of designing effective distributional policies to safeguard the poor when education, health and housing are privately provided; the state provision of services is also defended on the grounds of the taxpayers' interest in the kind of goods consumed by the poor as opposed to redistribution in cash alone. However, there has been increased acceptance of the proposition that the existence of market failure does not inevitably and sufficiently prove the case for state involvement or provision on efficiency grounds, and that state provision is not a guarantee of superior efficiency.

THE MID-1970S WATERSHED

Somewhat separate from, but complementary to, the doctrinal disputes over the appropriate role of the state has been the debate over the contribution of the growth of public spending to Britain's poor industrial performance. A number of writers, with rather different viewpoints on the role of state spending, contributed to an IEA symposium in 1975. It was held in the aftermath of large-scale public sector strikes and during a sharp recession. The papers illustrate well the way in which British economists reacted to the bleak prospect facing the country at that time. The symposium, entitled 'Crisis '75', emphasised the long-term weakness of the British economy. A common view, expressed by Wilfred Beckerman ('Last Straw or Turning Point?'), was 'The crisis has been coming for a long time, particularly for the British economy'. As part of a new approach to rejuvenating industry, several contributors argued in favour of a tougher approach towards public spending (especially schemes of industrial support, which found wide disfavour). Victor Morgan advocated 'a government committed to do much less and to do it more effectively'.

This became the central theme of policy towards public spending after 1979. It was supported by Bacon and Eltis (1976), whose case for a massive turnaround in policy towards government expenditure was all the more persuasive because it did not appear to be based on *a priori* objections to public spending but on the pragmatic argument that in practice the growth of government, under both Conservative and Labour administrations, had damaged Britain's economic performance. Their analysis contrasted market and non-market sectors, with the former creating an economic surplus which was consumed by the latter at the expense of net exports and investment. Lower investment meant lower productivity and lower growth prospects: 'since 1961 Britain has unwittingly started to become one of the world's high non-market expenditure and low investment economies and since 1970 the ill effects have begun. What has gone wrong since then is only a foretaste of the chaos to come if the country fails to accept the need for new policies.' They advocated major cuts in public spending, cuts in the numbers and relative pay of public servants, large reductions in industrial subsidies and in the state ownership of assets, efficiency drives in government services, and cuts in taxation. They warned that these policies would need to be applied for many years before Britain's economic performance improved; they also warned that unless industrial investment and net exports rose there would be large-scale unemployment.

Others disputed this diagnosis. They blamed Britain's longer-term economic ills on poor industrial management; weak non-price competitiveness (poor quality, servicing, and delivery schedules for exports); poor industrial relations associated with social and class tensions; lack of

technological innovation; the low status of technical training and occupations, and insufficient industrial training. An analysis along these lines by
Gomulka (1979) concluded that but for government deficits and employment, unemployment would have been even higher than it was. Thus,
whereas the Bacon and Eltis line of reasoning blames the growth of public
spending for Britain's poor economic performance, others see this as using
public spending as a scapegoat for private industry's weaknesses. In any
event, the Bacon and Eltis view was well received by those concerned to halt
the growth of public spending.

The 1980 Brookings review of British economic performance concluded
that problems of the sort noted by Gomulka were endemic and deeply
rooted in social and political attitudes and institutions and, as such, beyond
the reach of conventional economic (including budgetary) management
(Caves and Krause, 1980).

PUBLIC SPENDING AND GDP IN BRITAIN AND OTHER COUNTRIES

Several international comparisons of government spending in Britain and
broadly comparable countries have shown that, over the 1960s and 1970s as
a whole, the share of general government spending in GDP and the rate of
growth of government spending relative to GDP (that is the elasticity of
expenditure with respect to GDP) in the United Kingdom were both about,
or even below, the average for OECD countries (OECD, 1978). However,
the elasticity of United Kingdom revenue with respect to GDP was lower
than that for expenditure, so that deficits rose faster here than elsewhere on
average (Saunders and Klau, 1985). It was also the case that, although the
British share of government consumption in GDP was close to the average
for industrialised countries, it spent more than might be expected,
especially on defence, in relation to its own relatively low level of *per capita*
income (Levitt, 1984).

Comparisons of the composition of spending in the United Kingdom and
the average of advanced OECD countries suggest that Britain spends an
above average share of GDP on defence and public administration, but
below average on education, health, social security and economic services
(Saunders and Klau, 1985).

Such international comparisons of public spending are fraught with
statistical difficulties. They omit differences in fiscal support through tax
expenditures (that is, the Exchequer cost of tax deductions), which are
probably more important in other countries than in the United Kingdom,
for example through tax exemptions for private health insurance. It is also
the case that comparisons of spending often make no allowance for
differences between countries in the relationship between the prices of
public services and prices generally. The ratio of the pay of British public

servants to British incomes generally is lower than the comparable ratio for many other western advanced economies, with the result that the relative price of public spending, with respect to average domestic prices, is lower in the United Kingdom than in many other countries.[1] For example, the number of teachers represents a larger share of real national resources (for example, skilled labour) in the United Kingdom than conventional comparisons at market prices suggest. Similarly, a given expenditure share on health care will purchase a larger share of real resources in the United Kingdom, where health care is relatively cheap, than in the United States where health care is relatively expensive.

'BAUMOL'S DISEASE'

The Bacon and Eltis explanation of poor British productivity growth in terms of excessive government spending contains an echo of Baumol's theoretical analysis and prognosis, although they do not refer to it. Baumol's argument is relevant to much of the work discussed in this book, so it is appropriate to summarise his analysis (Baumol, 1967).

Baumol contrasted two sectors. In one, inputs such as labour are the means of producing a distinct final product (as in manufacturing) and productivity grows over time. In the other, the input is seen as an end in itself because the quality of output is judged in terms of the volume of input; either for this reason or because of the intrinsic labour-intensive nature of production (a violin trio cannot be reduced to a duet or solo and remain the same product), productivity growth is nil or close to it. In these circumstances if the constant productivity sector attempts to maintain a constant share in the volume of national output it will absorb resources from the progressive sector and 'the growth rate of the economy will asymptotically approach zero'; if pay in the constant productivity sector grows in line with pay in the progressive sector, where the impact of wage rises is offset by productivity increases, costs in the constant productivity sector will rise 'cumulatively and without limit'. Baumol did not identify the constant productivity sector only with government services, suggesting that this sector also included many private services.

In practice our national income and output accounts show a long-run trend upwards in the price of government relative to GDP prices generally, and they record virtually no productivity increases for government. But this picture is the result of our accounting *conventions*: we do not measure much of government output other than in terms of input, so no productivity growth (when output grows faster than input) is possible by definition. The question, to which much of this book is directed, is whether we can measure government output more directly and what evidence there is for government productivity growth, actual and potential.

While it is true, as Baumol argued, that for *some* products no reduction in input is possible if the quality of output is to be maintained (as in certain musical performances) this is not generally true even in the arts (not to mention the development of electronic reproduction): concert halls need maintenance staff and museums need curators, whose work could be made more productive. The same is obviously true of most government services.

THEORIES OF THE GROWTH OF PUBLIC SPENDING

While it is not our intention to provide an exhaustive survey of the theories which have been put forward to explain the growth of public spending, a brief guide is in order. Some of the theories have implications for the efficiency with which public spending is managed.

In strict neo-classical theory the problem of explaining the growth of public spending does not arise: the price mechanism acting through the behaviour of private producers and consumers leaves no role for the state. Recognition of the minimum role of the state in producing pure public goods (defence, law and order) alone cannot explain more than a fraction of the actual growth of public spending; those who favour a minimalist role for the state view the growth of spending as the result of political or bureaucratic distortions, operating on the demand for or supply of public services and transfers.

A demand-side view which did not regard the growth of public spending as a political or economic distortion was that of Adolf Wagner. 'Wagner's Law' both predicts and advocates the growth of public spending (as a share of national income) on social services and transfers, on infrastructure, and on a range of economic services. As societies get richer more needs to be spent to alleviate social and industrial stress and because citizens expect more and better public services. A considerable literature exists presenting tests of Wagner's Law by comparing total government spending as a share of GDP across countries or over time. We would simply note here that Wagner's Law is not helpful in determining how the state should conduct itself to ensure that its services cannot be provided more efficiently by the price mechanism operating in the private sector nor how it should ensure that the services it does provide are produced as efficiently as possible.

Another demand-side approach is that of 'public choice' models, such as that of Buchanan and Tullock (1962), which explain growth in terms of the effective lobbying by coalitions of voters who gain from specific expenditure, the financing burden of which largely falls on others (the generality of taxpayers) who, at the margin, either tolerate or do not perceive their net burden; expenditure is predicted to grow until the median voter objects. However Musgrave (1985) has emphasised the role of anti-tax lobbies and concluded that the outcome of pro- and anti-spending lobbying cannot be determined *a priori*. To the extent that pro-spending lobbies are successful from time to time at least, their concern to gain from redistribution might imply weak interest in the efficiency of the services from which they gain so long as the costs are borne by others. Lindbeck (1985) has recently stressed the role of special interest groups in the growth of 'horizontal' redistribution: that is, not to low income groups, but to others who are able to organise themselves to gain or retain transfers and subsidies (farmers, home owners). Where politicians, eager for votes, may align themselves with such lobbies, demand- and supply-side explanations of the growth of spending coincide.

A supply-side model which is in tune with much recent popular and political opinion is the Niskanen (1971) model, which emphasises the role of senior officials in expanding government spending and employment, to demonstrate and to increase their own status. It is a rather simplified view of the bureaucracy and ignores the countervailing power of finance departments, the role of exclusivity as opposed to size as a badge of status, the possibility that officials are rewarded for prudence rather than extravagance, the strong sense of public service held by most officials, and the likelihood that officials in growing departments are simply implementing policies for public expenditure growth determined by their political masters.

In a persuasive rejection of the popular critique of officials, Musgrave (op.cit.) has argued that 'the quality of the budgetary process and the technical expertise of the personnel involved has improved over time rather than worsened. While reality does not match the picture of an idealised civil servant, neither is it reflected by the now popular caricature of heavy-handed bureaucrats imposing their interests on the public'.

Reviewing the swings in political fashions and the broad cultural climate within which governments operate, Wildavsky's (1985) explanation of differences in public spending over time (and between countries) is that they reflect the varying relative fortunes of broad egalitarian and competitive principles and feelings among the public.

Musgrave's conclusion seems to be consistent with that view: 'Quite possibly the public, by and large and subject to correction over time, gets what it wants'. To ensure that it does, he advocates more and better information about the costs and performance of government.

PLAN OF THE BOOK

Against this background the book first examines the growth and pattern of public spending since the 1960s (Chapter 2), and the prospects for the next ten years in Chapter 3, in order to provide a setting for the examination of government output and performance.

Chapter 4 presents an outline of the problems associated with the interpretation of the concept of the output of public services; and this is followed by a discussion of certain aspects of the measurement of changes in government output and productivity in Chapter 5. The next three chapters consider the problems of applying these ideas in the specific cases of public administration in the United Kingdom and United States (Chapters 6 and 7 respectively) and defence procurement (Chapter 8).

The general questions of defining and measuring relative efficiency within government services are introduced in Chapter 9. The remaining chapters consider the particular cases of the locally administered education, health and police services, and illustrate a number of quantitative techniques.

These issues are of interest to economists and non-economists alike. We have attempted to discuss them in a manner which will be intelligible to both, although in a few places unavoidably technical questions do arise, especially concerning the measurement of relative efficiency. Economics has an important contribution to make to the management of public spending and the analytical procedures it suggests are of real practical value. Wherever possible these procedures are described in non-technical language in the main text, but some of the detail is presented in technical appendices.

There are a number of important themes which we do not explore. One is the whole area of local government spending, its finance and control, and the way in which central government formulae for determining local needs are arrived at. Another is that of the distributional aims and effects of spending programmes, to the extent that social security spending is intended to relieve poverty, or to concentrate spending where it is needed most, or the education and health programmes are intended to improve the access to the services concerned and to raise the educational attainment and health status of the less well-off. An important aspect of the growth of spending and of 'performance measurement' with respect to these aims is left aside in our discussion below (see, for example, Atkinson, Hills and LeGrand, 1986, for an examination of these themes).

Part I

THE GROWTH OF GOVERNMENT EXPENDITURE

2

PAST TRENDS IN THE GROWTH AND COMPOSITION OF GOVERNMENT SPENDING

Government spending for our purposes includes central and local government but excludes the nationalised industries (other than government grants to them). First we discuss total government spending, and the contexts in which different definitions of that total are appropriate. The composition of spending by economic category is also considered, since concern about spending growth might relate either to its financing or to the extent of state control over real resources. In different contexts different price deflators are also needed; the tendency for the cost of public services to rise faster than prices generally, the relative price effect, is briefly considered; it is largely the result of national accounting conventions and is not necessarily evidence of relatively poor productivity growth. We then go on to examine the growth of spending between 1969 and 1984 in terms of the behaviour of total spending, its economic composition, and by major programme. Periods of restraint and expansion followed one another, neither type of period being uniquely associated with a particular political party in office. The contrast between governments with respect to the growth and shares of particular spending programmes is found to be much less marked, in the period covered, than political rhetoric might suggest.

TOTAL SPENDING

Total government spending can be looked at in a number of ways: the most comprehensive definition is that used in the national income accounts, that is total general government spending, which conforms to international national accounting conventions. For expenditure planning and control purposes a more restricted definitition is currently used: the planning total. This excludes interest payments, on the grounds that they are not susceptible to forward planning and control in the same way as departmental programmes; interest payments nonetheless enter the government's financing requirement and some open-ended departmental spending, especially benefits for the unemployed, has proved to be difficult to forecast and control. The planning total is also net of the proceeds of the sale of assets under the current privatisation programme, such as shares in British Telecom, which are treated as negative spending rather than a means of financing a given total.[1] After certain other adjustments, the planning total amounts to approximately 85 per cent of general government spending in national accounts terms, or almost 40 per cent of GDP at factor cost.

Estimates, the traditional basis of parliamentary control and audit, account for only three-quarters of the planning total. The difference arises largely in two ways: first, because whereas public spending in the planning total includes all social security spending however it is financed, the estimates only include tax financed expenditure, which is just over one-third of total social security spending, and not expenditure financed by national insurance contributions; secondly, although all local government expenditure is included in the planning total, only central government spending on the rate support grant, amounting to 60 per cent of local government spending, enters the estimates.

Governments can often choose between providing a cash grant or offering a tax reduction to families or firms they wish to assist, for example to support the cost of children or to encourage particular forms, or locations, of investment by firms. The cash grant counts as public spending but the tax allowance, often called a tax expenditure, does not. Examples of comparable expenditures and tax allowances include child benefit, which is a cash payment, and the previous child tax allowances; and cash investment grants and investment allowances which are set against corporation tax liability. It is not our purpose to discuss the relative allocational or distributional effects of grants and allowances, but simply to note that a switch between a cash expenditure and an equivalent tax expenditure alters the public expenditure total (whether in national accounts, the planning total or estimates terms) but not the government's financial deficit.

The composition of public spending

The composition of spending may be looked at in terms of the split between central or local spending authorities, between programmes, or between economic categories (table 2.1). We are not concerned with central–local relationships here. The allocation between programmes is the principal focus of political and popular debate over relative public spending priorities, to which we return below, but for important aspects of the debate about the appropriate division between public and private uses of resources the distinction between economic categories is relevant. A broad distinction may be made between public spending on goods and services on the one hand, and cash transfers on the other. The former category represents the state's direct control over real economic resources, whereas cash transfers, such as social security or interest payments, are spent by the recipients as they choose.

Table 2.1 *Total public spending in 1984*

Percentage shares

	Total of current spending	GDP at current market price
Total general government expenditure (£140 bn)	100	46
Planning total	86	39
Supply estimates	62	29
Local authorities	24	11
By economic category		
Goods and services		
Current expenditure on goods and services [a]	48 ⎫ 52	21
Gross domestic fixed capital formation	4 ⎭	2
Transfers		
Current grants to private sector	31 ⎫	13
Debt interest	11 ⎪ 48	5
Subsidies	5 ⎪	2
Current grants abroad [b]	1 ⎭	

Sources: NIESR estimates, derived from 1985 Public Expenditure White Paper, 1985 Financial Statement and Budget Report and 1985 Supply Estimates.
[a] Of which 60 per cent is wages.
[b] For example, overseas aid, EEC budget contributions.
Note: 'Total general government expenditure' is the national accounts definition, which includes interest payments and does not net off the proceeds of selling shares in public corporations: the 'planning total' excludes interest and asset sales.

Public spending as a share of GDP

We might be interested in the share of public spending in GDP because of concern about the extent of administrative control over the use of productive resources or because of concern about the financing implications of public spending.

In the first case, where we are concerned about the use of productive resources, we need to concentrate on spending on goods and services, which table 2.1 indicates represents just over half the total or 21 per cent of GDP. In the second case of concern about financing we include all public spending, irrespective of composition, as a share of GDP.

For measuring changes in government spending over time, allowance for the effect of price changes needs to be made. The process of general inflation in the economy as a whole is indicated by the growth of the GDP price deflator. Government spending deflated by the GDP deflator is described as spending in '*real*' or '*cost*' *terms*; the latter phrase indicating that it is a broad measure of the opportunity cost of public spending in terms of other uses of GDP foregone after allowing for price increases generally. Measured in these terms, public spending represents the same percentage of GDP at constant prices as its share when both public spending and GDP are measured at current prices.

The growth of public spending in real terms is composed of changes in the volume of inputs (especially the numbers employed in the case of spending on goods and services) and changes in the relative prices of those inputs. However, it is often interesting and useful to examine changes in the volume of inputs alone, for which purpose we need to remove the effect of increases in *their* prices, which might not be the same as the increase in GDP prices generally. The deflation of public spending on goods and services by their 'own' price deflators produces expenditure at *constant prices* or in volume terms. In the case of cash transfer payments (such as social security) we are often interested in the amount spent in terms of its purchasing power, and for this purpose we can deflate the cash figures by the consumer price deflator, to arrive at expenditure at constant prices.

In practice there has been a tendency for the price of the inputs into government current expenditure on goods and services to rise faster than GDP prices generally, at least over the medium to long term.

Table 2.2 illustrates these points. Current expenditure on goods and services rose as a share of GDP at current prices over the period 1964–84 but the share in volume terms at constant (1980) prices was virtually unchanged: the increased share at current prices was thus virtually wholly attributable to higher relative prices rather than an increased share in the volume of GDP consumed by this category of government spending. In the case of investment, the share of GDP fell irrespective of the price base of the comparison (and this remains the case after adding back the proceeds of council house sales and other capital receipts which are treated as negative spending in the national accounts). On the other hand, spending on transfers rose as a percentage of GDP irrespective of the price basis. Therefore the increase in government spending as a share of GDP at current prices (which is equivalent to an increased percentage in real terms) is accounted for by the relative price effect on the one hand, and the increased volume of spending on transfers on the other.

The relative price effect (RPE)

There is considerable difficulty in measuring the output of government services. United Kingdom national accounting practice is to measure output movements in government services very largely by changes in the numbers employed, that is with no provision for productivity growth. To

Table 2.2 *General government share in GDP*

Percentages

	1964		1984	
	Current prices	1980 prices	Current prices	1980 prices
Current goods and services	16.5	20.7	21.8	20.8
Investment[a]	8.6	9.0	3.4	3.7
Transfers[b]	13.1	12.0	20.6	20.0
Total	38.2	41.7	45.8	44.5
Excluding transfers	25.1	29.7	25.2	24.5

Source: National Income Blue Books and NIESR estimates.
[a] Includes gross domestic fixed capital formation, capital grants and net lending deflated by the GDFC cost index.
[b] Includes debt interest which is deflated by the consumer price index.

the extent that government input prices, especially wages, rise in line with prices and wages in the rest of the economy where productivity growth is measured, it follows that relative prices will rise. But since the RPE very largely reflects national accounting conventions its existence is not confirmation of the presence of 'Baumol's Disease'. According to Baumol (see Chapter 1) the labour-intensive nature of government services implies virtually no scope for productivity increases. However, as we argue later, there is in fact abundant evidence of productivity growth in many government services. The RPE is partly, perhaps entirely, the result of current conventions. A further, more detailed disaggregation of expenditure growth is provided at the end of this chapter.

THE PATTERN OF CHANGE SINCE 1969

The pattern of changes in public spending since 1969, the last full year of the 1964–70 Labour administration, is described below first in terms of total spending, then by economic composition and finally by functional programme.

The behaviour of total spending

Details of spending both in real terms and in volume terms, by economic category and by function, are shown in Appendix tables A1.1 to A1.6. Total general government spending is summarised in table 2.3; it seems to display a pattern of biennial changes. The years 1969–71 were years of tight constraint, following the balance of payments and debt crises of the 1960s and the election in 1970 of a new administration committed to reducing taxation and the role of the state. During 1971–3, in the face of rising unemployment and against the background of the tripartite talks with

Table 2.3 *The growth of general government expenditure* [a]

	Volume[b] terms	Real terms[c]
1969–71	1.3	2.3
1971–3	5.0	6.5
1973–4	7.0	12.0
1974–5	3.0	3.2
1975–7	−4.0	−4.5
1977–9	4.5	4.3
1979–81	0.7	1.0
1981–3	1.8	2.5

Source: National Income Blue Books, NIESR estimates.
[a] Annual averages.
[b] Deflated by the price of inputs.
[c] Deflated by general inflation.

industry and the unions, expenditure accelerated (the Barber Boom); this growth was reinforced during 1973–5 especially following the March 1974 general election and the arrival of the new Labour administration, members of which were determined to compensate for the tight budgetary constraints on social and industrial programmes which they had often faced in the 1960s. However, the following two years saw cuts in spending in the face of the exchange and debt crisis of 1976 and as part of the negotiations with the IMF. Subsequently spending recovered in 1977–9. Expenditure grew more slowly in the following two years than during any comparable period shown (apart from the 1976–7 cuts), following the election in 1979 of the Conservative administration under a leadership committed to cutting the share of government spending in GDP, reducing borrowing, and cutting taxes, somewhat along the lines of 1970–1 policies. The next two years demonstrate a modest acceleration in spending, but 1984 saw a significant deceleration (see Appendix tables A1.2 and A1.3).

Three things stand out from the picture outlined so far. One is that the Conservative and Labour administrations of the 1970s were virtually mirror images of one another: under the former, rapid growth followed tight restraint, under the latter, cuts followed rapid growth. The second is that neither rapid growth nor tight restraints in the 1970s were peculiar to government by a particular party, although the Conservative party is generally thought to prefer restraint and the Labour party is generally thought to prefer growth in state spending. The third point is the contrast between the considerable volatility in volume spending up to 1979 (table 2.3) and the relative stability of total spending in the 1980s, perhaps because public expenditure was no longer being used as an instrument of demand management. Prior to that, spending was on more than one occasion increased to boost demand and employment, as an instrument of short-term demand management, or in an attempt to win union support for wage restraint, social spending being presented as providing a social wage comparable to earnings. At other times spending was cut in order to increase confidence in the government's monetary and fiscal management. Since 1979 spending has been more stable, despite increased unemployment; we return to some of these themes in Chapter 3 below.

Spending priorities

Table 2.4 summarises the directional changes in programme spending in the two-year periods used in the account of total spending shown in table 2.3. Law and order demonstrates the most stable pattern, irrespective of party in office, although it is noticeable that its share grew in periods of overall restraint and was stable in periods of overall growth. Some programmes increased their share in the first three sub-periods to 1975, which seems to have been something of a watershed because their share has

Table 2.4 *Changes in shares in total general government spending*[a]

	1969–71	1971–3	1973–5	1975–7	1977–9	1979–83
Programmes						
Defence	−	−	−	+	−	+
Law and order	+	=	=	+	=	+
Education	+	+	+	−	−	−
Health	+	=	+	+	−	+
Personal social services	+	+	+	=	=	+
Social security	−	−	−	+	+	+
Housing	−	+	+	−	−	−
Employment	+	−	+	+	−	+
Industry and trade	−	−	+	−	+	−
Transport and roads	+	−	=	−	=	−
Economic categories						
Current expenditure						
on goods and services	+	+	+	=	+	+
Current grants to persons	+	+	+	+	+	+
GDFC[b]	=	+	−	−	−	−
Subsidies	=	+	+	−	+	=
Capital finance[c]						
private sector	=	=	−	−	=	+
public corporations	=	−	+	−	+	−
Debt interest	−	+	+	+	+	+

Source: Appendix tables A.1.1 to A.1.6.
[a] Definitions of symbols: + increased, − reduced, = unchanged share.
[b] Gross domestic fixed capital formation.
[c] Capital grants and net lending.
Note: The functional classification of spending in the National Accounts, on which the upper half of this table is based, changed in 1984 so that a consistent series beyond 1983 is not possible.

been cut ever since (education and housing) or their growth has been more moderate (health and personal social services). On the other hand, social security had a falling share to 1975 but its share has risen steadily since. Other programmes show a much more volatile picture: defence had a falling share in most of the period, with a slight increase during 1975–7 and a more marked increase after 1979 (reflecting the previous Labour administration's acceptance of a NATO target of 3 per cent real growth); employment demonstrates increases in periods of overall constraint, although it also grew from 1973–5; the share of transport and roads increased only during 1969–71; industry and trade took an increased share only in the periods of expenditure growth in the mid- and late-1970s, that is, under Labour administrations, otherwise the share has been cut, including in the Labour years 1975–7.

If the sub-periods are compared some similarities and contrasts emerge. Although there was a change of government in March 1974, the periods of rapid overall expansion of the 1970s, 1971–3 and 1973–5, demonstrate considerable similarity, except for the change from falling to rising or stable shares for some industrial programmes. On the other hand, the period of cuts, 1975–7, shows a reversal of the preceding period for many programmes. The final period of restraint, 1979–83, shows a remarkably similar pattern to that of 1975–7, despite the change in administration. Since 1979 the share of defence has grown, but this partly reflects previous commitments; education and housing have continued to fall; social security has continued to rise; law and order, health and personal social services, and employment have increased their share; the industrial and transport programmes have taken a falling share.

Taking account of the shares of individual expenditure programmes in total spending, it is difficult to discern any major differences in priorities between the years since 1979 and the 1975–9 period (apart from cuts in industrial support and transport spending). But there are some important changes since 1971–5: greater priority for defence and less for housing, a greater share for social security but a smaller share for education. For other programmes the changes in shares after 1979 were either minor as for health and law and order, or the pre-1975 picture was too unstable to present a clear contrast as for employment, industry and transport, although in the latter two cases 1979 does represent a clear break with the 1973–5 and 1977–9 pattern.

However the pattern by programme described above obscures changes in approach *within* programmes, for example the encouragement of the contracting-out or privatisation of certain ancillary services such as catering, cleaning and maintenance in education and health since 1979. Changes within the social security budget, which were of greater importance in expenditure terms, are commented upon further in the next chapter.

Programmes differ in the extent to which governments are free to vary them in the short run. Thus in the cases of education, health and social security, publicly stated policy commitments, statutory requirements, demographic influences, and the activities of pressure groups (which are more effective for some programmes than for others) constrain the scope for large change without major legislation. However, variations in the rate of real growth of resources per client are often open to the government and in the case of some services productivity improvements are claimed, which can have large cumulative effects over a period of years. Defence is a matter for domestic political judgement but in practice alliance commitments, presssures from major allies, changes in the perceived level or risk of external threat, and domestic industrial/employment considerations impose important constraints. Law and order, employment and agricultural spending offer some flexibility but are constrained, respectively, by the need to respond to rising recorded crime or unemployment and membership of the EEC Common Agricultural Policy. It is mainly in the fields of housing, transport and industrial support that governments have had the greatest margin for manoeuvre, especially since 1979. This is in spite of the problems of rising homelessness, the deteriorating housing stock, rising road traffic and deteriorating road surfaces, and the collapse of much of manufacturing capacity.

By and large, with the exceptions noted above, the contrast between Conservative and Labour administrations since 1969 has not been as great as is sometimes either claimed or believed. Some other studies of programme shares have reached somewhat similar conclusions including one which allowed for demographic and other influences outside the government's control (Dunne *et al.*, 1984). Atkinson, Hills and LeGrand (1986), in their review of welfare state spending 1970–1985, concluded '. . . the overall impression is one of continuity rather than rapid change of direction'.

Traditionally, Labour governments are committed to redistribution and industrial subsidies, whilst Conservative governments are concerned about defence, law and order, and the role of markets. But Conservative governments also have a record of concern for poverty relief and for the provision of 'merit goods' (to use Musgrave's term) such as subsidised education and health services, even though a preference for market solutions implies that any transfers should be in cash rather than in kind. Moreover, the higher the level of unemployment and the greater the number of retirement pensioners, the more will tend to be spent on cash social security benefits, *irrespective* of party in power: a high share for cash transfers is not, by itself, evidence of a preference for market solutions.

Those who favour market solutions will encourage a higher share of spending, within a given total, for public goods like defence and a lower share for services such as education and health which the market could provide. But non-marketeers, or even Labour governments, may favour spending on public goods. Britain's initial commitment to 3 per cent real spending growth on defence, for example, was undertaken by Labour.

A further complication is that concern over the provision of a service need not, at the margin, imply an increased provision of resources if efficiency can be improved. A government committed to raising efficiency may decide to meet rising, or constant, output targets by a less than proportionate increase, or even reductions, in the volume of inputs. So it is difficult to relate differences in resource provision to *output* priorities, if the scope for efficiency gains differs substantially between programmes. The recent decision by a Conservative government to reverse the growth in defence spending, in the hope of securing major efficiency improvements in the equipment procurement process and in defence support services, does not necessarily imply a weaker priority for defence. It is conceivable that a different government concerned to use United Kingdom defence procurement as a means of boosting domestic employment, for example by increased spending on warship procurement in areas of high unemployment, might spend more on defence, without any change in priorities with respect to defence *per se*, if it also took a more relaxed view of the need to raise efficiency and labour productivity in the United Kingdom industries supplying defence equipment.

Given the somewhat blurred nature of the differences between the Labour and Conservative governments outlined above, the fact that over the years since 1979 as a whole total spending has grown, and given the greater emphasis on efficiency gains, for example in defence, the absence of sharp contrasts in programme shares is not very surprising, political rhetoric apart. Indeed, some might argue that the main watershed on public spending was not so much 1979 as 1976, when the contradiction between public spending aspirations and the macroeconomic constraints became brutally explicit. Total spending has been much more tightly controlled ever since. This has induced a more stringent approach to priorities between programmes, and particularly tight constraints on certain programmes, especially education, housing, industrial support and transport, irrespective of the party in office. This is not meant to understate the differences between political parties. The constraints associated with and subsequent to the 1976 debt and exchange crisis were a matter of regret for the Labour administration, which saw many of its spending aspirations thwarted. The constraints since 1979 have been a deliberate policy choice, perhaps reflecting perceived macroeconomic constraints, but also associated with a desire to reduce the role of the state, tax burdens and government borrowing, and to strengthen financial management in government.

Table 2.5 *Composition of the growth in general government current expenditure 1962–72 and 1972–82*

Percentages

	1962–72	1972–82
Growth in volume terms	38	41
Growth in real terms	48	48
Composition of growth at current prices:		
volume	26[a]	9[c]
to offset higher GDP prices	46[b]	60[d]
to offset higher relative prices	9	6[d]
effect of higher prices on volume increase	19	25
total	100	100

Sources: National Income Blue Books; NIESR calculations (see Levitt, M.S., 'The growth of government expenditure', *National Institute Economic Review*, no. 108, May 1984).
[a] At 1962 prices.
[b] Given 1962 volumes.
[c] At 1972 prices.
[d] Given 1972 volumes.

Decomposition of growth into volume and price changes

The growth of public spending at current prices may be decomposed into the effect of growth in input volume, the effect of price increases on initial volumes, and the additional combined effects of increased volumes at increased prices. The latter 'interaction effect' can represent a large proportion of total growth; for example in the periods 1962–72 and 1972-82 we have estimated that it accounted for up to a quarter of overall growth (table 2.5).

Whereas table 2.5 above summarises the decomposition of public spending in cash terms, table 2.6 below presents results of a decomposition of spending growth in real terms for more recent periods. Being an analysis of growth after allowing for general GDP price increases, the only price changes included are in relative prices; as they are much smaller than the inflationary price increases of table 2.5 it follows that the interaction effects will be small.

The price deflator for government final consumption rose faster than GDP prices in both periods; that is, its RPE was positive. The deflators for current grants and subsidies (the consumer price index) and for investment (the gross domestic fixed capital formation price index) rose more slowly than GDP prices in both periods; that is, their RPEs were negative.

The period 1974–83 has been split into two sub-periods. Taking 1974–9 first we note that the volume growth (that is, using the separate price deflators for each category) was larger than growth in real terms (that is, deflating by the GDP deflator). This was because the effect of the fall in the

Table 2.6 *Decomposition of changes in general government spending 1974–9 and 1979–84*

Percentages

	Final consumption	Current grants	Investment	Subsidies	Debt interest	Other	Total
1974–9							
Change in real terms[a]	*10*	*26*	*−39*	*−30*	*17*	*37*	*3*
Accounted for by change in							
Volume[b]	95	120	95	90	100	100	153
RPE	5	−16	8	13	0	0	−56
Interaction	0	−4	−3	−3	0	0	3
	100	100	100	100	100	100	100
1979–84							
Change in real terms[a]	*14*	*29*	*−30*	*10*	*14*	*−62*	*9*
Accounted for by change in							
Volume[b]	47	106	80	114	100	100	75
RPE	50	5	27	−13	0	0	21
Interaction	3	−1	−7	−1	0	0	4
	100	100	100	100	100	100	100

Sources: as table 2.3.

[a] Derived by deflating cash change by change in GDP deflator.

[b] At constant input prices derived by deflating final consumption by general government final consumption index, current grants and subsidies by consumption deflator, investments (gross domestic fixed capital formation, capital lending and grants) by the GDFCF index.

relative price of current grants, subsidies and investment exceeded the normal RPE on final consumption. Final consumption rose faster in real terms than at constant own prices, demonstrating a positive, but small RPE. Spending on current grants rose, but its RPE was negative, so volume benefit growth (that is, growth in the volume of consumer goods that the benefits could finance) was greater than expenditure in real terms. Spending on investment and subsidies fell, but their RPEs were also negative, so that they fell by less in volume terms than in real terms.

In the second sub-period, 1979–84, overall growth exceeded growth in 1974–9 on both measures. Growth in real terms was faster than in volume terms, reflecting a large positive RPE (accounting for half of its growth) which exceeded the negative RPEs for other categories. As in the earlier period spending on current grants rose faster than final consumption; both grew faster than during 1974–9; in contrast to the earlier period subsidies rose; as in the earlier period investment was cut, although by a smaller proportion. Debt interest continued to rise, but more slowly.

Three principal themes emerge from this chapter. One is that the contrasts between Conservative and Labour administrations have not been as marked as one might expect. Another is that the growth of the share of government spending on goods and services in GDP is a reflection of the relative price effect rather than a growing share in volume terms. The third is that the relative price effect is the result of national accounting conventions and does not necessarily tell us anything about relative productivity growth of government vis-à-vis the rest of the economy.

3

RECENT POLICIES AND LONGER-TERM PROSPECTS FOR SPENDING

INTRODUCTION

The basis of expenditure policy after 1979 was the government's overall economic strategy. Key elements included reductions in the Public Sector Borrowing Requirement to relieve the domestic pressure on interest rates, lower tax rates, reductions in the state's ownership of assets, and tight constraints on the real level of total public spending. The 1980 Public Expenditure White Paper stated 'The government intend to reduce public expenditure progressively in volume terms over the next four years'. Subsequently the aim was stated to be one of holding the level constant in real terms.

If the relative price effect was expected to be positive (the normal situation over a run of years in the 1960s and 1970s), this would also have amounted to an intention to reduce spending in volume terms. In fact spending has risen in both volume and in real terms, but it has fallen as a proportion of GDP since 1982/3 and the aim in practice has been to accept modest increases in the amount of spending while reducing its share in total national resources.

The focus in recent years has been on cutting the planning total which is measured after asset sales, which are treated as negative spending rather than, as several outside commentators (including the House of Commons Treasury and Civil Service Committee) prefer, a means of financing government. Here the main emphasis is on spending by department, and the total of departmental spending (that is, all expenditure for which departments take policy responsibility, whether or not the expenditure is incurred by departments themselves, local authorities or public corporations).

DEVELOPMENTS SINCE 1978/9

Table 3.1 illustrates spending growth by department from 1978/9 to 1985/6 in real terms, that is, after allowing for general inflation. Intentions to the contrary notwithstanding, total departmental spending has grown, by 10 per cent in real terms.

In the case of *education*, expenditure fell marginally between 1978/9 and

Table 3.1 *Public expenditure trends and plans*[a]

£bn, 1985/6 real terms

	1978/9 Actual	1985/6 Actual	1989/90 Plan
Education and science	17.9	17.5	19.0
Health and personal social services	17.4	20.7	22.6
Social security	32.0	42.8	44.7
Defence	14.1	18.0	17.1
Agriculture, fisheries and food	1.5	2.4	2.2
Home office	3.8	5.3	5.8
Employment	2.0	3.4	3.8
Energy	1.0	0.7	− 0.2
Trade and industry	4.5	1.8	0.9
Transport	4.9	4.6	4.5
Housing	6.7	2.8	2.7
Other	18.2	16.3	16.8
Reserve	..	..	6.6
Total departmental expenditure	124.0	136.3	146.5

Sources: 1986 and 1987 Public Expenditure White Papers.
[a] The education, health and social security figures refer to the United Kingdom as a whole.

1985/6. School pupil numbers have fallen but because of lags in the adjustment of numbers of teachers and the building stock, unit costs have risen. However, this does not necessarily mean improved quality of provision: under-utilised buildings still require maintenance and fuel expenditure, and falling rolls make curriculum organisation difficult. In further and higher education unit costs have been reduced, as student numbers have risen faster than the volume of resources. We estimate a reduction of 3 per cent for universities and 12 per cent in advanced further education between 1980/1 and 1983/4 in real terms; and the purchasing power of student awards fell by 12 per cent between 1979/80 and 1985/6. Universities have expressed concern about the closure of departments and the possible closure of entire universities.

Spending on *health and personal social services* rose by 18 per cent between 1978/9 and 1985/6; an important influence has been the growing number of elderly people in the population (the over-75s cost, on average, over six times the cost of those of working age). In addition the emergence of new treatments and technical advances tend to raise costs, by some $\frac{1}{2}$ per cent annually in *volume* terms. We estimate (Levitt and Joyce, 1987) that during the first half of the 1980s the demographic changes required 0.7 per cent annual growth at constant prices (*before* allowing for efficiency savings, the cost of medical advances, or relative price effects) for hospital, community health and local authority social services as a whole, and actual growth at constant prices was 1.4 per cent; but for hospitals the growth of spending just matched the demographic requirement. The extent to which productivity improvements have offset the pressures associated with the cost of medical advances for hospitals has been a matter of dispute (House of Commons Social Services Committee, Session 1985–6). There are numerous pressures to increase provision of resources to reduce waiting times, to level up less well-endowed regions without drawing resources away from the Thames regions and London districts in the 'RAWP' process (Resource Allocation Working Party) for redistributing resources, and to improve provision for community care.

Social Security spending rose by one third in real terms from 1978/9 to 1985/6. Expenditure on the elderly rose by over a quarter (in real terms), on family support by half, and on the unemployed by one and three-quarters; as well as the impact of unemployment and increases in the numbers of the retired, this higher spending also reflects increased take-up of means-tested benefits as economic pressures on low income families have risen, increases in the numbers claiming disability benefits, increases in the number of one-parent families, and increases in board and lodging payments for the homeless and the elderly in private or voluntary homes. While over the period as a whole the real purchasing power of some benefits (such as retirement benefits) has increased, the 1980 Social Security Act ended the link between pensions and earnings (which was not always maintained in practice in the 1970s) and the Earnings Related Supplement has been abolished. Present practice is to uprate national insurance and supplementary benefits in line with prices, but some unpledged benefits, notably child benefit, have been reduced in real terms. The taxation of unemployment benefit has been introduced, so that a given income bears the same tax whether it is in the form of wages or benefit. Short-term benefits have been uprated more slowly than long-term benefits; there have been changes in the period over which price changes, upon which upratings are based, have been measured. Waiting periods, during which benefits cannot be drawn, have been extended for certain benefits and restrictions on the scale and duration of benefit for certain young claimants have been extended. These changes notwithstanding, spending has risen considerably in the face of increased unemployment and growing numbers of the retired, and numerous pressures exist to extend entitlement and to increase the value of benefits.

Defence expenditure grew in line with the United Kingdom commitment to the NATO aim of 3 per cent real growth, which expired in 1985/6. Over the period as a whole defence prices grew faster than GDP prices generally, on the basis of existing accounting conventions. The defence RPE partly reflects the cost of improved performance by equipment of higher specifications. On the other hand, the commitment to fund spending planned in terms of constant input prices, whereby any actual price increases had to be financed, cannot have been conducive to cost containment or improved productivity in the manufacture of the equipment involved. Some of the industries concerned demonstrated relatively poor performance and the National Audit Office has frequently pointed to the scope for improvements in cost containment.

Spending on other programmes presents many contrasts. Spending on agriculture, home office and employment programmes grew relatively rapidly in response, respectively, to the effect of changes in world food prices on support under the CAP, pressures to spend more on law and order in the context of rising recorded crime, and the extension of special employment and training measures in the face of rising unemployment, together with mounting evidence of unfavourable comparisons between industrial training in Britain and in other countries. On the other hand spending on housing, industrial support, transport (where spending on roads has risen while rail and bus subsidies have been cut) and energy have all been tightly restrained. This is in line with the wish to reduce state asset ownership and state support for trading activities, and with the improved financial performance of some nationalised industries.

RECENT PLANS

Prior to the November 1986 Autumn Statement, the plans had each been for broadly flat spending, in real terms, between the year in which the plan was announced and the final year to which it referred. In practice, as table 3.2. shows, the spending outturn tended to exceed the amount originally planned and successive plans were frequently revised upwards. The largest excess of spending over plan was for the 1983/4 outturn compared to the amount originally planned in 1980; the overshoot amounted to almost £9 billion or 7 per cent of the initial plan. In the two subsequent years the excess over initial plans was relatively small, but from 1986/7 onwards larger differences between outturn and earlier plans will emerge. This is because of the increase in planned spending for the second half of the 1980s announced in the 1986 Autumn Statement, the details of which were spelt out in the 1987 Public Expenditure White Paper. To the extent that even these plans are exceeded, in line with much previous experience, the difference between outturn and earlier plans will be even greater. However, it should be noted that general government spending as a share of GNP has fallen from $45\frac{3}{4}$ to $43\frac{1}{4}$ per cent between 1983/4 and 1986/7 (Public Expenditure White Paper, 1987).

The unplanned increases in spending since 1980 (that is, by comparison with original plans) reflect a number of influences. The most important has been the much greater increase in demand-led social security spending than the government anticipated. Another has been the difficulty of controlling

Table 3.2 *Plans and outturns in cost terms: planning totals*

£bn, 1985/6 real terms

	1983/4	1984/5	1985/6	1986/7	1987/8	1988/9	1989/90
Plan in White Paper:							
1980, *Cmnd* 7841	124.2						
1981, *Cmnd* 8175	125.5						
1982, *Cmnd* 8494	133.3	135.4					
1983, *Cmnd* 8789	132.1	134.1	132.3				
1984, *Cmnd* 9143	133.0	134.1	132.1	132.8			
1985, *Cmnd* 9428	*132.9*	135.9	132.1	132.8	132.6		
1986, *Cmnd* 9702	*132.9*	137.4	134.2	135.2	134.8	134.6	
1987, *Cm* 56	*133.0*	*137.6*	*133.6*	136.5	139.3	139.7	142.1

Sources: 1986 and 1987 Public Expenditure White Papers and NIESR estimates.
Note: The outturn figures for each year are shown in italics.

local government spending, which has tended to exceed plans by more in absolute terms than has been the case for central government spending.

Leaving aside the comparison between plans and outturn and turning to the increase in spending outturns *per se*, the main influences have been: the large increase in social security spending, mainly reflecting increases in the numbers unemployed and retired but also increased take-up, and increased spending on the disabled; the commitment to 3 per cent volume growth in defence spending until 1985/6; and growing pressures on the health services. Spending on these three large programmes grew by £16 billion between 1978/9 and 1985/6, in real terms (see table 3.1). Pressures on law and order, employment and agricultural spending, added a further £3.5 billion. The increase in total departmental spending was only kept to £12 billion by cuts in education, environmental, housing and industrial spending, and by tight constraints on manpower numbers and pay.

The increases in spending plans for the later 1980s announced in the 1986 Autumn Statement reflected increased acknowledgement of some of the concerns which emerged in the mid-1980s about the quality of education in particular, the need to provide for some real increases in public service pay, and for levels of actual local authority spending higher than those originally planned. Nevertheless, the planned constraints on programmes such as defence, health and housing, remained very tight in relation to the pressures to spend more, and policy towards public spending on industry remained restrictive. The average annual planned growth between 1985/6 and 1989/90 in departmental spending was only slightly greater than actual growth of 1.6 per cent between 1978/9 and 1985/6. Nonetheless, the 1986 Autumn Statement did represent a change towards greater realism by comparison with the tightly constrained plans previously announced.

According to our estimates the 1987 plans for health spending were for a rise in excess of the amount needed to meet demographic trends alone, before allowing for possible relative price increases on the one hand or productivity improvements on the other. Defence spending faced cuts in cost terms and, unless significant efficiency improvements were achieved, the more so in terms of input volumes: this does not mean a cut in the total stock of defence equipment (to believe otherwise is to confuse stocks and flows) so long as annual procurement exceeds depreciation. For these programmes improvements in efficiency are essential to maintain the effectiveness and quality of service in the face of tight budgetary constraints.

The 1987 plans for social security spending implied the uprating of retirement pensions broadly in line with prices, but also the likelihood of real cuts in child benefits. There were to be major structural changes in social security, particularly for income-related benefits (broadly revenue) neutral) and for the national insurance scheme, where the main effects would build up only gradually for the remainder of the century.

Three programmes, agriculture, employment, home office, have grown rapidly since 1978/9. In contrast to recent rapid growth, a fall in spending on agriculture was planned although developments in world food prices and the Common Agricultural Policy could threaten the viability of these plans. Spending on employment programmes was to grow more slowly than in recent years, reflecting a forecast levelling off or modest reduction in unemployment. Spending on home office law and order programmes has increased at a much faster rate than spending generally since 1978/9, partly as a response to concern about rising recorded crime (although the relationship between police resources and recorded crime is a complicated one, see Chapter 12); it had been planned to level off or even fall despite projections of further increases in recorded crime but the 1986 Autumn Statement, in recognition of these trends, revised previous plans upwards although the effectiveness of the spending needs to be improved.

The fall in housing expenditure was to continue in spite of pressures associated with an estimated £20 billion bill for repairs to existing houses, and the contrast between the constraints on local authority spending on residential accommodation (for the elderly and homeless) and the rise of un-cash-limited social security spending on private (and voluntary) accommodation. Trade and industry faced continued cuts. Transport spending would fall as operating subsidies were reduced for publicly owned operations. It was intended that energy would become a net source of finance.

LONGER-TERM PROSPECTS

The Treasury's 1984 Green Paper (HM Treasury, 1984), on the longer-term outlook for public spending, emphasised the financing implications of spending. It stressed the need to decide what could be afforded before setting out the plans for particular programmes, and it questioned why total spending should rise at all. The Green Paper did not make projections of individual programmes, although it outlined sources of pressure for higher spending, for example those arising from demographic change, and the rising cost of sophisticated defence and health equipment. It considered the implications for taxation of either holding total spending flat in real terms, or of allowing it to grow by 1 per cent annually after 1988/9. Either would represent a break with the past, when public spending had normally risen both absolutely and as a share of GDP.

A number of commentators disagreed with the Green Paper view that it was first necessary to determine what could be afforded in total before deciding what should be spent on each programme: they argued that the total should be arrived at in the light of an analysis of the case for spending, programme by programme (O'Higgins and Patterson, 1985). The Green Paper preference for holding spending broadly flat in real terms reflected the absolute priority awarded to cutting taxation and borrowing. A different view is that there is a trade-off between increased spending and reduced taxation, and that the judgement to be made on total spending should be reached after taking into account the case for spending on each programme and not vice versa. On the other hand the merit of the Green Paper approach is that it would provide greater incentives to set priorities and to increase efficiency than would exist with a more relaxed approach to financing constraints.

The question of what can be afforded is not one which permits any simple mechanical answer; it is largely a political issue. It is reasonable for governments to set a target for financing, and sometimes this might require spending to grow more slowly than GDP, for example, if it is believed that tight constraints on taxation and borrowing will improve the performance of the economy. But even so voters may actually prefer higher taxation, slower economic growth and more public spending, or they may believe that the inducement to faster economic growth will turn out to be weaker than anticipated. On the other hand governments might adopt a less restrictive approach, letting spending rise at the maximum rate they can finance, even though this might be faster than the rate of growth of United Kingdom GDP. This approach also requires political judgement: taxpayers and lenders may turn out to be less tolerant than government assumed.

An important new element in the outlook, stressed in the Green Paper, is the downturn in revenue from North Sea oil. Public expenditure growth in line with GNP would now require increases to the burden of non-North Sea taxes.

PROJECTIONS AND TARGETS FOR REVENUE AND TOTAL SPENDING

There is no mechanical method for determining what must be spent on any individual programme. In the case of the social programmes, where demographic influences are important, it is possible to project the spending needed to maintain a given standard of service, leaving aside possible efficiency gains on the one hand or relative price changes on the other. But, as numerous OECD studies have shown, demographic changes alone account for only a fraction of increased spending on social programmes. In practice, increases in the volume of provision per beneficiary and extensions in the coverage of these programmes have been very important and will be in the future. As for programmes such as defence, agricultural and industrial support, spending on law and order, housing and so on, the scope for judgement about future prospects is even greater.

In the projections shown in table 3.4, two approaches have been adopted to the longer-term spending outlook. In one case constraints have been imposed from the top downward, working from financial targets for borrowing, taxation and other spending. In the other case, projections of the individual programmes have been made from the bottom upward, on the basis of alternative assumptions, for example, about social security upratings. The two sets of results are then compared and some possible trade-offs among programmes, and between spending and taxation, are discussed. GNP is assumed to grow in line with productive potential, at an average annual rate of 1.8 per cent, from 1985 to the year 2000. This estimate is taken from Savage and Biswas (1986). It takes into account the projected slowing down in the growth of the population of working age, an assumed downturn in North Sea oil production, and productivity growth of 2 per cent per year, which is below that achieved in the 1960s but in line with trends since 1973. GNP growth on this trend basis is invariant with respect to our alternative public spending projections, between which there are no price or income differences. Alternative expenditure and revenue projections are not intended to represent government by different political parties; the revenue projections are based on the 1985/6 share of non-North Sea taxes in GNP on the one hand, as a starting point, and a range of projections for North Sea revenue on the other.

North Sea revenues are an important element in the revenue outlook because the volume of production, the cost of extracting oil, and the price of oil are all subject to uncertainty. Savage and Biswas suggested that possible reductions in the volume of production and reduced tax-take from increasingly costly and less profitable production might offset the impact on revenue of a gradual recovery in oil prices. Oil revenues were projected to fall from 3.5 per cent of GNP in 1985 to somewhere in the range of 0.2 per cent in 1995.

For government borrowing we simply assume that budget deficits are a constant proportion of GNP (which is less restrictive than policies between 1979 and 1986 which aimed to reduce the share of government borrowing in GNP). We also assume that interest rates are such that interest payments on outstanding debt grow in line with GNP.

Table 3.3 *Total revenue and expenditure*

£bn at 1985/6 cost terms

	1985/6	1995/6	
Expenditure			
Departmental spending	137	163 ⎫	Constant
			GNP
Net interest	5	6 ⎭	shares
Total	142	169	
Revenue			
North Sea taxes	12	0–7	(projection)
Non-North Sea taxes	120	142	(target)
Financial deficit	10	12	(target)
Total	142	154–161	
Excess spending	0	15–8	

Sources: The overall revenue and GNP projections are derived from work by Savage and Biswas (1986); the individual programme projections use methods described elsewhere (Levitt and Joyce, 1984).

On the basis of these assumptions, a projection is shown in table 3.3 in which departmental spending and non-North Sea revenues both grow in line with GNP up to the mid-1990s. Excess spending in the region of £8–15 billion emerges. If the financing targets are to be achieved, annual expenditure growth needs to be restricted to 0.75–1.4 per cent in real terms compared with 1.6 per cent over the period 1978/9 to 1985/6. This means that *either* departmental spending must be constrained to somewhere in the region of £148–158 billion, *or* the revenue from non-North Sea taxes must be increased by between 5 and 10 per cent, *or* the financial deficit must be virtually doubled, *or* some combination of all these things will be needed.

SPENDING BY PROGRAMME

We now consider some illustrative projections for spending on individual programmes. The estimates for the main social programmes have been built up from an examination of the demographic and other influences on them but the projections for the other programmes are much more subjective in nature and derived from extrapolations of spending beyond the levels shown in table 3.1 after 1989/90. Two illustrative cases are shown in table 3.4 where Case I is more tightly constrained than Case II.

Pay assumptions

Pay is such an important element of public expenditure, representing about one-third of the total, that it is useful to set out at the beginning what we

Table 3.4 *Expenditure projections, 1995–6*

£bn, 1985–6 cost terms

	Case I	Case II
Social programmes		
Education	21	22
Health and personal social services	24	26
Social security	47	54
Total	92	102
Defence	17	20
Agriculture, employment, home office	16	21
Energy, trade and industry, transport, housing	8	18
Other	15	16
Total	148	177

have assumed. Case I assumes that public sector pay rises only in line with general inflation, falling behind the private sector until 1989/90, but then increases in line with private earnings until 1995/6. The cost of real earnings growth after 1989/90 is added to departmental spending totals. Case II assumes that pay rises in line with private earnings over the entire ten-year period, and also that the cost of increased real pay is met in full (Levitt and Joyce, 1987, and Trinder, 1987).

Social programmes: education, health and social security
The projections for education and science were calculated by combining the latest official estimates of future pupil/student numbers with the appropriate unit costs in each educational sector. It was assumed throughout that capital expenditure remains a constant proportion of expenditure on education and that the science budget remains at its present level in cost terms. None of the variants allows for any time lags or extra costs which might be associated with changing the workforce in line with pupil/student numbers; nor is there any allowance for any improvement or extension of provision such as growth in courses on science and technology and the expansion of adult education. Cases I and II assume existing participation rates for those above and below the school leaving age, and that the numbers in higher education are in the middle of the range estimated by the Department of Education and Science. Pay is assumed to remain a constant proportion of the education and science budget up to 1989/90 and thereafter to grow in line with private earnings. In Case II we have allowed for an increase in the participation of the under-fives to 50 per cent and for higher education numbers to be at the top end of the range of recent official projections.

The projections for *health and personal social services* take into account the official demographic projections and our estimates of the costs of health care for different age groups, which are particularly high for the elderly and the very young. We have also allowed for the additional pressures arising from medical advance which the Department of Health and Social Security assumes adds $\frac{1}{2}$ per cent per annum to the hospital and community health services budget. Capital expenditure is assumed to remain a constant proportion of the total programme. Case I makes no allowance for a relative price effect (RPE) on non-pay costs. Case II allows for an RPE of 1 per cent; if productivity grows, this is tantamount to providing an extra volume of resources (for example for non-Thames regions, for expanding the provision of renal dialysis, and so on). Both illustrative cases assume there is no significant change in the real level or composition of health charges and that any efficiency savings are used to improve service provision rather than to reduce expenditure levels.

In the projections for *social security*, demographic trends (especially of the elderly and children), social trends (for example, the growth in the number of one-parent families) and the build-up of benefits under the state earnings-related pension scheme (SERPS) are key elements together with assumptions about benefit uprating and the possible effects of the proposed changes in social security. We assume that the increase in earnings-related benefits reduces expenditure on means-tested benefits by 20 per cent, and that the structural changes in the latter benefits proposed in the 'Reform of Social Security' (Department of Health and Social Security, 1985) are broadly revenue-neutral. For national insurance benefits we have taken the Government Actuary Department's projections to 1993/4 and extended them in line with the build-up of SERPS, and the population projection. The assumption of an unchanged unemployment rate at 13 per cent is the same as the official one which underlies the estimates in table 3.1. Constant take-up is assumed for means-tested benefits; it is estimated that an increase to 100 per cent could add £2.5 billion to expenditure in 1995/6. Case I assumes that benefits are uprated in line with prices and Case II assumes uprating in line with real earnings.

Defence

It is assumed that the recent rapid increases in defence spending will not continue over the next decade. Case I assumes that spending stays flat in cost terms at its planned 1989/90 level, while Case II assumes the adoption of 3 per cent growth in real terms after 1989/90.

Agriculture, employment, home office

Expenditure on each of these programmes has grown considerably since 1978/9 but current plans are for more modest growth or even cuts. Case I assumes that spending represents a balance between 1986 plans and growth since 1978/9; and Case II assumes that spending is higher, growing at the same rate as during 1978/9 to 1985/6, for example, reflecting failure to reform CAP or alternatively increased spending on national food subsidies to hold down prices, higher spending on employment and training and increased spending on law and order as a response to higher levels of recorded crime without improved efficiency and effectiveness.

Other programmes

Recent policy has been for spending on *energy, trade and industry, transport and housing* to be cut, but there are numerous pressures to spend more. Case I extrapolates spending held at the levels planned for 1989/90 announced in the 1986 Autumn Statement, Case II assumes a return to 1978/9 levels.

Other programmes are held at levels planned for 1989/90 as announced in the 1986 Autumn Statement, apart from the effect of pay increases.

The effect of these assumptions is to produce the illustrative expenditure projections for the mid-1990s shown in table 3.4. This is the result of a 'bottom up' approach to expenditure planning. This can now be compared with the 'top down' approach of table 3.3.

OVERALL FINANCING TARGETS AND PROGRAMME SPENDING

Quite fortuitously Case I produces total expenditure equal to the amount permitted by the bottom end of the range of revenue projections, £148 billion. The expenditure policies needed to achieve this involve a widening gap between public service pay and pay elsewhere for the remainder of the present decade, no real uprating in social security benefits, very little scope for increases in the provision of health services other than those implied by demographic change except insofar as efficiency is improved, no real increases in the volume of defence spending following planned cuts to the end of the decade unless efficiency improves, and the maintenance of very tight constraints on the programmes for public housing and industrial support. Total spending on this basis is consistent with holding the share on non-North Sea oil revenues in GNP constant at its 1985/6 level, that is to say with no reduction in average tax rates, if North Sea taxes turn out to be at the bottom of a projected range. If North Sea revenues were at the upper end of the projected range then expenditure could be raised or non-North Sea taxes reduced by £10 billion.

Case II produces total expenditure £20 billion above the upper end of the revenue range implied by the more optimistic North Sea revenue projections; it is also £30 billion above the lower revenue projection and the Case I total. It could be financed by a 20 per cent increase in non-North Sea taxes or by trebling the financial deficit.

A third of the difference between Cases I and II is due to higher spending on social programmes and another third is due to increased support for industrial and housing programmes, with the remaining third scattered over the other programmes. If North Sea revenues were at the upper end of the projected range, then either non-North Sea taxes could be cut by £10 billion or spending could be increased on the social programmes to take them up to Case II levels, or industrial housing spending could be raised to the Case II amount. A different political stance could involve raising spending on defence, agriculture, employment, and home office programmes to Case II levels, leaving a further £2 billion for extra spending on the social, industrial and housing programmes or for tax cuts.

Clearly, Cases I and II do not exhaust all the possibilities. One strategy would be to relax the revenue constraint and to permit total department spending to grow in line with GNP, to £163 billion which, fortuitously, is the mid-point between Cases I and II. A very different approach would be to hold spending flat at 1989/90 planned levels, permitting non-North Sea taxes to be reduced by between £2 and £12 billion. This would imply even tighter constraints on programmes than Case I and the experience of trying to hold spending level in the first half of the 1980s suggests that this would be both unpopular and very difficult to achieve. On the other hand, with the abandonment of the commitment to 3 per cent real growth in defence spending and the cessation of the very rapid rise in social security spending on the unemployed, the difficulties could be easier than those facing government in the first half of the 1980s.

Even if one were to leave aside the very restrictive policy of trying to hold total spending flat in cost terms after 1989/90 it is clear that very tight constraints will be needed on all programmes if North Sea revenues decline by anything within the projected range and if GNP grows no faster than productive potential.

CONCLUSIONS

Policies towards public spending in the first half of the 1980s were intended to hold the amount spent broadly level in cost terms after allowing for general inflation. In practice outturn exceeded plan in virtually every year and plans were revised upwards. A much more substantial upward revision was presented in the 1986 Autumn Statement, which reflected acknowledgement of public concern about public services, especially education, and greater realism about the pressures on programmes. The upward revision in plans nonetheless implied the maintenance of very tight constraints on virtually every programme.

Looking forward to the mid-1990s is clearly a hazardous enterprise, given all the uncertainties bearing on public spending. The analysis above

suggests that if GNP were to grow no faster than productive potential and if
financing targets were adopted which permitted non-North Sea taxes and
budget deficits to grow no faster than GNP, then public spending would need
to grow more slowly than GNP and even more slowly than in the period since
1980, a period when expenditure plans were very tightly constrained.

However, the discussion so far has been entirely in terms of spending on
inputs, whereas the purpose of spending is to achieve outputs in terms of
policy goals. The outlook is such that unless there are substantial increases
in tax revenues it will be difficult to maintain or improve the effectiveness of
public services unless productivity in the public sector rises. If productivity
in that half of government spending represented by goods and services were
to increase by just 1 per cent annually over the period to the mid-1990s it
would yield savings equal to the difference between spending permitted by
the middle of the range tax projections, £153 billion, and the amount of
spending needed to increase service outputs *without* efficiency savings and
transfer payments in line with GNP, £163 billion. The remainder of this
book is devoted to a discussion of efficiency and productivity issues.

Part II

GOVERNMENT OUTPUT AND PRODUCTIVITY

4

THE MEANING OF OUTPUT AND EFFICIENCY IN PUBLIC SERVICES

THE NOTION OF 'OUTPUT' IN PUBLIC SERVICES

The production of public services can be regarded as a process running from the purchase of *inputs*, such as labour, through the *activities* undertaken, namely what public servants *do*, such as read claim forms, perform surgical operations, deliver lectures and patrol streets, to the *social consequences* of those activities, such as poverty relieved, better health, improved knowledge and less crime. The definition of inputs and activities is straightforward in principle, if not always in practice, and the activities can be regarded as giving rise to intermediate measures of output in the form of benefits paid, patients treated, children taught, or criminals caught. The social consequences in terms of better health, knowledge, and reduced crime correspond to the final outputs of policy. They are more problematical not only because influences external to government are important, but also because the kind of output intended is not always clear.

Output in public services is rarely defined precisely. Different citizens and different groups – clients, professionals, managers and politicians – may have different ideas about the intended final output of any given service. Ultimate outputs are often rather nebulous and multi-dimensional: education involves the acquisition and development of various cognitive and non-cognitive skills; health care includes the alleviation of different conditions, which vary in the distress and incapacity they create, and the prevention of further ill-health; the police service maintains public order and deters crimes which vary in their severity. In each case the precise relationship between the intermediate output and final output is far from obvious given the social influences external to government also at work. There is, moreover, no simple way in which either the final or the intermediate outputs of any given service can be aggregated by assigning relative values as weights to the separate elements of the service (for example, the teaching of different subjects, the development of non-cognitive personal and social skills) because these values are not known. So we usually have to rely on imperfect, incomplete proxy indicators of final outputs, such as examination results, the recorded crime rate, the mortality rate and so on. However, some of the studies of health output discussed below attempt to provide measures of final output using a methodology which permits the aggregation of the final outputs of a variety of health activities; it is derived from a psychometric approach to the evaluation of public preferences.

The output of any good or service must often be measured along a number of dimensions, for example the number of payments of social security benefit on time and of the correct amount is a more useful indicator of intermediate output than simply the number of benefits paid. Where goods are sold in a private market, differences in their various aspects, such as in their quality, are normally reflected in their relative prices. In the measurement of government output there is a risk of focussing on single indicators which cover only one aspect of the service provided. This can distort behaviour if it becomes directed towards maximising the one dimensional indicator to the neglect of everything else. Nove (1961) has given numerous examples of Soviet indicators with these flaws, for example the one ton nail which incorporated a factory's entire monthly nail output target defined in terms of weight alone, the window glass or roofing material which was too thin to use, because the output target was set in terms of square metres, the cloth which was too narrow because the output target was set in terms of its length, the target for the unloading of bricks for a transport undertaking where the bricks were unloaded so quickly that many of them broke. In a number of instances noted below these problems may occur in measures of output being developed in Britain because of ambiguities in their interpretation and lack of clear weights to attach to the various dimensions of output (such as timeliness and accuracy in benefit payments).

WHY MEASURE OUTPUT?

Put at its simplest, an efficient allocation of resources is one where the greatest possible output is obtained from the available resources, or given output is produced with least resource input. It is impossible to say whether the use of resources is more efficient in one situation than in another if we have no means of comparing their outputs and only have information on costs. Thus the need to have information about output has its roots in well-established microeconomic principles.

In the particular case of public expenditure, information about output is needed in order to evaluate the extent to which the spending is achieving its aim. The mere existence of spending, provided in response to expressions of social concern, is no guarantee that government is effectively achieving the social objectives which it quotes to justify the expenditure. Likewise, information on output is needed to compare the extent to which goals are being met in one year by comparison with another, or in one local (education, health, or police) authority compared with another. In order to plan expenditure, staff and other resources, information is needed about intended or expected levels of output. The managers of expenditure programmes need information on output in order to evaluate their own performance in meeting the objectives they face, to evaluate the relative performance of their subordinate management units, to develop measures of their efficiency over time, to plan and budget their resources, and to understand, if expenditure departs from that planned, whether this is due to a difference from expected levels of output or costs or productivity.

Therefore, information on output is needed on the one hand by voters, parliament, and the external auditors of government (such as the National Audit Office) to evaluate the performance of government and, on the other, by government itself to plan and manage its resources and to assess its own performance. All this seems self-evident and uncontroversial. But in practice information about government output and performance in attaining policy goals has rarely been available, either to the public at large or within government itself. One reason for this has been that goverments are often loathe to state their aims with sufficient precision and in a form which permits the quantitative assessment of their output and perform-ance. Another is that officials and lobbies outside government often tend to assess government performance in areas of social, industrial or military concern almost exclusively in terms of the resources made available, that is, inputs rather than outputs.

PRODUCTIVITY

Increases in productivity require that the volume of output should rise faster than the volume of input. If we measure the volume of output in terms of input volumes, such as the number of employees in the public service, logically there can be *no* measured increase in productivity. This statistical consequence of national accounting conventions is often mistakenly taken as confirmation of Baumol's (1967) hypothesis of zero productivity growth, and of the inefficiency of government asserted to exist by those like Niskanen (1971) who emphasise the inertia of the bureaucracy and its perversion of electors' preferences.

Government spending departments and the interest groups who lobby for public spending on particular services have also supported the view that government productivity growth is low and cannot be improved, in order to justify bids for higher spending. We have noted in Chapter 3 above that in the case of several public expenditure programmes, such as education, health, law and order, and defence, recent policy has been to emphasise the scope for, and the need to achieve, increases in efficiency. Several of the pressure groups associated with these programmes (whether as consumers or suppliers of manpower or equipment) have expressed scepticism about what productivity improvements can and will be achieved. To the extent that such groups are in a position to influence the outcome, then of course these pessimistic prophesies might be self-fulfilling.

IMPROVED MEASURES OF GOVERNMENT OUTPUT

The development of measures of output is an essential element in recent efforts to improve the management of government services in the United Kingdom in recent years. Within government itself, these efforts include: the Financial Management Initiative (FMI), launched in September 1982 with the publication of *Efficiency and Effectiveness in the Civil Service(Cmnd 8616)*, which emphasised the need for clear objectives and information about costs and performance; 'efficiency scrutinies' of a wide variety of activities within several departments; reviews of administrative running costs, personnel policy, the use of accommodation and of the procurement of materials and services across several departments; the strengthening and extension of investment appraisal. In the case of local authority services the Audit Commission was established in 1982 to review costs, efficiency and effectiveness and its work has included comparisons of performance across local authorities. The external scrutiny of government has been strengthened by the replacement, in 1983, of the Exchequer and Audit Department by the National Audit Office, which is responsible to Parliament, and which has emphasised the need to develop more and better measures of output and performance, for example in its reports *The Financial Management Initiative* (1986) and *Financial Reporting to Parliament* (1986). The National Audit Office acknowledged that measures of output and performance were being developed, although the pace and extent of progress varies across departments; however it accepted that formidable difficulties are often present and it does not propose any measures of its own.

In fact it is possible to measure what *most* public servants do, in terms of the intermediate outputs they produce. The vast majority are involved in such activities as assessing and collecting taxes, paying social security benefits, providing support services to the armed forces, providing medical treatments and lessons, patrolling the streets to deter crime, and so on. Greater difficulties arise when we want to measure the 'final' outputs of such processes or activities.

In the next four chapters we consider the problems of measuring government output and productivity, and the available evidence on productivity growth over time. The efficiency with which resources are used, and the extent of variations in efficiency within government among different management units providing similar services, are discussed in Part III.

5

GOVERNMENT OUTPUT AND PRODUCTIVITY IN THE NATIONAL INCOME ACCOUNTS

General government expenditure on goods and services in the United Kingdom is comparable in size to the whole of manufacturing output and employment in government is very little lower than that in manufacturing. But, whereas a considerable effort is devoted to measuring changes in the real output of manufacturing, very little is done to measure changes in government output. The paucity of measures of the real output of government partly reflects genuine conceptual and empirical problems, but it also reflects the low priority hitherto attached to improved measurement. Although interest in government output is now greater than it has been in countries such as the United Kingdom and the United States, official statistical resources have been tightly constrained, and in the United States until recently it has been felt to be more profitable to devote those scarce resources to matters which raise fewer problems.

However, present accounting conventions can create a misleading impression of government efficiency and they tend to exaggerate the resource requirements of several expenditure programmes, as noted in Chapter 2. Also, as several other chapters indicate, much more could be done in practice to improve the measurement of real changes in government output.

Below we first consider existing conventions and their purpose; then an earlier attempt by the United Kingdom to measure government output and the reasons for the change to present conventions are discussed; next we present some estimates of changes in real output in the education and health services on alternative conventions; finally we consider the implications of these estimates and the analyses of performance in public administration in defence procurement, and in the United States federal productivity measurement system, for national income accounting.

A possible source of misunderstanding arising from differences in terminology needs to be noted. Earlier chapters on the growth of public spending have used the description 'public spending in real terms' in the sense used by recent United Kingdom Public Expenditure White Papers, that is, money expenditure deflated by the GDP price index. However, the national accounting literature, in many countries and over many decades, has used the concept of 'real product' to mean a measure where inputs and outputs are deflated by their *own* price indices to arrive at volume measures. The term 'real product' is used in the latter sense in this chapter.

PRESENT CONVENTIONS

The traditional purposes of national income accounting include the measurement of changes in the aggregate value of national output (in money terms and in volume terms at constant prices), the provision of a basis for economic forecasting and for the economic analyses of the behaviour of different sectors of the economy on a consistent basis. A considerable literature exists on the amplification of these topics (see Hill, 1971, Searle and Waite, 1980, Mark, 1980, Hagen and Budd, 1958, Jaszi, 1958, and Kendrick, 1958), but one theme running through this literature and most clearly expressed twenty years ago is 'The treatment of government services in the accounts is less satisfactory . . . than that of any other component of gross national product' (Hagen and Budd, 1958). This statement remains largely true today, although the treatment of financial services (another sector of considerable importance) also leaves immense scope for improvement.

One important use to which national accounts estimates of real product are sometimes put is to examine trends in productivity in terms of changes in the ratio of the volume of output at constant prices to changes in the volume of inputs at constant prices.

Whereas several hundred statistical measures of the volume of manufacturing output are used to derive changes in real manufacturing output, national accounting practice is to measure output movements in the general government sector very largely by changes in the numbers employed (Hill, 1979); it follows that by convention there is no increase in productivity. To the extent that the pay of public servants and the costs of other inputs tend to move in line with pay and prices in the rest of the economy (where productivity grows), the relative cost of government services will tend to rise. This tendency, the relative price effect, sometimes known as Baumol's disease, was discussed in Chapter 1. It has, according to Baumol, pessimistic implications for financing public services (and the arts) where, he argued, their labour-intensive nature made productivity increases difficult (Baumol, 1967). But the labour-intensive nature of public services, as with many private services, is a red herring: significant productivity improvements are possible in public services and have been achieved. As for the accounting conventions, they are sometimes defended on the grounds that the nature of the final output (for example, health and education) is hard to define and measure, especially when it is not sold, and in any event the government is a consumer not a producer.

This argument seems to assume that constant price GDP is meant to be an indicator of national economic welfare or consumer satisfaction. It is not. It is more limited in scope and is intended to record, as far as possible, the growth of the real volume of production.[1] Although government services are in a sense partially intermediate products, or perhaps inputs with respect to final consumer citizen satisfaction which we cannot always precisely define, the same is often true of private production as Jaszi (1958) emphasised: expenditure on private security services is not an end in itself; a meal in an expensive restaurant might be an input to promote a sale to a prospective client, to meet a nutritional need, or a form of entertainment. Nor does it always follow that additional private spending is associated with increased consumer satisfaction: increased spending on private medicine might be attributable to an increase in ill-health or in the incidence of a shameful disease for which private treatment is sought.

Although the absence of a price does not determine the measurability, in physical units, of changes in the volume of production, a price needs to be imputed if the good is to be included in the GDP – otherwise it would be deemed to be of no value; real changes in GDP are not the same as physical changes in production: the production of effluent, the number of robberies, are excluded. Information about prices is required in order to aggregate together volume indicators for more than one product. In the absence of actual market prices for most general government services a price has to be imputed, on the basis of input costs. This procedure implicitly assumes that, in some sense, the marginal value of such services to consumers, society at large or taxpayers is equated to their marginal cost by a rational, well-informed, efficient government. Other possibilities exist, for example, where analogous private alternatives are available of comparable quality their prices could be used. Leaving the issue of price and value aside, the major flaw in measuring real output by reference to input prices and volumes is that there is no reason in principle why input and output volumes should change equally: unless there really are no productivity increases, and constant returns exist, in the production of government services. In practice these are merely assumptions. Further, the implicit assumption of a rational well-informed government, which strives to minimise costs of production and to equate marginal values with marginal costs, requires that it knows the volumes of services it is producing and their values. However, existing national accounts conventions largely eschew any attempt at such measurement, although most public servants do things which can be measured, one way or another, in volume terms: they collect taxes, pay social security benefits, repair military equipment, feed troops, teach children, extract teeth, treat the sick, and so on.

A possible justification for present conventions is the argument that government is merely a consumer of goods and services, hence the description of non-transfer general government expenditure as final consumption in some of the national accounts tables. However, the government is also treated as a producer in the sectoral income and output tables. In short, the boundary which distinguishes between production and consumption is not consistently drawn for government services.

Most of what public servants *do* can be measured. Intermediate output can be measured with reference to the number of children taught, patients treated, benefits paid, and so on. But a number of problems arise. If we define output on the basis of some index which we might broadly call quality (for example, examination pass rates in the case of education), a simple approach in terms of the throughput of pupils, patient numbers and so on is insufficient. Instead, we might make an assumption about the relationship between the ratio of teachers to pupils or doctors to patients on the one hand, and the index of quality on the other. This was the general approach behind the United Kingdom practice in the 1950s (see below). It has been advocated more recently by some writers (Marris, 1983 and Hill, 1979) but the relationship between staffing ratios and quality may not be a simple one. We need to take account of the contribution of external (socio-economic) factors as well.

These considerations might imply that unless we can *estimate* the relationship between staffing ratios and quality (which needs to be carefully defined) it is better to ignore it. This could also be justified on the grounds that considerations of quality come close to defining output not in terms of what public servants do but with respect to ultimate consequences, which lies beyond the scope of national accounting anyway. On the other hand, quality is a problem in the measurement of much private sector output as well as government services and the existence of problems is not sufficient reason to ignore it.

A related problem concerns changes in the specification of equipment especially in the defence and health programmes. The measurement of the output of such goods in terms of their input costs alone will exaggerate cost increases associated with equipment of superior performance. Many years ago Kendrick (1958) proposed that this problem might be overcome by the construction of 'pseudo prices'. Specifications for the products in question would be carefully spelt out and over a period of years contractors invited to submit tenders for their manufacture, which need not in fact take place. This would distinguish cost increases for equipment of a given specification from increases associated with specification changes. (It is unlikely, however, that manufacturers would make a serious attempt to participate in the costly work involved in quoting 'pseudo prices' for hypothetical equipment.) The cardinal points system recently adopted for United Kingdom defence procurement is another attempt to relate prices more clearly to specification. Where a specification change occurs and the identifiable cost of that change is accepted by a spending department acting under a budget constraint (and provided that competition among producers exists) it can be deemed to represent increased output.

Another problem concerns double-counting and aggregation. In a manufacturing process involving several stages (for example smelting iron ore, rolling steel sheets, pressing the sheets into car body panels, casting engine blocks, assembling and wiring a complete car) the value-added at each stage can be summed to arrive at the value-added of the motor industry. In addition the industry's productivity can be established by weighting the productivity of each stage by its value-added. In the case of a government service involving several processes (for example reading claim forms; typing, distributing and filing responses; issuing payment cheques or payment books; checking accuracy, and so on) no measures of value-added are available at each stage. In the case of the United States federal productivity measurement system, for example no netting-off of services consumed within each agency, to avoid double counting, is undertaken. The aggregate productivity of each agency is arrived at by weighting the component productivity indicators for each sub-function within an agency by their relative man-years of labour input. The result is a weighted average measure of productivity, not a true measure of productivity for a given agency or government as a whole. However, in principle it might be possible to weight the contributions at each stage (and for each agency) on the basis of their relative costs in some base period in order to construct productivity measures over time. Another possibility, within an agency, would be to establish the weights to attach to each stage or process by estimating a production function (a regression equation which explains movements in a final output indicator in terms of indicators of each input, where the coefficients estimated for each input are then used as weights).

Clearly numerous problems exist. They are not all unique to government. To a greater or lesser degree they could be overcome. However, present conventions have the merit of being unambiguous: they simply count inputs.

UNITED KINGDOM ATTEMPTS TO MEASURE GOVERNMENT OUTPUT

There was a time when the United Kingdom national accounts did attempt to measure the physical volume of government output, despite all the problems '. . . even a crude measure of output is assumed to be preferable to an index based on total cost, at constant prices, of the factors of production . . . the latter method is only used .. . e.g. in public administration, where it is difficult to conceive of any sensible measure of service rendered' (Central Statistical Office, 1956). The administration of national insurance was measured by the numbers insured and receiving benefits, hospital services by numbers of staff and patients, education by pupils and teachers, that is, a mixture of input and 'output' indicators very much along the lines proposed recently (by authors who do not refer to the earlier work) (Marris, 1983).

The series based on this approach in the 1950s and early 1960s were heavily criticised. The relative weights for the various indicators used, such as teachers and pupils, were said to be arbitrary. Different, equally plausible, weights gave different results. Some of the indicators had a very indirect link with the outputs they were meant to reflect and the important issue of quality changes was troublesome. Half the total weight for schools was, arbitrarily, assigned to teachers, so that a reduction in pupil–teacher ratios was shared between reduced productivity and presumed higher quality. The same applied with the patient–doctor ratio. The new system of public expenditure planning introduced in the mid-1960s was based on *input* volumes in relation to available national resources, at constant prices. It was confusing, as well as politically tendentious, to have two series, particularly as government sought to reduce pupil–teacher and patient–doctor ratios. For all these reasons the old approach was scrapped, and the present conventions were adopted.

EDUCATION AND HEALTH

A subsequent analysis by Beales (1967) measured output under the old and new conventions (table 5.1). The new indicators allowed departments to claim faster increases in output (as their manpower increased relative to their client groups). Beales said that would not always necessarily be the case.

We have used the old weights and, where still available, the old indicators to recalculate education and health output for 1978–83. However, it is clearly inappropriate to use 1950s weights to examine output three decades later and some of the indicators are no longer appropriate even where they are still available, so we have also used revised weights and indicators. Our results, including a comparison with expenditure in the Blue Book at 1980 prices, are in table 5.2.

In the case of education, the old indicators included pupil or student numbers for the various education sectors and, in the case of schools, teacher numbers; teachers had the same weight as pupils; the origin of all the weights is obscure. The case for including a weight for teachers is that

Table 5.1 *Education and health output, 1958–63*

	Education		Health	
	Old indicators	Present conventions	Old indicators	Present conventions
1958	100.0	100.0	100.0	100.0
1963	113.5	119.4	106.2	109.2

Source: Beales (1967).

Table 5.2 *Education and health output, 1978–83*

Method		1978–83 % change
Local authority education output		
Original (1956) national accounts indicators and weights A		−8.8
Revised weights A		−5.1
B		−7.0
Blue Book expenditure at 1980 prices[a]		0.5
NHS output		
Original (1956) national accounts and weights C		3.6
Indicators and weights	D	9.0
Revised indicators and weights	C	2.0
	D	9.5
Blue Book expenditure at 1980 prices[a]		8.1

Source: United Kingdom National Accounts, 1984 and 1985 editions, Central Statistical Office.
Note: Variant A assigns equal weights to pupils and teachers; variant B assigns zero weights to teachers; variant C uses average occupied beds; variant D uses in-patient cases.
[a] That is, final consumption.

the number of pupils per teacher is intended to provide an approximate indicator of quality. Fewer pupils per teacher involves better education, therefore the total weight for schools in output should be split between teachers and pupils. The precise relationship between the pupil–teacher ratio and education quality is a matter of debate. We illustrate the effect of using equal weights and, in our revised indicator, the effect of ignoring the quality argument (that is, no weight for teachers). The old output approach included universities but, because existing Blue Book figures for education spending at constant prices refer to local authority spending, to permit a comparison with the Blue Book we have dropped universities. Our revised weights refer to the share of each education sector in local authority education expenditure in 1980/1; the weights for nursery, primary and special schools are lower, and the weight for further education higher, than in the 1956 weights. Whereas the Blue Book shows a modest rise in education spending at 1980 prices, our activity-based output series show a fall – especially if we exclude teachers – reflecting falling school rolls. The Blue Book series will reflect the increasing seniority and qualifications of the teacher stock which score as additional output.

Ideally, we would like to find some objective basis for the relative weights attached to teachers and to pupils. The number of pupils measures the throughput of the service, but the ratio of teachers to pupils affects its quality. So we really need to know the relationship between the quality of education and that ratio. Needless to say this is a controversial issue. One way of resolving it would be by reference to the kind of cross-section studies described in Chapter 10. There we try to estimate the effect of extra teaching staff on examination performance. As it happens, the results we present there would support variant A, rather than variant B. The quality of education, it seems, rises with the staff to pupil ratio, but not in proportion.

Turning to health spending, a mixture of indirect indicators of output (in-patient beds, out-patient attendances, sight tests, dental treatments) and inputs (hospital staff, number of general practitioners) were used in the 1950s. Some indicators are no longer relevant (for example, those dealing with mental illness and the community health service) especially as a result of national health service reorganisation, and we have substituted new indicators while, as far as possible, retaining the old weights for the health services in question. In this way we have recalculated health service output 1978–83 using the old approach. However, the source of the original weights is obscure and we have also calculated revised weights, on the basis of each service's share in 1980/1 health expenditure. To complete the revision we have also incorporated additional indicators where the old indicators were inadequate, for example, for the community health service, where the old approach ignored home nursing. As in the case of education a problem arises over the treatment of staff costs. On an expenditure share basis hospital staff costs would receive a very high weight, which is inappropriate to an attempt to measure output rather than input. As a compromise, the total hospital in-patient weight represents the share of hospital in-patient costs in health spending, and the weight is divided equally between full-time equivalent staff numbers and in-patient numbers. An important problem concerns the appropriate indicator for hospital patients. In the 1950s the number of occupied hospital beds was used as the indicator of activity or output, but the number of cases seems to reflect output more closely (although there is the problem of readmissions, see Chapter 11). As table 5.1 shows, output in terms of cases has risen more rapidly than inputs (so productivity has grown), although the opposite is true if we retain the beds approach.

This attempt to apply the 1950s conventions to recent data shows up their weaknesses and ambiguity. Different patterns of weights give very different results. For example, does it make most sense to give equal weights to teachers and pupils? Do expenditure shares in the base year, which reflect *costs*, adequately reflect social *values* for different health services? One can conceive many other weighting systems. On the other hand the existing conventions tell us almost nothing about output in terms of what public servants do. They ignore the whole problem of productivity, and create the impression, via the government relative price effect, that public services are relatively inefficient irrespective of whether they are or not in reality.

Evidence for the growth of productivity in public administration is described below in Chapter 6, where output is defined in terms of the processing of tax and benefit payments. The national accounts simply take expenditure on inputs, especially employment, as the basis for measuring changes in real output and no productivity growth is possible with such conventions. This is despite the possibility of even more refined official measurement than that presented in this book. Government administration is not unique in the paucity of output or productivity measurement in the national income accounts: private financial services are an analogous area. Banks and insurance companies use hundreds, or even thousands, of volume activity measures for internal productivity measurement but the national accounts measure insurance output solely in terms of the deflated value of premium income. For banks a low weight is attached to the number of transactions but the main output indicators refer to the deflated value of financial transactions and to the number of employees.

However, the admittedly very aggregative evidence of Chapter 6 suggests annual productivity growth for public administration (and retail banking) in the region of $2\frac{1}{2}$ per cent, on the basis of staff–client ratios. If the real output of public administration were reckoned in terms of the number of transactions, or clients, or some weighted average of all the clerical and other processes involved, it would be a relatively straightforward job to alter the national accounts. The rationale is that the public servants involved are providing a cash handling and executive service of a kind which can be measured. The question of quality arises. How would changes in error rates or delays in payment be handled? The value of errors in terms of the aggregate sum of cash wrongly collected or paid could be used to abate or raise output (for example increased errors equal to 1 per cent of the total would reduce real output by 1 per cent). Changes in timeliness are no problem: faster or slower payments directly alter the number of transactions anyway so the indicator used to measure the volume of output needs no adjustment.

Defence spending can be divided into three broad categories: support services (payroll maintenance, catering, vehicle repair, and so on), equipment manufacture and procurement, and military training or operations by the armed forces. Support services in the United Kingdom account for around one-third of the civil service. The services in question are probably those with the closest analogues to private production. Information about activities and costs is sparse in the public domain and,

the Comptroller General has reported, often for internal purposes also
(National Audit Office, 1984). But in principle a good deal of quantification of output and productivity is possible: over time, and for comparisons
between official establishments performing similar functions, and with
private analogues.

Turning to equipment manufacture and procurement, amounting to
almost half the defence budget, and of the same order of magnitude of the
entire gross domestic capital formation of manufacturing industry, volume
changes are derived by deflating cash spending by indices of input prices of
manufactures. This procedure makes no allowance for any increase in the
volume of equipment output permitted by the productivity growth of
manufactures, nor for increases in the output of service from the equipment
itself when performance improves as a result of higher specifications. On the
other hand the convention exaggerates the increase in the price of defence
equipment if by price we refer to goods of constant quality.

When contracts were preponderantly awarded on a cost-plus basis in
conditions of zero, or very limited, competition, the convention of scoring
zero productivity improvements in equipment manufacture probably
reflected reality (see Chapter 8). With greater competition and more fixed
price contracts, that situation should change, so that the use of contractors'
input prices to deflate cash expenditure on equipment will understate the
volume of equipment. We need direct measures of equipment volume to
cope with this problem, and with the separate issue of measuring the
increased output from equipment of superior performance. The way ahead
is to specify given characteristics of equipment, to measure changes in the
volume of such equipment wherever possible *or*, if it were practical, to adopt
Kendrick's 'psuedo price' approach when equipment of superior performance is introduced. That is, the difference between the price which
manufacturers would charge to produce the older (replaced) equipment
and the price of the higher specification goods would be used to measure
changes in output associated with new specifications; existing conventions
treat the price difference misleadingly as a cost increase. The new cardinal
points system for specifying the performance of defence equipment and for
establishing contract prices could be adapted to this purpose.

THE UNITED STATES FEDERAL PRODUCTIVITY MEASUREMENT SYSTEM

The American national accounts ignore the federal productivity measurement system, which involves over 3,000 indicators of intermediate output,
collected by the Bureau of Labor Statistics, and which is described more
fully in Chapter 7. Professional responsibility for the United States national
accounts rests with the Bureau of Economic Analysis at the Department of

Commerce. The Bureau's views were made available at a conference organised by the National Bureau of Economic Research in 1977. They do not seem to have changed since, and the debate continues (Searle and Waite, 1980).

The United States accountants recognise that a choice needs to be made over the definition of government output in terms of whether it involves direct measures of what government does or the evaluation of what it ultimately achieves in terms of policy goals. Considering whether the federal measurement system should be used in the national accounts 'Our answer is *no* if government output in the national accounts is viewed as . . . the ultimate public goods and services which government provides such as national security, education . . . *Maybe* if one views government output more variously . . . as processes, such as passports issued. . . .' (Searle and Waite, 1980). They accept that for the private sector ultimate consequences or welfare effects are ignored anyway. 'In the private sector, changes in output are measured in terms of physical units and not in terms of consequences, although consequences are a factor in determining relative values . . . in the market place.' They had accepted, therefore, that the difficulty of defining, measuring and valuing the ultimate, consequential output of government need *not* be decisive. However, more recently, the difficulty of defining and quantifying output in terms of final objective such as national defence, educational performance and so on seems to have re-emerged as a major hurdle.[2]

The question also arises whether the system is adequate for a more limited treatment of government in the national accounts, where existing conventional measures would be adjusted by the Bureau of Labor Statistics productivity series without claiming that *ultimate* outputs were being measured. The Bureau's answer is still 'no', or at any rate 'not yet'. On the other hand the treatment of government as a consumer, in the national accounts, whereby no productivity relationship arises anyway, does imply a degree of inconsistency in the approach to possible changes in accounting conventions.

The Bureau's view appears to be that although there is considerable merit in attempts to measure the productivity of specific functions in particular agencies or services, serious problems arise in attempting to derive an indicator for the whole of general government. Coverage is incomplete (about 55 per cent overall) and patchy even within agencies. There is said to be a serious risk of double counting because intermediate services are aggregated together with final outputs into which they are fed even within the same agency and, *a fortiori*, over government as a whole. The quality of the data supplied by agencies is suspect. If the BLS series were adopted, revisions to historical series could be required and in any event their incorporation would place additional burdens on professional resources which are under pressure from tight budgetary and manpower constraints. If these constraints were relaxed there are other issues to which additional resources could be profitably devoted which raise fewer serious conceptual problems.

All the officials concerned seem to accept that the deficiencies in the data could be reduced with more resources and greater priority for more accurate and more comprehensive measurement. (For example, adjustments for coverage could be made and a separation between intermediate outputs within agencies and agency final outputs could permit aggregation of only the latter.) Problems of double counting, allowance for quality changes, and defects in the validity of the basic data are all amenable to remedy. In the meantime, the question boils down to one of choosing the lesser evil: is the convention of ignoring productivity increases, despite, albeit imperfect, evidence of their existence, preferable to one of making some allowance for them? For the foreseeable future the zero option looks likely to remain in force. However, it is an intention of the current Federal productivity initiative that before too long the increased quantity and quality of productivity data will be incorporated in the national accounts, particularly as the BLS productivity trends look quite reasonable.

CONCLUSIONS

We have shown some examples of output measurement conventions for education, health, and public administration. Results for education and health have been compared with those obtainable under 1956 conventions and under present, input-based, conventions. In the case of education, where throughput in the form of pupils has fallen, output fell on the basis of activity data whereas the national accounts show a slight increase. Cross-section comparisons of the contribution of teaching expenditure to examination performance (on the lines of Chapter 10) might provide the basis of a less arbitrary treatment of the relative weights to attach to pupil numbers and teaching inputs if a quality-adjusted output approach were adopted. For health, the comparison depends on whether the output indicator includes in-patient beds or cases: in the former instance output grew more slowly than the national accounts constant price series, whereas cases show faster output growth than the national accounts. The comparison of public administration with analogous private financial services shows a relatively favourable picture for the public services illustrated. The emphasis on better output measurement for internal management purposes in public administration (and in financial services) is providing better indicators of output and productivity. The discussion of the American federal productivity measurement system shows what might be done on a comprehensive scale in other countries; the flaws in that system are largely amenable to improvement, with sufficient priority and resources. The discussion of defence support services and of equipment also suggests that much more quantification of output (and more realistic price deflators) is desirable than has been common.

Given the considerable emphasis on improving productivity in the public sector, and the existence of a growing body of evidence that productivity is improving, the resolution with which the national accounts appear to affirm the absence of productivity growth in government looks increasingly anachronistic.

6

PRODUCTIVITY IN UNITED KINGDOM PUBLIC
ADMINISTRATION AND LARGE FIRMS

In September 1982 the government launched a 'Financial Management Initiative' (Treasury and Civil Service Committee, 1982). Its central theme was the promotion of a system and a culture in which managers, at all levels, would have clear objectives and information about their performance towards achieving those objectives, and clear responsibility for ensuring value for money from the resources they directly control and programmes upon which they advise. Action plans were prepared for departments and progress reports have appeared (HM Treasury, 1983, and Public Finance Foundation, 1985). The initial emphasis in the initiative was on running costs, where staff costs are the largest element. Associated developments included the wider application of investment appraisal.

This chapter makes some comparisons in the approach to measuring productivity in public administration with that of a number of private sector financial service organisations. In the public sector it concentrates on the running costs of departments which are broadly representative of government executive operations, employ a large number of people and have private sector analogues. These departments are involved in the payment of benefits, the collection of revenue, and employment services. Together they employ around 190,000 officials, or 40 per cent of the non-industrial civil service.[1] The private sector organisations which have been examined include five financial institutions and the non-production, non-sales, work of a further three large companies.

The clear impression to emerge from discussions with private firms is one of variety in the approaches adopted and wide variations in the rigour with which productivity and performance are measured and pursued. This is hardly surprising, given the mixed performance of the private sector. Best practice within government probably compares favourably with much practice outside; on the other hand, best professional practice in general, a hazy concept admittedly, is probably rather rare in both sectors.

Insofar as workforce complements and productivity measurement for large clerical operations are concerned, systems such as those operated by the Departments of Employment and Health and Social Security have many features in common with those reported by firms. On the other hand, the extent of continuous precise work measurement and costing in some firms goes well beyond that in government. The results of such analyses are regarded as crucial in setting workforce complements, a major element in budgets and in setting well-informed targets for improvements in productivity and expenses. They are also used in monthly (or even weekly) monitoring and control, and in making detailed comparisons between management units, regions and, where possible, competitors.

Private firms, like departments, have struggled with the problem of assessing the output of managers and professional services outside the sales and production areas: the problems are not unique to the Civil Service. Some firms have not made much progress, others rely on internal charging arrangements; others have elaborate activity analysis and time budgeting systems; and others use peer reviews. All the firms in the enquiry agreed that at the end of the day subjective judgement is important, but some have gone further than others – and government departments – in reducing the area where judgement alone applies.

Some firms seem to have much greater expectations that their top management are familiar with the details of the operations they manage than has been usual in parts of the Civil Service in the past. Most firms visited expected their employees to share the benefit of productivity improvements; some linked senior management pay to the movement in their subordinates' pay. There is no link between productivity and pay in the Civil Service; senior management pay and pay for the rest are determined by different arrangements.

Precise productivity and cost comparisons over time and between branches, requiring detailed time and cost analyses for very many activities, are rare in government departments but a number of firms have invested heavily in the systems and technologies. In a number of companies the systems have been established by firm top management within two to three years. Government departments, which do not have profit as a yardstick, have a greater need for disaggregated information. They need moreover, better data on, and explanations of, *aggregate* measures of performance than they have at present, as the building blocks are not there to permit other than very crude measures. Aggregate measures require the weighting together of separate output volume indicators within a department, such as those relating to the different taxes collected or the different benefits paid, perhaps using their relative costs in a base period. However the relative weights to be attached to, say, the timeliness and accuracy of benefit payments require political judgement. Nevertheless, the staff complementing systems operated by the Departments of Employment and Health and Social Security have a lot in common with those found in some insurance companies; and their approach to reporting the volume and value of work done, and to measures of timeliness and accuracy, although not as detailed as in some firms, compares favourably with much outside practice. The Inland Revenue is improving the data on the use of staff time; this, together with computerisation of the main clerical operations, will permit local productivity comparisons by the end of the decade.

Firms, like departments, vary in the extent to which internal 'league tables' of relative performance are prepared and circulated; the conflict between the possible incentive effect and the demoralising effect of such comparisons seems common to both sectors.[2] However, a number of firms see the circulation of internal comparisons as an essential feature of an open style of management.[3] In some firms the data-processing and systems departments are given precise targets for improving the performance of the rest of the company. In government such branches are heavily involved in installing new systems but this may be a once-for-all reform. It is not so clear that they have a commitment to continuing improvement of the system and its software at a targeted rate (of time or cost) over the longer term. Investment appraisal, the monitoring of projects during implementation, and *ex post* evaluation are part of the same disciplined approach in some firms; in government getting an appraisal done before the event is the main concern and *ex post* evaluation is rare. One reason given for the rarity of *ex post* evaluation is that 'the external environment has changed'. Few firms in the private sector said that they found this an acceptable argument: the effects of such changes have to be quantified. At least one firm expects, as a matter of course, that its managers will quantify in monthly reports the effects of changes in the external environment, as well as new data, on costs and output. A number of firms use internal charging arrangements, whereby consumers of services are expected to bargain with their internal suppliers: in some cases they are free to go outside the firm even when internal services are available. Such an approach has been rare in government, although charging is now the norm for services provided by central agencies, such as office accommodation, publicity and stationery, and is growing for computer services. Possibly the biggest difference is that at least some private firms see change as a way of life, whereas in government it is usual to expect *ad hoc* changes to be digested before new norms are established.

THE PRIVATE FIRMS

The firms examined included two banks, four insurance companies, one retail and manufacturing firm, one United States-owned manufacturing company, and one conglomerate company. The emphasis was on the work of staff not involved in production or sales (Levitt, 1985).

Most of the firms had clear targets, laid down by the chief executive, as to sales and profits, staff numbers and running costs. The running cost target acts as a cash limit. Corporate plans, when translated into detailed plans for each part of the firm, set output targets and cash limits for operating divisions and central head office support divisions. Most firms have formal staff complementing systems, sometimes involving detailed periodic work measurement analysis for their large clerical operations. In one large financial institution up to 20,000 elements of work, and in another 6,000, are measured and costed in terms of staff time and in cash, then aggregated by office, area, and the type of business involved. In some cases the base complement was settled several years ago as a result of work measurement which has not been repeated, for industrial relations reasons; actual complement each year is settled on the basis of forecast workload and productivity growth since the base year. In some companies very detailed continuous work measurement is undertaken with time spent on specified tasks precisely recorded, although this need not involve many staff in operating the system. Most firms seem to have a planning system which is built up by successive bids and scrutinies up the hierarchy. These staff complementing systems often involve setting standards of labour input for specific tasks. One firm has a system by which all the work of all the staff is broken down into activities defined according to a company-wide system. This permits comparisons across departments and over time, notwithstanding the fact that different parts of the firm do different things which involve different mixes of activities. The others have a broadly similar approach for their civil service-like operations.

Most of the firms were managed on the basis of a mix of profit centres and cost centres (the latter being, for example, the top management group as a whole and various central services). They varied in the extent to which internal charging was practised. Two firms had encouraged operating divisions to shop around outside for services available from internal sources and the internal service groups had been encouraged to offer their wares outside; in one case this seemed to threaten corporate cohesiveness but another found it worked well.

The assessment of the output and productivity of different sorts of staff had some common elements, for routine clerical operations, but varied for supervisory and professional groups. All firms said that there were limits to what quantification could contribute in the assessment of management performance. Where work done can be counted this seems to be commonly done, but there are variations in the extent to which timeliness and accuracy are continously monitored; in some important instances clerical operations also involve judgements, which are more subjectively assessed. Some firms simply assume that the output and productivity of supervisory and professional groups moves proportionately with the output and productivity of the staff where measurement is practised. Others make an *ex ante* estimate of the time to be spent on specified tasks, actual time is monitored and the quality of the work is assessed subjectively. In the case of profit centre managers, financial indicators of performance are used. One firm said policy is to reduce as far as possible the scope where judgement is needed, for all levels of management assessment. The same firm outperforms its United States parent – itself widely believed to be one of the best-managed firms in the United States.

Modern management science stresses the role of peer group assessment. A number of firms have periodic meetings of managers doing similar things with a view to debating performance but one firm expected its top managers to review one another's performance critically at monthly meetings. Another said, 'The fact that the firm is involved in providing a financial service makes little difference: a lot of the work can be analysed in the same way as if we were building cars'. Another firm expects its directors and top managers to be thoroughly familiar with all the operations of the company; it is policy for each board member to make a site visit every week; as in some other firms, the job appraisal review for each manager lasts up to half a day at least once a year and includes a detailed discussion of the performance of his subordinates. Another firm has biennial opinion surveys of managers by their subordinates.

Several firms commented on regional variations in output and productivity. Some circulate periodic comparisons within the firm. Most of the firms have regular monthly monitoring of performance and costs against plan and previous periods. In two firms managers are also expected to indicate possible future risks which might alter performance or costs and to quantify their effects if they arise.

Although all the firms have a general aim of productivity growth, change is a way of life, but in practice ways of achieving it vary. Simplification of procedures (even at the cost of some central control or information), new technology, better organisation and harder work all contribute, but their separate contributions are not usually estimated. In one firm attempts to set targets had proved unhelpful and produced under-achievement; they had gone over to a version of zero base budgeting whereby economies were identified in the course of considering whether an entire activity should continue to exist in future. Another firm said their new chief executive had set the aim of levelling up the worst regions and areas to the best. In others, precise productivity improvement targets, including an explanation of exactly how they were to be achieved, were expected from managers in their annual budgeting and planning exercise. All the firms mentioned the role of computer technology and improved systems as sources of higher productivity; two firms seem to have specific targets for their automated data processing and management service staff either to develop software to reduce the operating costs of other parts of the firm or to improve the speed of operations.

In most firms new investments were subject not only to initial appraisal but also to monitoring during implementation and rigorous *ex-post* audits which were found to be a valuable discipline on the initial appraisers and to contribute to the learning process.

A number of companies said that all staff, including top management, shared in productivity gains on a uniform basis, with equal percentage pay rises. This was said to promote harmony in industrial relations, corporate loyalty, and a willingness to move within the firm between activities offering different scope for productivity improvements. In other firms, although the entire pay structure moved in a way which maintained differentials, individuals were paid in relation to the pay scale or a point on the scale, according to individual performance as assessed annually. One firm said nobody could move more than half way up the scale appropriate to their grade on the basis of seniority alone.

GOVERNMENT DEPARTMENTS

In the Inland Revenue, parts of the Department of Employment (Levitt, 1985) and the social security side of the Department of Health and Social Security, complementing is undertaken on the basis of a forecast of workload on the one hand (for example the number of tax codings and different types of benefit claimants) and on the other indicators of the manpower requirement for a given unit of workload, derived from periodic work measurement samples. Indicators of the actual allocation of manpower among different activities is highly aggregative, given the variety of work commonly undertaken in a given tax or benefit office; likewise costs cannot usually be precisely allocated among different types of work such as different taxes and benefits.

Work measurement is undertaken periodically in the Department of Health and Social Security via 'activity sampling' to establish the relative manpower requirements of different sorts of work, and national indicators (divisors) are established. The aim is to review the base complement in relation to total workload triennially. Broadly, in the Department of Employment comparable systems operate for the unemployment benefit service and redundancy payment offices. Each year, when managers bid for staff and plans are finalised, the Manpower Services Commission expects to see improvements in output per staff unit (that is improved productivity) as a regular feature of bids.

The three departments, or parts of them, reviewed here have systems for reporting (at local, regional and national level) indicators of the volume of work done (tax codings, investigation visits, benefits paid, trainees placed, and so on) and indicators of staff in post; this monitoring often includes a comparison with plan and previous periods. However, in the absence of precise, continuous work measurement it is not always possible to allocate staff time to each activity nor to cost each activity. This means that comparisons over time which take into account changes in the mix of work, or between regions and areas, are not possible except at a highly aggregative level. The indicators available, such as the ratio of administrative costs to tax yield or benefit expenditure and the number of staff to taxpayers or claimants, all show significant improvements.

Plans are in hand in all departments to introduce more refined work measurement and costing systems, but it is not always clear how they will be used. Nor is it clear exactly what is envisaged for the measurement or assessment of performance outside the area of large scale clerical operations.

A summary picture of the relative momentum in unit costs or in staff workload is provided in table 6.1 below. More detail is shown in the annual Public Expenditure White Paper, where measures of administrative performance are now a regular feature of the separate departmental chapters. But in principle measures of productivity need to be based on a benchmark initial *level* of productivity, taking into account all the relevant dimensions of the output in question. In the case of financial services these dimensions include the accuracy with which the tax or benefit due is assessed, and the timeliness with which transactions are handled.

In the case of social security payments the picture is mixed. The clearance times shown in the 1987 Public Expenditure White Paper (Cm 56–II) show a volatile pattern for retirement pension claims but no change for callers at local offices for supplementary benefits. Published error rates for supplementary benefit have fallen but for sickness and maternity benefits error rates have risen. In the Department of Employment, clearance times for handling unemployment benefit claims have improved considerably in recent years, while the number of claims handled per member of staff has also risen. No measures of take-up rates, that is, the proportion of those deemed eligible to claim benefit who in fact do so, are provided in the White Paper, although such analyses are published in Social Security Statistics.

PUBLIC–PRIVATE COMPARISONS OF PRODUCTIVITY

We have noted the highly aggregative nature of the available data on workload and productivity available for certain government departments. Nonetheless it seems worthwhile to see what comparisons might be drawn with private sector activities of a broadly similar nature, and for this purpose financial services have been chosen. Like the activities of the Inland Revenue, the Department of Employment group and the social

Table 6.1 *Public-private comparisons*

Average annual percentage changes

Comparison of staff–client ratios	
Six London clearing banks, number of accounts per employee	2.50
Three Scottish clearing banks	3.74
Building Societies, numbers of accounts per head	4.07
C and E, number of VAT traders per head, VAT staff	3.87
IR, number of income taxpayers per head (all staff)	2.55
Cost ratios	
Life insurance, ratio of expenses to premium income	+0.5
C and E, ratio of administrative costs to revenue	−5.0
IR, cost–yield ratio	−3.3
DHSS, ratio of administrative expenses to benefit expenditure	−4.0

Sources: Lines 1, 2, and 3, *Abstract of Banking Statistics*, vol. 1, 1984; 4 and 5, 1978/9–1982/3, *Cmnd* 9143; 6, *Life Insurance in the UK 1979–83*, Life Offices Association, 1982 (excludes investment income); 6, 1978/9–1983/4, *Cmnd* 9143; 7, 1978/9–1982/3, *Cmnd* 9143 (note the influence of increased VAT); 8, 1978/9–1982/3, *Cmnd* 9143 (contributory and non-contributory benefits).

security work they involve large clerical and cash handling operations: as with government, the publicly available data are highly aggregated.

In the case of banks an attempt was made in 1982 to compare the productivity and financial performance of individual London clearing banks with one another and with foreign banks using data on profits, assets, staff costs and staff numbers; the author judged performance to be poor (Fanning, 1982). Another study which incorporated some data on physical measures of work came to an opposite conclusion (Frazer, 1982). Our comparisons use some recently published data on the number of accounts and on staff numbers, for the London and Scottish clearers; this is not broken down by individual banks; no unit cost data are available.

In the case of British insurance companies previous productivity studies have relied on financial data, which is more readily available than volume data, for example on numbers of transactions (Johnston and Murphy, 1957). However, recent studies in North America, where insurance companies' statutory reporting includes data on the volume of different categories of business done, have used volume and financial information (Hirshhorn and Geehan, 1977 and Geehan, 1977). Our comparisons use some United Kingdom information on the ratio of management expenses to premium income.

Some aggregated data are also available for building societies as a group. This makes possible the construction of an index of the ratio of numbers of staff to indicators of the volume of business, for example number of deposits, new advances, although without relative weights to reflect differences in the time required for different types of business.

The results are reported in Table 6.1. The basic data are very aggregated, the nature of the work differs considerably between all the institutions covered, the time periods are not identical, external influences (in financial markets, the state of the economy, economic policy) have different effects on the institutions shown, no comparisons of quality, for example timeliness, accuracy, are available. Subject to these important caveats the striking thing is the degree of similarity between the government departments and private financial institutions with respect to the broad indicators shown. There is no overwhelming evidence that the government departments considered are markedly inferior in their performance to private institutions, despite significant differences in the financial incentives to the staff concerned. This is not to say that either or both are maximising their potential performance.

POSSIBLE DEVELOPMENTS

Several firms have emphasised the importance they attach to detailed data on indicators of work done, manpower, and a wide variety of running costs for use in setting staff complements, budgets, and efficiency targets, and for monitoring and control, and making comparisons. There are many activities within government where more could be done to measure volumes of work, its precise cost and the precise manpower involved. Such indicators would permit better comparisons with targets, over time, between establishments and with private firms. A great deal more information seems to be produced by the private sector than by government departments, both for its own internal management and accounting purposes and to meet various government administrative and statistical requirements; the results permit reasonably comprehensive and consistent comparisons to be made over time and between sectors. It seems likely that, within government, more should be done to obtain data on activities common to several departments and on major departmental activities, especially where data for private analogues including 'quality' measures exist or might be obtained. This could be done on a sample basis. A number of possibilities are listed in note 4 to this chapter.

A related consideration is whether data on performance and productivity should continue to be provided at the pace and with the coverage departments find useful internally, or whether a more comprehensive continuous system should be devised, or whether periodic centrally initiated *ad hoc* reviews suffice. There may be some lessons in the more centrally managed American system discussed in the next chapter.

Departments are developing systems which will, and to some extent already do, throw up large quantities of detailed information relating to different types of work such as different taxes or benefits in different locations and over time. It is not clear how the detail will be reduced to useful aggregate measures nor how it will be analysed in ways which permit the influence of difference in work-mix or location to be explained. Techniques such as regression analyses or data envelope analyses, of the kind discussed in Chapter 9, should have a contribution to make.

7

MEASURING CHANGES IN CENTRAL GOVERNMENT PRODUCTIVITY IN THE UNITED STATES

Since 1973 the United States Department of Labor's Bureau of Labor Statistics has operated a productivity measurement programme covering two-thirds of federal civilian employees, built up from 3,500 indicators, with average measures of federal productivity back to 1967. The series are not used in the construction of the national income and product accounts (which conventionally rely on government employment data); nor are the data much used for management purposes (although the basic micro data might have been prepared for agency management purposes). The series owes its existence to a management initiative of the early 1970s which, like so many others in the United States or elsewhere, went out of fashion, especially because it did not attract or retain the commitment of senior officials. The series has been maintained by the division of the Bureau responsible for the measurement of productivity throughout the United States economy.

Interest in productivity measurement for management and budgeting purposes has recently revived. President Reagan announced a series of initiatives, collectively known as 'Reform '88', to improve government management, which included a productivity improvement programme intended to secure productivity gains in federal agencies averaging 3 per cent annually for several years ahead. Top level teams were established to oversee the programme, annual reports to Congress were promised: the General Accounting Office was asked to monitor achievements for Congress, and new efforts on productivity measurement were introduced. A key element in the background to the new initiative is the existence of the massive federal budget deficit, which will exert pressure for some years to come, not to mention the Gramm-Rudman Act, which puts a ceiling on the federal deficit.[1]

The main emphasis in this chapter is on the measurement of changes in productivity but we also discuss a comparison of productivity levels within the social security administration and discuss the Reagan management initiatives on federal productivity.

THE FEDERAL PRODUCTIVITY MEASUREMENT SYSTEM

The conceptual approach[2]

The Bureau of Labor Statistics (BLS) indicators are intended to relate the labour inputs of federal bodies to the goods and services they produce. 'This measurement approach does not, however, determine whether these products should be produced or relate them to some desired goal' (Mark, 1981). In other words, the indicators do not attempt to assess the effectiveness of agency activities in securing policy goals (Bradford, Malt and Oates, 1969); the measures are of what public servants do, for example arrest drug dealers, rather than the consequences of their actions such as the impact on drug addiction (Burkhead and Ross, 1974). Although this is a limitation, the final consequences of much private production of goods and services are also often not known, but this does not inhibit attempts at measurement quite as much as it does in government.

The gap between the Bureau's measures of goods and services produced by public servants on the one hand and possible indicators of consequential outputs varies between activities. In the case of enterprise agencies such as the postal service, indicators of the volume of mail delivered are closer to final outputs than, say, indicators of student-class-contact-hours to the final output of federal training programmes. Although the aim is to measure outputs final to the management units and agencies involved, leaving aside consequential effects relevant to ultimate policy goals, a number of problems remain.

One problem is the risk of double counting. The data are built up according to functional groups which are common to several agencies and include paying invoices, processing claims, paying benefits, typing services. In a manufacturing process involving several stages (for example, smelting iron ore, sheet steel pressing, engine casting, engine assembly, car assembly), the productivity of the intermediate stages can be weighted by the value-added at each stage to arrive at an aggregate measure which takes into account the contribution of each stage to final output. In the measurement of government output no measures of the value-added at each stage are available. The various indicators available refer to the final outputs of each agency and function and to the intermediate activities consumed within each agency or function. These are weighted together in proportion to the man-years involved in the production of each output, whether final or intermediate, to arrive at an overall weighted average for the federal government. No netting-off to avoid double counting is possible. For this reason the data are probably more useful for examining productivity changes in a given homogeneous function, whether over time or across agencies (but see below) than for examining average productivity for a given agency involving several functions or, except in very broad terms, federal government as a whole.

In accordance with statistical good practice, the products are intended to be homogeneous within a given category or function, but in practice difficult cases of heterogeneity can arise. For example, an indicator such as meals served per head of catering staff in each of the armed services is a useful indicator for comparisons over time and across the services; but the indicator for aero-engines overhauled, without specifying type or the extent of the overhaul, is less useful. Similarly, the combination of water inspection visits and arrests for drug offences in the overall indicator of 'regulation, compliance and enforcement' seems less useful. And insofar as the detailed product mix within a given function changes over time, the value of the time-series is diminished further. On the other hand the problem of establishing homogeneity is not confined to government output: problems of heterogeneity within product categories are present in much private sector output, of both goods and services, also.

Finally, the question of quality changes arises. The system does not seem to specify a given standard of, for example, timeliness or accuracy for processes such as clearing invoices or paying social security benefits. Sometimes the basic concept of quality gives rise to difficulties. For example, the easing of regulations on the scrutiny of applications for broadcasting stations permits faster throughput; but it is not clear whether the new throughput represents a productivity increase (resulting from simpler administrative procedures) or a different quality of product. However, the problem of allowing for quality changes is not confined to government output; it arises in the case of private output also, especially in the most rapidly changing electronic and aerospace industries.

The view of the Bureau of Labor Statistics appears to be that many of the problems associated with double-counting, product heterogeneity and quality changes are not insuperable nor peculiar to public as opposed to private production. More detailed data, permitting more rigorous netting-off, finer weighting systems and more refined product definition would go a long way towards overcoming such deficiencies as do arise. But improvements would require more resources and greater priority for productivity measurement than it has commanded in recent years. We return to these issues on page 76 below.

Coverage and structure

The federal government employs just over five million people of whom almost three million are civilians, the rest being military. The measurement indices, available back to 1967, cover 1.9 million federal civilian employees in 54 agencies and are built up from over 3,000 output measures (Bureau of Labor Statistics, 1985).

Table 7.1 *Federal productivity measurement program: coverage by employee-year, fiscal year 1984*

	Total employee years ('000s)	Per cent covered
Cabinet departments		
Agriculture	112.2	55.3
Commerce	32.9	47.2
Defence	1094.2	39.3
Education	5.4	47.7
Energy	15.8	39.7
Health and human services	145.7	85.3
Housing and urban development	12.6	67.4
Interior	77.4	28.8
Justice	62.0	95.5
Labour	18.4	63.9
State	25.2	18.5
Transport	63.4	81.4
Treasury	129.5	89.0
Other (illustrative)		
General services administration	26.3	66.8
Veterans' administration	224.1	96.1
Environmental protection agency	11.5	18.0
US information agency	8.5	15.7
Office of personnel management	5.9	76.9
Postal service	725.1	100.0
Tennessee Valley authority	36.7	94.3
All other executive branch	88.0	37.5
Total executive branch	2920.8	66.8
(excluding postal service)	2195.7	55.8
Non-executive branch		
General accounting office	5.0	1.2
Government printing office	5.9	100.0
Library of Congress	5.3	64.9
US courts	16.4	100.0

Source: Federal government productivity summary data fiscal years 1967–84, US Department of Labor.

The data do not represent a random sample of government outputs; they are supplied on a voluntary basis and coverage across agencies and within any given agency is rather mixed. An important component of total coverage is the federal postal service, an enterprise, not a non-trading activity.

Total coverage in 1984 (table 7.1) represents two-thirds of federal civilian employment; coverage falls to 56 per cent if the postal service is excluded; coverage is below average in defence and 72 per cent on average for the remainder of civil employment.

The structure of the federal productivity measurement system is based on the grouping of agency measures into 28 functions having common characteristics across reporting agencies. Therefore a given function will relate to several agencies and a given agency will be covered by several functions. Details of the coverage of the system including several examples of output indicators are shown in Appendix 3. A very wide range of unambiguous indicators of work are included, such as insurance premia collected, grants made, invoices paid, product samples analysed, arrests made, pay-checks issued, vehicle fleet miles driven, patients treated. However, differences in the difficulty or complexity of similarly classified activities such as legal opinions, answers to Congressional inquiries, aero-engine repairs, are not allowed for; nor are differences in the timeliness or accuracy of certain activities: for example, improved productivity might be at the expense of reduced timeliness or accuracy in benefit payments, equipment overhaul, legal opinions or message transmission. However, the new productivity improvement programme requires a base-line or bench-mark of service quality to be set for future productivity measurement.

Comparisons for a given function across agencies do not seem to have been a major feature hitherto. However, the 1986 initiative on productivity improvement and measurement required the comparison of productivity between common functions across Federal government.

Results

Over the period 1967–83, the average annual increase in output per federal employee was 1.5 per cent, compared with 1.4 per cent for the private sector on a net final output basis. Unit labour costs rose by 6.7 per cent a year. For the sample as a whole, productivity rose faster and unit labour costs rose more slowly in 1977–83 (by 1.7 per cent and 5.6 per cent respectively) than in 1967–83, so that performance in these terms improved in the later years (Fisk, 1985).

The BLS recognises that productivity comparisons between the public and private sectors are of interest, but is cautious about the scope for using the data in this way. In particular, whereas the private sector index relates to net output of the whole sector, the government index is for gross output (with some double counting) of a non-random sample. It considers that more useful comparisons might be made for specific, comparable services but so far no comparisons appear to be available publicly.

Management interest

In a review of the development of the federal productivity measurement system in 1983, the Comptroller General of the United States reported to Congress that '. . . for the most part government efforts have lacked consistent leadership and have been largely disjointed, short-lived and ineffective' (General Accounting Office, 1983). But he claimed that a number of agencies had been stimulated to develop their own measurement systems helped by the BLS and that a government-wide focus for productivity measurement had been provided. However, because of the lack of clear encouragement from the centre, the management portion of the programme was leaderless and the future of the programme was in doubt. More recently in 1986, in reviewing management initiatives, including productivity improvement, the Comptroller General told Congress that commitments to reform had waxed and waned over the years.[3]

The Office of Management and Budget, in an annex to the 1983 report, denied that there was a lack of central interest in productivity improvements and said that they needed to be viewed as part of an attempt to improve management generally and not something to focus upon in isolation. But a number of officials appeared to believe that agency managers were in a 'no win' position: if losses in productivity were reported management abilities might be questioned; if gains were reported, resources might be transferred elsewhere.[4] To the extent that these arguments have force they reflect differences in objectives: agency managers would prefer to raise their volume of service while retaining their staff and other resources; the Office of Management and Budget and the Treasury need to consider other public expenditure claims, the scope for tax reductions, and the need to reduce the federal deficit.

It is also possible that agencies, and management units within agencies, are reluctant to support the system because those which may look like relatively poor performers may believe that their absolute level of productivity is relatively high: it is harder to demonstrate a large improvement in productivity if one's starting level is relatively high, and vice versa. This points to a genuine weakness in the system, common to many measures of productivity trends: the absence of an explicit benchmark level against which trends are measured. The development of benchmarks would require a major investment of effort, although something could be done on a limited scale.

The Comptroller General's report in 1983 also revealed widespread lack of interest within agencies in improved systems for monitoring their costs and performance and laid part of the blame for this on the lack of top level support; in some agencies 'top management officials candidly told us they were unaware of their departments' productivity directives' (General Accounting Office, 1983). Given the lack of top management interest in productivity improvement, it is not surprising that there was little interest in productivity measurement and that, although productivity measurement data was generated, the data were not used in agency management. It was suggested that one possible reason why these measures were ignored was that they were reported separately, outside the management and budget process. It was noted that this picture was changing, for example the Internal Revenue Service was integrating its productivity programme and its management system.

Agencies have sometimes said that they find the BLS series too broad brush for internal management purposes and that the requirement of fitting measures into a broad functional framework across the whole of federal government is too aggregative to be useful. However, there is nothing in the system to prevent agencies developing their own, more refined indicators. An alternative might have been to let agencies develop measures at their own pace and to report them centrally when they were ready rather than to initiate a centralised system. But that might have produced even slower progress.

Potentially, productivity and unit cost indicators of the sort covered by the federal productivity measurement system could be used to compare performance over time, between management units undertaking similar tasks, for setting less arbitrary manpower ceilings and for budgets; in short, as a management tool in resource allocation and output monitoring. An example of the use of productivity and unit cost data is provided by official analyses of local offices of the social security administration. A feature of this work is that it includes a comparison of productivity levels across management units; these have at least as much intrinsic interest as indices of productivity changes over time, particularly in view of the absence of explicit benchmarks. The Bureau of Labor Statistics has regularly investigated variations in the growth and levels of productivity in social security administration among six states; in 1972–9 it found a range of average annual productivity trends from plus 4.7 per cent in one state to minus 3.1 per cent in another (where the productivity trends refer to changes in the volume of work handled divided by changes in the number of employee-years of input) (Fisk, 1983). The time required to process initial claims for benefit varied by 370 per cent; unit labour requirements within one state varied by 200 per cent between local offices. It concluded that most of the difference in performance was attributable to conditions within the control of State authorities, that is after allowing for demographic and socio-economic factors outside their control.

The General Accounting Office has also undertaken detailed analyses of local social security offices; its most recent report covers over 260 offices in the best administrative region (Atlanta). Each local office handles a mix of benefits including those which are means-tested and those dependent on previous social security contributions; up to 50 different types of claims may be handled, including those where benefits vary according to family size and ages. After allowing for differences in the mix of work, levels of productivity in some offices were found to be almost *double* the levels elsewhere and 50 per cent above average; the most productive offices achieved their performance without deterioration in timeliness or accuracy. The poor performers pointed to local demographic and socio-economic circumstances outside their control as the explanation, but the General Accounting Office found no statistically significant explanation of variations in performance along these lines (General Accounting Office, 1985). Instead, factors within management control, (internal procedures, automation and staffing arrangements), were found to provide the main explanation.

Social security managers argued that some local offices in especially difficult circumstances (for example Bronx, Watts) faced special problems. However, the General Accounting Office appear to take the view that, while special performance standards could be set for such offices, cross-section comparisons are useful for the bulk of the remaining 1,200 offices and common performance standards could be set.

THE FEDERAL PRODUCTIVITY IMPROVEMENT PROGRAM

Background

The Reagan administration, like the Conservative government in Britain, was determined to attack what it regarded as civil service mismanagement and waste. The growth of the federal deficit and the Gramm-Rudman Act provided an incentive and urgency to the implementation of reforms. A number of steps were taken in the early 1980s to this end and in 1985 the President sent a message to Congress to elicit their support for legislation on productivity issues. Management reviews of agencies' internal management procedures were announced and productivity improvements were to be integrated into agencies' budgets. The announced aim was a 20 per cent productivity improvement target between 1986 and 1991. Several actions to improve productivity were announced as part of the President's Productivity Improvement Program. The 1987 Budget repeated the emphases on productivity management and measurement and spelled out the proposed reforms in more detail.

In short, the management reforms are intended to be connected to the 'oxygen supply' of the budget process. Previous management initiatives, for example PPBS (and programme analysis and review in the United Kingdom), never quite achieved this. The officials, procedures and information systems were separate from the public expenditure budgeting machinery. It is too soon to judge what will be achieved or whether the reforms will prove more durable than previous management initiatives.

The Executive Order

The Executive Order, issued by the President in February 1986 (Executive Order, 1986) and supplemented by guidelines to agencies, set out the aims of the federal productivity improvement programme and the actions to be undertaken to implement it.

In order to achieve an improvement in productivity of 20 per cent, at a given level of quality of service, by 1991, each agency was required to develop and submit annually a productivity plan stating productivity goals, actions to improve efficiency and the methods to be used to measure the improvements. Agencies were required to define standards of quality (for example timeliness and accuracy) in 1986 to serve as the baseline from which to measure subsequent productivity improvements. Planned improvements were to be taken into account in agency budgets, and achievements were to be monitored by the Office of Management and Budget which was instructed to report to Congress annually on achievements and future plans.

The requirement of an explicit plan, the reference to private sector comparisons, the appointment of an accountable official, the proposed integration with budgets together with annual reporting all represent potentially major practical developments.

An important element in the productivity improvement programme was the emphasis on simplicity. Agencies themselves choose areas for improvement which are easy to define and measure, possibly starting with pilot schemes. The suggestion was that routine, repetitive activities should be chosen first. Otherwise, agencies might choose different areas that are difficult to measure so that adequate assessment of whether or not true improvements were acheived would be hard to make.

Another potentially significant aspect of the programme was the intention to develop common performance standards for functions common to several agencies. The Executive Order said that the President's Council on Management Improvement would select 'common functions for which common performance standards can be developed across government' (Executive Order, 1986). This development, amounting to the establishment of benchmark productivity levels, would represent a major step in the developement of productivity in government if it were to be achieved.

Productivity measurement

The new initiative proceeded from the belief that much of what government does is measurable. According to an official responsible for the new initiative 'more than half the work in the civilian side of government involves various forms of processing paper: claims, checks [cheques], grants, contracts, loans, licences, passports, etc. All of these are relatively routine . . . and can be relatively easily measured' (Ewing, 1986). In accordance with this approach, the emphasis was on measuring what could be measured in simple terms, rather than on discussions of fundamental conceptual issues which arise in difficult areas.

Bulletin 87–12, issued in May 1987, makes it clear the new initiative will be integrated with the BLS system and that the Office of Management and Budget will jointly issue the call for data. This represents a major boost to the status of the FPMS.

There appears to be no provision for analysis of the sources of productivity growth and their separate contribution, for example more equipment per worker, investment in training, changes in the scale of operations, changes in the mix, or in the output mix, new administrative procedures and so on. However, such analysis has not been undertaken anywhere else on a significant scale, in government or even in private service sectors.

The federal productivity measurement system provides evidence of reasonable productivity growth in government. It shows what might be done in other countries interested in developing measures of government output and productivity. It is subject to a number of technical weaknesses, it does not include measures of quality, and its use has been limited. Its deficiencies could be largely overcome if productivity improvement and management were to command sufficient, sustained, priority. Recent initiatives might secure this, but it is at present too soon to judge their success.

8

DEFENCE PROCUREMENT

In recent years a major source of the growth of total public expenditure in both Britain and the United States has been defence spending. This has been partly the result of increased purchases of volumes of inputs, measured at constant input prices; but it also reflects the tendency for the price of defence inputs to rise more than prices generally, so that the share of defence in GDP has risen even faster at current prices (which are what matter for financing expenditure) than in volume terms.

One possible explanation of the faster rise in defence equipment prices than in prices generally is the increased sophistication of defence technology, so that new warships or aeroplanes can be a multiple of the cost of the earlier generations which they replace (Kirkpatrick and Pugh, 1983). Spending on equipment now accounts for 45 per cent of the defence budget (Ministry of Defence, 1986). It is very nearly one and a half times the amount spent by the whole of manufacturing industry on investment in plant and machinery (£8.6 billion and £6.0 billion respectively in 1984/5).

There is something in the sophistication argument. But we also need to consider how we measure defence prices, and the industrial performance of the industries supplying the equipment. This chapter suggests that their record with respect to investment per worker, productivity and resistance to wage pressures has tended to be worse than for manufacturing industry generally. This has reflected weak competitive pressures, cost-plus contracts, and the lack of incentive to contain costs when public spending plans have involved commitment to volume growth targets. Competition is being increased, more rigorous planning of equipment requirements and closer control over contracts are being introduced. There are some signs that these developments are having an effect, although their full potential remains to be demonstrated and achieved.

DEFENCE PRICES IN THE NATIONAL INCOME ACCOUNTS

Table 8.1 illustrates the movement in defence prices with respect to prices generally as indicated by the GDP deflator: the difference between the two series reflects the defence relative price effect (RPE), as it emerges from the accounting conventions: its trend is clearly up, although in some years it falls (as in 1985).

Table 8.1 *Defence relative price effects*

	Defence deflator/ GDP deflator (1)	Defence procurement deflator/ manufacturing price index (2)
1964	75.15	79.9
1965	75.89	79.3
1966	77.35	80.6
1967	77.58	82.4
1968	79.79	84.6
1969	79.99	85.4
1970	84.70	88.3
1971	87.02	86.9
1972	89.26	92.6
1973	93.15	96.0
1974	98.61	96.0
1975	96.36	97.4
1976	100.58	101.0
1977	98.26	96.5
1978	98.95	99.9
1979	100.58	100.1
1980	100.00	100.0
1981	99.25	103.1
1982	102.48	105.4
1983	103.96	106.8
1984	105.96	107.6
1985	104.55	103.3

Sources: Column (1) National Income Blue Book; Column (2), CSO for the procurement deflator, *Monthly Digest of Statistics* for manufacturing prices.

For government expenditure generally a positive RPE is a normal feature, for the familiar reason that, in the absence of measures of output, no productivity growth can be registered to offset the rise in unit input costs (especially labour), which have tended to move broadly in line with input costs (such as wages) in the rest of the economy. In the case of defence, another important influence is said to be the rising cost of increasingly sophisticated equipment. Table 8.1 also illustrates the growth in relative procurement costs for defence vis-à-vis manufacturing prices generally.

The national accounting conventions do not allow for improved productivity in the production of defence equipment,[1] nor do they allow for the improved effectiveness in use of the more sophisticated equipment when it is deployed. While it is true that more sophisticated, advanced generations of a given type of tank, ship, or warplane cost more per unit than the less sophisticated, older types, it does not necessarily follow that the relative unit cost of standard equipment necessarily rises, and there is some American evidence that it does not (US Department of Commerce, 1982). Insofar as the newer types are more effective than the old, in other words their 'output' is greater, their additional cost is for an increased quantity of defence effectiveness rather than an increased cost of a given amount, so that to call it an RPE rather than increased output is misleading.

Examination of Appendix tables A1.2 and A1.3 suggests another influence on defence costs. It is noticeable that during 1970–4, when the government sought to relax the previous administration's constraints on defence spending, the volume of defence inputs continued to fall. But in real terms expenditure rose, that is the relative price of defence, as conventionally measured, rose. This suggests that in periods when the constraints on defence spending are relaxed, costs may rise. This may be because of improved armed forces' pay, the initiation of new equipment programmes with high development costs, or simply weaker cost control. This must be especially true when objectives are actually set for defence spending in volume terms. Thus the commitment to the NATO aim of 3 per cent volume growth adopted by the last Labour administration in 1978 (for implementation in 1979) can have done nothing to strengthen the incentives for cost restraint among contractors; the cash cost of the volume programme had to be made available.

INDUSTRIAL PERFORMANCE AND DEFENCE PROCUREMENT

Defence spending must have an important effect on the performance of the industries from which equipment is purchased. It is therefore appropriate to consider which industries depend most heavily on defence contracts, the impact of defence contracts on industry's approach to competitive civilian markets, the investment and productivity performance of industries dependent on defence contracts, and their import and export performance.

The industrial composition of procurement

Table 8.2 sets out the recent industrial composition of domestic procurement; excluding expenditure on buildings and land, the items account for 85 per cent of all non-personnel expenditure; 95 per cent of expenditure on equipment is within the United Kingdom. Apart from petroleum products, the largest and fastest growing expenditure in the period 1979/80 to 1982/3 was on aerospace, followed by electronics (to which we return below).

An official detailed analysis of the 1978 industrial composition of defence spending, including the employment it directly generates, and an analysis of sales per worker employed has been published by Pite (1980), using otherwise unpublished Ministry of Defence data. He estimated that 218,000 jobs had been directly generated in manufacturing industries by defence procurement, equivalent to 3 per cent of total manufacturing employment. By comparing Pite's data on defence contracts with overall data on turnover and employment for the industries involved, it is possible to estimate the relative importance of defence contracts to the different

Table 8.2 *Industrial composition of United Kingdom procurement*

Industry	SIC (1980)[a] group	1982/3 % share	Expenditure growth 1979/80 to 1982/3[b]
Aerospace	364	30.0	34.6
Electronics	344,345	18.6	33.2
Ordnance, small arms, explosives	256(part),329	7.5	20.9
Shipbuilding, repair	361	7.4	12.4
Other mechanical and marine engineering	320–328	5.0	13.1
Motor vehicles and parts	351–353	2.9	9.0
Instrument engineering	371–374	2.0	3.0
Other electrical engineering	341–348	1.8 ⎫	11.7
Data processing	330	1.0 ⎭	
Petroleum products[c]	140	13.2	54.6
Solid-fuel, electricity, gas	111,120		
Water[c]	161–170	2.5	10.9
Food and clothing[c]	411–429 431–456	2.9	−13.4
Other		4.9	10.3
Total		100	25.7

Source: Statement on Defence Estimates, Ministry of Defence (HMSO), 1985 and own estimates.
[a] SIC = official Standard Industrial Classification.
[b] 1979/80 cost terms.
[c] Includes purchases abroad.

industries concerned. The results are in table 8.3. They show that, for the year in question, defence work accounted for almost half of aerospace equipment sales, a third of radio, radar and electronic capital goods, a fifth of shipbuilding, but only 8 per cent of instrument engineering and 5 per cent of radio and electronic components.

A comparison of defence shares in sales per head and in employment (table 8.3) shows that sales per employee in defence work are broadly equal to non-defence sales in the case of aerospace and radio, radar and electronic capital goods, somewhat higher for radio components, slightly lower for instruments, and much lower in shipbuilding. Pite used sales per employee as an indicator of productivity, an issue discussed below.

The case of electronics

'One of the fundamental problems of the industry is that its strength is more related to primarily military dominated demand than to the broad consumer mass market' (Soete, 1985). This remark, by the author of a recent international comparison of the electronics industry in Britain and competitor economies, provides a useful introduction to a discussion of the electronics industry. Military demand provides a large market for the

Table 8.3 *The relative importance of United Kingdom defence contracts in total sales and employment, 1978*

Percentage shares

Industry	(Old) SIC	Sales	Employment	Sales[a] per head
Scientific and industrial instruments	354	8.2	8.9	90.7
Radio electronic components	364	5.2	4.7	108.6
Radio, radar and electronic capital goods	367	33.2	33.1	100.2
Shipbuilding and marine engineering	370	21.2	33.3	54.0
Aerospace equipment	383	46.8	46.7	100.7

Source: Derived from data on defence sales and related employment in Pite (1980), and from industry total sales and employment, Business Monitor (HMSO) (pre-1980 Industrial Classification).
[a] As % of non-defence. Defence sales are related to employees involved in defence work only, non-defence sales related to those involved in non-defence work only.

industry. This might induce valuable spin-off in civilian uses; on the other hand the presence of massive demand for defence work might weaken the incentive to compete in the more open, competitive, civil market.

Table 8.3 indicates that within the electronics and communications industry defence work is much more important in capital goods than in components; this also appears to be true of military expenditure on electronics and telecommunications in other countries (Soete, 1985). The British industry is the largest in Europe, and the capital goods sector is more than double the size of that in Germany or France.

The share of government expenditure on electronics R and D in the private sector (that is excluding in-house official establishments) rose from 37 per cent in 1968 to 54 per cent in 1981. With over 90 per cent of government electronics R and D expenditure being on defence, it is notable that government spending on electronics R and D is higher in absolute terms, and a higher proportion of public plus private funding, than in Japan, Germany or France, where private firms themselves spend considerably more on R and D than British firms spend (table 8.4).

The relatively large involvement of government in the electronics industry, both as an equipment purchaser and as a customer for R and D, might be thought to influence the industry's performance. One indicator of relative performance, vis-à-vis foreign competitors, is the industry's share in foreign patents taken out in a third country: the United States. Soete shows that the British share of electrical and electronic patents fell from 16 per cent in 1971 to 8.2 per cent and that of telecommunications patents from 15.5

Table 8.4 *R and D expenditure in electrical and electronic engineering, 1979*
£m

	US	Japan	Germany	France	UK
Total	7,927	2,833	3,119	1,408	1,035
of which:					
per cent public funded	43.0	0.8	13.5	26.6	56.8

Source: Soete (1985).

per cent in 1971 to 9.8 per cent in 1981. This implies a relatively poor performance in terms of capacity to innovate. However, Soete's data do not permit an assessment of the relative importance of British and other patents in terms of the sales value of the items involved, nor do they distinguish between civil and military applications.

What can be said about the spin-off in civilian uses of military spending on electronics? The former government chief scientist, Sir Euan Maddock, has examined the performance of several British firms in the electronics industry (National Economic Development Council, 1983). He distinguished four types of firms, running from A, almost wholly concerned with defence contracts, to D, wholly civil, but where the Ministry of Defence bought some products off the shelf.

He found that type A firms had no independent long-run objectives, but relied on Ministry requirements; they admitted they lacked competitive entrepreneurial skills; they felt uncomfortable with civil customers, who tended to operate with shorter time scales, to be less prepared to pay in advance for development costs, and to offer no long-term guarantee of work; civil work involved greater exposure to competition. 'It has to be faced that the likelihood of type A companies making a major contribution in the civil areas (other than aerospace) is vanishingly small . . . Type B companies are more likely to generate civil business, but there are very few such companies . . . Type C companies are more likely to make efficient commercial use of skills . . . Type D companies are aimed at civil markets but they are outside the main defence market.' In short, heavy dependence on defence contracts is unlikely to induce much civil spin-off, or much of an incentive to innovate unless the Ministry picks up the bill.

Investment and productivity

Leaving aside shipbuilding, table 8.5 demonstrates that in virtually every case the sub-sector identified as being a significant recipient of defence contracts invested less per employee than the rest of the industry of which it is part. In the case of electrical engineering, the components sector (where

Government output and productivity

Table 8.5 *Investment per employee, 1978*

£

	Net capital expenditure	Plant and machinery
All manufacturing	831	661
Order VIII Instrument engineering	878	662
of which SIC 354 Scientific and industrial instruments	586	435
Order IX Electrical engineering	598	485
of which SIC 364 Radio and electrical components	676	591
367 Radio, radar capital goods	480	415
Order X Shipbuilding and marine engineering (SIC 370)	441	239
Order XI Vehicles, transport	767	593
of which SIC 383 Aerospace equipment	448	356

Source: Business Monitor.

defence contracts were only a twentieth of output) invested more per employee than the industry average, but the capital goods sector (which sells a third of its output to the Ministry of Defence) invested much less than the industry average. In the case of shipbuilding, where defence work accounted for a fifth of output and a third of employment, investment in plant and machinery was under half the average for manufacturing as a whole. Aerospace, the industry identified as being most dependent on defence work, invested little over half the average for manufacturing generally and its parent order, XI. To the extent that investment involves embodied technical progress, these results imply the possibility of relatively poor productivity growth for the industries most dependent on defence work.

Table 8.6 presents data on productivity growth 1970–81 for the industries classified as in Pite's analysis of defence contracts, which we used in table 8.3. Apart from aerospace, productivity growth in groups where defence contracts are important is much lower than for the industrial average for radio capital goods and lower than its parent order for scientific instruments. Shipbuilding data do not distinguish between defence and civil construction/engineering but half the labour force was engaged in defence work; its productivity record is, uniquely, one of decline. Aerospace, with almost half output and employment accounted for by defence work, demonstrates productivity growth well above the manufacturing average.

The data for electronics capital goods and others (SIC groups 354, 367 and 370) show relatively poor productivity growth in industries where defence contracts are important. But they cannot distinguish between the

Table 8.6 *Growth of output per head, average annual per cent*[a]

	1970–5	1976–81	1970–81
All manufacturing	2.6	1.1	2.1
Order VIII Instrument engineering	4.5	2.8	3.4
of which SIC 354 Scientific and industrial instruments	2.6	2.3	2.5
Order IX Electrical engineering	4.9	3.6	4.2
of which SIC 364 Radio and electrical components	6.2	8.7	7.6
SIC 367 Radio, radar capital goods	1.6	− 0.6	0.8
Order X Shipbuilding and marine engineering (SIC 370)	0.6	− 2.4	− 1.2
Order XI Vehicles, transport	1.0	0.8	0.9
of which SIC 383 Aerospace equipment[b]	5.4	5.7	4.6

Sources: Output, Department of Industry; Employment, Department of Employment.
[a] Growth of index of production divided by index of employees in employment.
[b] The reason why productivity growth over 1970–81 is below that for the two sub-periods is that productivity *fell* by 6.3 per cent, 1975–7.

effect of possibly relatively short production runs which are sometimes said to be a feature of defence work and the effect of weak incentives to improve productivity: the latter may be the consequence of cost-plus contracts or because defence expenditure was planned on a volume basis with weak incentives to economy.

Import penetration and export performance

Table 8.7 sets out some data on import penetration ratios in 1970 and 1979, and the percentage change in those ratios over the period. A low ratio might imply a very competitive domestic industry, or lack of openness in the market for the goods in question, for example non-competitive contracts. Export performance is indicated simply by the ratio of exports to total United Kingdom producers' sales. A low ratio for import penetration *and* a low export ratio will indicate lack of openness: that is a home market dominated by domestic supplies and hence defence industries with less need to export to maintain turnover than industries with major import competition.

In the cases of scientific and industrial instruments (354) and radio and radar capital goods (367), the import *and* export ratios were lower, in 1979, than in the parent sectors (VIII and IX). Aerospace had a lower import penetration than vehicles as a whole, but its export performance ratio was equivalent to that for vehicles in 1979 and had risen almost twice as fast since 1970, suggesting openness to the forces of foreign competition. Shipbuilding had higher import penetration than manufacturing as a whole. Over the period 1970-9, the industries identified as being particu-

Table 8.7 *Import penetration and export performance 1970–9, per cent*

	Imports/ Home demand			Exports/ UK producers' sales		
	1970	1979	% change	1970	1979	% change
All manufacturing	17	26	53	18	24	33
Order VIII Instrument engineering	34	56	65	42	57	36
of which SIC 354 Scientific and industrial instruments	29	42	45	37	45	22
Order IX Electrical engineering	18	38	111	23	38	65
of which SIC 364 Radio and electrical components	30	53	77	28	52	86
SIC 367 Radio, radar capital goods	15	22	47	27	30	11
Order X Shipbuilding and marine engineering[a]	43	36	−16	29	36	24
Order XI Vehicles, transport	11	40	264	32	42	31
of which SIC 383 Aerospace equipment[a,b]	16	33	106	26	41	58

Source: Hewer (1980).
[a] Certain restricted items excluded.
[b] According to SDE approximately only one ninth of aerospace exports are recorded in the Customs and Excise tariff.

larly dependent on defence contracts experienced rising import penetration, but the increase was significantly less than for their parent sector (except for shipbuilding, where import penetration fell).

Between 1970 and 1979 two sub-sectors, 354 and 367, had much less success in raising their export sales ratios than their parent sectors; and like shipbuilding they did much less well than manufacturing. Aerospace clearly out-performed vehicles and manufacturing as a whole.

THE CONTRACTUAL RELATIONSHIP

The Ministry of Defence emphasised its intention to improve value for money in defence procurement by encouraging greater competition in the letting of contracts in the 1985 Statement on the Defence Estimates. It acknowledged that in the past there had been too much reliance on cost-plus contracts, which offer little incentive to contractors to minimise costs, and too little competition. It also expressed the hope that costs would be contained by more collaborative projects with allies, which help to share the costs of R and D and to stimulate economies of scale in production by widening the market for the units produced.

In practice, greater competition among firms within the United Kingdom can be difficult to arrange when the nature of the equipment is such that very few producers have the skill to develop and produce it, or where development costs would be too great for it to be economical for more than one producer to be involved. However, the option of buying from abroad and of collaboration may exist; even if development is undertaken by a single producer subsequent production might be possible by other firms, after competitive tendering.

Collaboration *per se* does not necessarily ensure a good deal for the United Kingdom. It depends on the terms of the collaborative arrangement and its subsequent management (National Audit Office, 1986). As for buying abroad, this can be unpopular if jobs are likely to be lost in the short term. But here it is essential to distinguish between the broad case for supporting British contractors on employment grounds (which is not a legitimate charge to a *defence* budget) and the purely military case for maintaining domestic industrial capability. In the latter case, the greater the strategic stocks and the shorter the war for which planning is undertaken, the weaker the military case for effectively subsidising domestic industrial capacity by paying prices above those offered by foreign producers.

The percentage by value of defence contracts placed by competitive arrangements rose from 38 per cent in 1983–4 to 60 per cent in 1985–6 (Ministry of Defence, 1986). This trend should produce cost savings. The Public Accounts Committee has noted that the return offered on non-competitive contracts in the early 1980s was high, by comparison with other industrial experience, because the target return aimed at was relatively high and because windfall profits above even the target rate (resulting from excessive inflation assumptions) were not recouped. Costs have been raised as a result of design changes introduced after orders have been placed. Production has been initiated before development has been completed in order to bring forward in-service dates, which usually have not been achieved anyway. There has been insufficient incentive for producers to restrain costs, all of which are met by the government, incurred before prices have been agreed; in 1983/4 half the work had been completed on 36 per cent (by value) of contracts placed under the profit formula before prices had been set. The Public Accounts Committee was especially critical of the inadequacy, as it saw the matter, of information available to government upon which to judge the return to contractors and to measure the capital devoted to defence contracts (National Audit Office, 1985). In a more recent review of progress the National Audit Office reported that although the Ministry of Defence had worthwhile improvements in hand it had not succeeded in overcoming the problems of cost escalation and delays (National Audit Office, 1986).

PROCUREMENT PRICES

A comparison of the movement in defence procurement prices with manufacturing prices provides a closer analogue than, for example, GDP prices. Table 8.1 shows that on this basis a relative price effect has also occurred. In order to make a more systematic comparison of defence procurement prices with manufacturing prices generally, an econometric analysis was undertaken.

The aim was to explain the movement in defence procurement prices $(CPRO)$ in terms of input costs and possible demand influences, and to compare the response of $CPRO$ to cost influences with that of manufacturing wholesale prices $(PWMF)$. No explicit allowance is made for the cost of capital services or for taxes which fall on producers' costs (for example national insurance contributions). Homogeneity was not imposed.

$CPRO$ depends on earnings (HE) measured by hourly earnings in manufacturing, productivity in manufacturing (Q), sterling import prices (PM), and demand influences, which affect profit margins, indicated by the volume of defence procurement at constant, own, prices $(PROV)$.

Measuring all variables in terms of the logs of their index numbers and estimating, we define $LCPRO$ as the log of $CPRO$ (and so on). The regression equations we estimate are:

$$LCPRO = a_1 + a_2\ LHE + a_3\ LQ + a_4\ LPM + a_5\ LPROV + U$$
$$\text{and } LPWMF = b_1 + b_2\ LHE + b_3\ LQ + b_4\ LPM + V$$

Table 8.8 reports the results. Annual data for 1963–82 were used: the most recent years when procurement has been most stringently controlled are not included. The results suggest that increases in earnings (LHE) have a rather stronger impact on defence prices than on manufacturing prices; offsetting productivity improvements are insignificant for defence prices, as measured; increases in import prices seem to have a rather larger impact on manufacturing than on defence prices. The effect of demand influences is positive but rather weakly determined for defence.

The results are summarised very broadly in table 8.9 and confirm that defence prices are (or were) insensitive to productivity growth (in reality or by virtue of the way they are measured).

Table 8.8 *Defence procurement (LCPRO) and manufacturing wholesale prices (LPWMF)*

	R^2	DW	C	LHE	LQ	LPM	LPRO
LPWMF	0.987	1.39	1.799	0.516	−0.415	0.506	
			t = 2.8	6.5	−2.5	4.4	
LCPRO	0.989	1.42	−4.633	0.606	−0.042	0.441	
			−8.9	9.1	−0.3	4.6	
LCPRO	0.995	1.49	−5.486	0.596	−0.106	0.475	0.119
			−5.7	8.6	−0.7	4.9	1.5

Notes: LHE = Hourly earnings in Manufacturing: LQ = Output per head in Manufacturing: LPM = Sterling import prices of manufacturers. All variables are logs of Index Numbers. Estimates from Cochrane–Orcutt iterative procedure.

Table 8.9 *Influences on defence procurement prices*

Response to a 1% rise in:	Defence prices	Manufacturing prices
Earnings	+0.6	+0.5
Productivity	−0.04	−0.4
Import prices	+0.45	+0.5
Volume of defence spending	+0.1	−

RECENT POLICIES

Since 1983 there has been much greater emphasis in the annual statement on the defence estimates on improved management and greater competition. There has been less reliance on cost-plus contracts with a view to improving value for money in defence procurement. The change from volume commitments to cash planning, under which the relative price effect needs to be financed from within the defence budget, has increased the impact of these developments. Table 8.1 demonstrates that the defence relative price effect with respect to either GDP prices or manufacturing prices fell in 1985. This might be evidence of the successful impact of recent procurement policies, although as in the past the volume measures to which they refer are hard to define and measure.

Many of the industries dependent on defence contracts demonstrate poor economic performance. This reflects the past weakness or even absence of pressures on them, and on the defence budget, to improve efficiency and to compete in the civil market. Aerospace, operating in a market more open to foreign competition, is an exception to this broad conclusion. Recent policies to secure better value for money should change the situation, but it is too soon to judge the extent to which their achievements will compensate for cuts in the defence budget.

Part III

EFFICIENCY AND RELATIVE PERFORMANCE

9

EFFICIENCY

ECONOMIC PRINCIPLES AND THE CONCEPT OF EFFICIENCY

The aim of management is to improve the efficiency with which resources are used. The definition and prerequisites of efficiency are a central concern of economic theory. This chapter is intended to outline some of the relevant economic principles and some of the quantitative procedures which can be used in estimating the relative performance of different management units. Later chapters illustrate the practical application of these concepts and techniques.

The first requirement of efficiency is that the maximum possible amount is produced with the resources used; or to put it another way, it must be impossible to reduce the volume of any input without reducing the volume of output. This is described as technical efficiency. The second requirement is that the cost of any given level of output is minimised by combining inputs in such a manner that one input cannot be substituted for another without raising the total cost. This is allocative efficiency. The third requirement is that the mix of outputs of different goods and services produced from the given resources maximises the benefit to consumers. This means that it is impossible to produce more of one good at the expense of another without reducing the total value of output to consumers. In the simple textbook world of perfect competition, efficiency is achieved by competition among cost-minimising firms for the custom of rational, well informed consumers who seek to get the greatest value for their money. In the production of government services the aim is to develop management and information systems which come as close as possible to maximising efficiency in the sense outlined above.

Technical and allocative efficiency

If we assume that there are constant returns to scale in production, so that a given proportionate change in all inputs produces an equi-proportionate change in output, then the minimum amount of inputs K and L required to produce a *unit* of output can be represented by points on a *unit isoquant* such as I in chart 9.1. All points above I use more of at least one input than is needed. At point A the ratio of K to L is identical to the ratio at all points along OA and, given this combination, B is the most technically efficient point. The ratio OB/OA equals the technical efficiency score for A; the closer A is to B along OA, the higher the score, with B scoring 100 per cent.

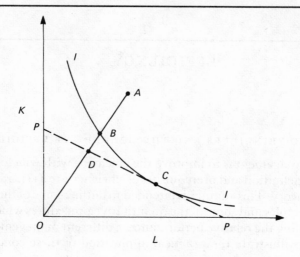

Chart 9.1 *Technical and allocative efficiency*

Suppose now that line P shows the available budget, all points along P have the same cost. Its slope reflects the relative prices of K and L. Although all points along I are technically efficient, only C is allocatively efficient: C represents the minimum cost combination of inputs. Point B costs too much because the unit of output could be produced at a cost of OD by substituting L for K. The *allocative efficiency score* for A is OD/OB, as B moves closer to C the score rises. Total efficiency is the product of technical and allocative efficiency, that is OD/OA.

The practical estimation of allocative efficiency is difficult: it requires data on the prices of all inputs, and it needs to take account of the possible movements over time in both prices and the responses of producers to such changes. We do *not* explore it further in the empirical work described later.

Input minimisation or output maximisation

Where perfect technical efficiency exists, it is impossible to reduce any input without reducing at least one output or to increase any output without increasing at least one input. Efficiency can be defined as either minimising costs, given output(s), or maximising output(s) holding costs constant. In theory it should be possible to measure the relative efficiency of a management unit in terms of an efficiency score. This could be defined as either the ratio of its actual output or, where there is more than one, some weighted average of them (see below) to its expected output (given its input(s) and after allowing for factors outside its control), namely, *output efficiency*, or the ratio of its expected input or, where there is more than one, some weighted combination of them (given its output and circumstances beyond its control), to its actual input, namely, *input efficiency*. The expected output or input would refer to the maximum possible output, given input, or the minimum possible input, given output, predicted from an observation of other management units. We could then go on to rank a set of managements according to their efficiency scores. However, as we explain below:

(a) the efficiency score of a given management in terms of its input efficiency will not in general equal its score in terms of output efficiency,

(b) the ranking of different managements may be different when assessed in terms of output efficiency and input efficiency.

Chart 9.2 below illustrates the simple case of one output Q and one input X (alternatively Q and X could be regarded as the weighted totals of composite outputs and inputs respectively). At point A actual output is oq and actual input is ox; the technically efficient production frontier is along $f(x)$. If the managers of A are encouraged to maximise output they should aim for output oq', given input ox; but if the managers intend to minimise inputs, given output, they should instead reduce inputs to ox'. The output efficiency score at A is oq/oq' but the input efficiency score is ox'/ox. There is no reason to suppose that these scores should coincide, unless the production frontier $f(x)$ is linear and at a slope of $45°$ indicating constant returns to scale when Q and X are measured in identical units. Further, except in the special case of a linear frontier, output efficiency scores and input efficiency scores might yield different rankings for inefficient authorities. Assuming that Q and X are measured in similar units, chart 9.2 suggests that under output maximisation authority A is technically more efficient than authority B, that is $oq/oq' > o\bar{q}/oq$.

But if the objective is input minimisation, authority B is more efficient, that is $ox'/ox < o\bar{x}/ox'$.

IMPLICATIONS OF EFFICIENCY CONSIDERATIONS FOR PERFORMANCE MEASUREMENT

If efficiency is to be improved we need to:

(a) define and, if possible, quantify the intended outputs and their associated costs;

(b) assess and if possible quantify the impact on output of a change in inputs after allowing for factors beyond the control of the management concerned;

(c) establish whether input minimisation or output maximisation is the objective in particular services;

(d) assess and if possible quantify the scope for improving technical efficiency; given the existing mix and volume of inputs, can output be increased or alternatively can total resources be reduced given output?

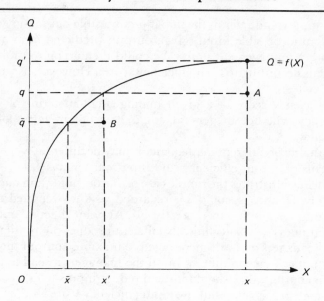

Chart 9.2 *The production frontier: diminishing returns*

(e) assess and if possible quantify the scope for improving allocative efficiency; given existing output, can inputs be substituted for one another so as to reduce total costs?

(f) assess and if possible quantify the extent to which efficiency can be improved by bringing the outlying worst performers near to the average or the best.

If efficiency is to be demonstrably improved in public services, considerable quantification of performance with respect to costs and outputs is required, along the lines outlined above. But such quantification is not sufficient to improve efficiency, it needs to be part of a coherent system of planning, management and budgeting which can serve to improve efficiency and which will take corrective action, as otherwise the collection and analysis of the data would be redundant. In practice there is considerable scope both for quantification and for the use of the results.

ESTIMATING AVERAGE RELATIONSHIPS: REGRESSION ANALYSIS

Regression analysis explains the variation in one data series in terms of variation in one or more other series; for example variation in output might be explained by variation in input, or by input together with other variables such as size of population or its social composition. The results of this kind of estimation take the form of an equation

$$y = a + bx + u$$

where, for each observation, y is the variable to be explained and x is the variable explaining it. The final term u is the unexplained variation in y. The values of a and b (which must be the same for all authorities) are chosen to minimise the variation of u, that is to explain as much as possible of the variation of y in terms of x. The method generalises, as multiple regression, to the case where x is replaced by a whole set of measured variables each having its own separate coefficient, b, to be estimated.

To use this approach we need to decide whether we are interested in divergences of actual from expected output, given costs, as in the outline of the method above, or differences between actual and expected costs, given output. This is because two regression models exist: one to minimise the unexplained variation in input, the other the variation in output, and the deviation from one regression equation will not equal the deviation from the other. Statistical procedures alone cannot say which is appropriate.

An important prior question is whether (a) differences in output (Q) are the result of differences in resource provision and perhaps demographic variation (P) (possibly after some standardisation for socio-economic factors), or (b), resources are allocated as a result of a policy towards output (as well as in accordance with demographic factors and so on)

$$R = c + dQ + eP + v$$

In the first instance the aim of behaviour in the authorities concerned is to maximise their outputs, given their resources which are provided in accordance with demographic influences but *not* performance targets. In the second case the aim is to minimise the costs of their outputs. A third possibility is that resources are provided as a result of a policy towards improving output as well as in accordance with demographic factors, but output reflects resource provision in an interactive, simultaneous system,

$$Q = a + bR + u$$
$$\text{and } R = c + dQ + eP + v$$

where Q = output, R = input, P = population or client group, u and v are random disturbances, and we have standardised for socio-economic factors. In this case policy towards output helps to determine resource provision, and differences in output reflect differences in resources, that is Q and R feed back onto one another.

ALLOWANCE FOR SOCIO-ECONOMIC INFLUENCES: MULTICOLLINEARITY

Differences in local socio-economic circumstances can produce differences in the ease with which different local managements can achieve similar outputs with similar resources. Also some programmes take account of socio-economic factors in the geographical allocation of resources. A large number of social influences might affect the extent to which resources and outputs are related. Variables such as household income, housing quality, occupational or skill levels of household heads, unemployment and ethnic origin, are often believed to have potentially important influences on behaviour. In statistical terms, the observed correlation between two variables (Q and R) may be due to the influence of a third (S) so that some form of standardisation is needed. The most common way to test for their influence is to include them in a regression equation of the form

$$Q = a + bR + cS_1, \ldots S_n + u$$

where $S_1 \ldots S_n$ are socio-economic indicators.

It is often difficult to measure these social influences individually. The picture is further complicated because they are often correlated with one another (for example, unemployment is correlated with low income and poor housing) so that their individual impacts are hard to disentangle from one another, and those which matter in reality might not appear to be statistically significant. One approach for incorporating social variables is to use the technique of step-wise regression which chooses those variables with the best statistical fit after trying out several separately or in combination.

The problem with this approach is that the precise choice of explanatory variables included in the final equation will sometimes be almost arbitrary. The variables selected might have little *a priori* superiority over those rejected, and the usual tests of statistical significance (which are intended to identify the likely impact of chance alone) have little meaning when such a selection process has been used.

Other approaches are possible, two of which we illustrate below. One is simply to take the total or average value of all the seemingly relevant socio-economic indicators and use that as a composite broad indicator of, for example, deprivation; certain indicators in the education and health fields follow this procedure. Some composite indicators assign equal weights to the individual social indicators chosen, others give them different weights according to some judgements of their relative importance.

Another approach is to use *principal component* analysis. This is a statistical procedure for transforming the initial set of variables into principal components which are weighted combinations of the original variables. The principal components emerge in a sequence such that the first explains the greatest possible variance among the original variables, the second explains the greatest possible variance in a component uncorrelated with the first and so on (Pidot, 1969).

RELATIVE PERFORMANCE

In examining differences in relative performance we need to be clear not only about whether we are referring to output or input efficiency, but also whether we mean performance relative to the average of all managements, or the average performance to be expected after allowing for differences in the socio-economic circumstances facing each local management, or the best possible performance demonstrated by outstanding local managements, after taking account of differences in their circumstances.

In this section we concentrate on average and average expected performance, frontier models of best practice are discussed in Appendices 2 and 3.

Regression analysis

A local management might spend more than the average but if its output is also more than average a simple comparison between its costs (or output) and average costs (or output) tell us nothing about its efficiency. Even if its output is much greater relative to average output than its costs are as a proportion of average costs, that tells us little: it might face especially favourable local cirumstances. One approach to judging relative performance is to examine the difference for each authority, between its actual costs, r_i, and $\hat{r}_i$ those predicted by a regression equation *or* the difference between actual and predicted output $(q_i - \hat{q}_i)$, as appropriate.

In the NHS performance indicator system, actual and expected average costs per in-patient case $(r_i - \hat{r}_i)$ are calculated for hospital in-patients. Expected costs take into account the mix of specialities in each hospital, the distinction between 'hotel' costs and treatment costs per case in each speciality, and length of stay.

The results of a comparison between actual and expected outputs or costs do not necessarily indicate good or bad peformance; the regression model might be misspecified, measurement errors might be present, chance alone can account for at least part of the residual. But they do provide managers with useful information, and an inducement, to help them to examine the performance of the units they manage, especially outliers, and to identify areas for improvement.

It is important to be clear whether the aim of the authorities under examination is to maximise their outputs given their inputs or to minimise their inputs given their outputs, that is whether the criterion is output or input efficiency. The principle of regression is to minimise the unexplained variation in the variable to be predicted given the explanatory variables. We might wish to provide the best explanation of Q, given R, or of R given Q. In the first case we want to minimise the unexplained variation in Q but in the second case we aim to measure the unexplained variation in R.

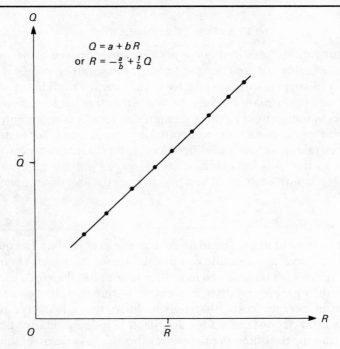

Chart 9.3 *Input and output: perfect correlation*

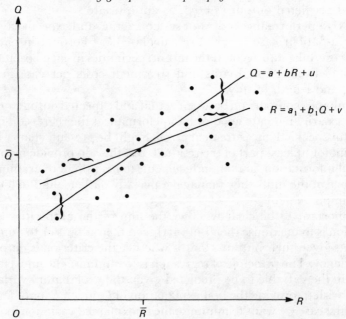

Chart 9.4 *Input and output: imperfect correlation*

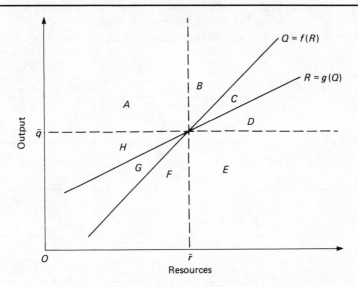

Chart 9.5 *Imperfect correlation and relative performance*

Regression equations can be represented by lines on a diagram. For example, the equation $Q = a + bR + u$ can be represented by a line plotting Q against R. In the case of perfect correlation between Q and R when there is a perfect fit for the regression equation, all points lie on the line, as in chart 9.3, but in general the points are scattered and subject to random (stochastic) influences as in chart 9.4. We can estimate either of two regression lines. One minimises the variation in Q, measured vertically, the other minimises the variation in R measured horizontally.

Chart 9.5 sets out zones A to H in which residuals might fall about two regression lines, $\bar{q}$ and $\bar{r}$ are mean output and mean unit cost respectively. Their properties are set out in table 9.1. Residuals for q are measured vertically; residuals for r are measured horizontally. It is clear that simple comparison of means produces the same impression of relative performance as inspection of residuals in only a few cases. Considering the comparison of residuals, then, if we believe costs determine output and we inspect $(q - \hat{q})$ then I.2 illustrates zones of relatively good performance and II.2 relatively poor performance; if we believe client numbers or output determines costs II.1 illustrates relatively good cost performance and I.1 is relatively poor. Taking output and costs together III.1 shows relatively good zones and III.2 relatively poor zones, IV illustrates ambiguous zones: high costs but high output, or low costs with low output, by comparison with expected values. The analysis could be extended by drawing boundaries, say ±1 standard error, about the regression lines and introducing further zones.

Table 9.1 *Relative performance*

Comparison type		Comparison with mean		Comparison with expected	
		Difference	Zone	Residual	Zone
I	1	$r > \bar{r}$	B, C, D, E	$r > \hat{r}$	D, E, F, G
	2	$q > \bar{q}$	A, B, C, D	$q > \hat{q}$	B, A, H, G
II	1	$r < \bar{r}$	A, H, G, F	$r < \hat{r}$	C, B, A, H
	2	$q < \bar{q}$	H, G, F, E	$q < \hat{q}$	C, D, E, F
III	1	$r < \bar{r}, q > \bar{q}$	A	$r < \hat{r}, q > \hat{q}$	H, A, B,
	2	$r > \bar{r}, q < \bar{q}$	E	$r > \hat{r}, q < \hat{q}$	F, E, D,
IV	1	$r < \bar{r}, q < \bar{q}$	H, G, F	$r < \hat{r}, q < \hat{q}$	C
	2	$r > \bar{r}, q > \bar{q}$	B, C, D	$r > \hat{r}, q > \hat{q}$	G

		Some comparisons with mean and expected	
			Zone
V	1	$r < \hat{r} > \bar{r}$	B, C
	2	$r > \hat{r} < \bar{r}$	G, F
	3	$q < \hat{q} > \bar{q}$	C, D
	4	$q > \hat{q} < \bar{q}$	H, G
VI	1	$q > \hat{q} > \bar{q}, r < \hat{r} < \bar{r}$	A
	2	$q < \hat{q} < \bar{q}, r < \hat{r} < \bar{r}$	E

Note: r = actual unit cost of authority i, $\bar{r}$ = mean unit cost of all authorities, $\hat{r}$ = 'expected' unit cost of authority i; likewise for outputs q, $\bar{q}$ and $\hat{q}$.

Interpretation of regression estimates

Regression equation estimates are presented in the chapters on education, health and police in the following form (numbers are hypothetical):

$$D = \begin{array}{cccc} & c & SOC & EXP \\ & 15 & -0.723 & 0.834 \\ & (3.72) & (2.02) & (1.65) \end{array}$$

$$R^2 = 0.67$$

(t values in brackets)

where D is the dependent variable, the variation in which we are explaining, in terms of differences in social circumstances SOC and public spending EXP. The proportion of the variation in D explained by the equation is shown by the coefficient of variation R^2: in the example above this is 67 per cent. The constant term C is measured in the same units as D; if D is expenditure in pounds per patient or pupil or police officer and so on, c, in the example, is £15; if D is the proportion of people in a locality with three or more GCE 'O' levels or hernias or burgled it means 15 per cent. The constant term depends on the expected value of D *before* allowing for differences in SOC and EXP. The coefficients for SOC and EXP respectively indicate the difference in D associated with a unit change in SOC, holding EXP constant and the difference in D associated with a unit change in EXP holding SOC constant.

SOC indicates the percentage of households with some particular socio-economic characteristics (for example, lacking certain housing amenities, or where the head is unemployed, or in high income groups). In the above example D is lower by £0.723 (if D is spending per patient/pupil and so on) for a one percentage point difference in SOC; if D is the number or percentage of people in an area with certain education or health characteristics it means that the number (or percentage) is lower by 0.723 for a 1 per cent point difference in SOC.

Likewise EXP is expenditure, in pounds, on some input (or all inputs); for example, if D is total spending per pupil and EXP is spending per teacher the example quoted above indicates that spending per pupil changes by £0.834 for every £1 difference in spending on teachers per pupil. Alternatively, if D refers to output, for example the proportion with Y GCE passes, it means that the proportion getting Y or more GCE passes is higher by 0.834 percentage points for every extra £1 spent.

It should be emphasised that the absolute sizes of the regression coefficients attached to SOC and EXP reflect the units in which they are measured; for instance if EXP is measured in hundreds of pounds the coefficient means that D changes by £83.4 for every £100 difference in spending, whereas if EXP is measured in units of one pound it means that D changes by £0.834 for every £1 difference in spending. However, if all the variables are measured in logarithms the coefficients show the percentage difference in D associated with a 1 per cent difference in SOC or EXP.

The t value is an indicator of the probability that chance alone is responsible for the statistical association found between the dependent variable and the variable to which the t value refers. The higher the t value the lower the probability that chance alone is responsible; the critical value of t depends on the size of the sample for any given level of probability. For a large sample a t value of about two or more means that there is at least a 5 per cent probability that chance alone is not the explanation.

RELATIVE EFFICIENCY AND BEST PRACTICE

In economic theory a production function, sometimes referred to as a production frontier, is a technological relationship which describes the maximum output that can be produced from any given combination of inputs, given the available technology. However, in much of the empirical literature on the subject, standard regression techniques are used to estimate what are, in effect, average production functions (where observations on actual output may lie either above or below the predictions of the model) as in the previous section. This distinction is particularly important if we are concerned with measuring efficiency because in that context we need to relate actual output to the maximum output that is potentially achievable, not just the average actually achieved.

The starting point for any discussion of frontier models is provided by the influential work of Farrell (1957). It was Farrell who proposed the ratio OB/OA in chart 9.1 as the measure of the technical inefficiency of a firm at point A. He proposed the ratio OD/OB as the best measure of allocative (what he called price) efficiency at point B. Overall efficiency at A is then defined as OD/OA, which is the ratio of costs at the most efficient point at D to their actual level at A, and is equal to the product of Farrell's measures of allocative and technical efficiency.

Numerous studies have attempted to apply the basic notions of Farrell's approach using a variety of models and estimating procedures. Some impose a particular framework on the frontier derived from specific theoretical considerations, some allow for random influences on the frontier. Appendix 3 provides a summary of the various approaches. The particular model which we used to estimate the efficiency scores of police authorities discussed in Chapter 12 below is that of data envelope analysis.

The main features of data envelope analysis are discussed in Appendix 2 but a summary is appropriate here.

It was suggested above that, in theory, efficiency scores can be calculated for each management unit the relative performance of which we want to assess, such as the local managements of a public service. These scores may indicate actual output as a percentage of maximum feasible output, given inputs, that is *output efficiency scores*; alternatively they may represent the *input efficiency scores* calculated as minimum possible inputs as a percentage of actual inputs, given output. In both cases scores of 100 per cent show maximum possible efficiency and the lower the score the greater the degree of inefficiency.

Regression analysis, which estimates the average output to be expected from a management unit, given its input (or average input, to be expected, given output) is, strictly speaking, inappropriate for this sort of evaluation. Thus in chart 9.6 below the solid line represents the average relationship, estimated by regression analysis, between input and output. Data envelope analysis mathematically estimates the frontier, shown by the broken line, representing the best possible performance represented by the outlying observations.

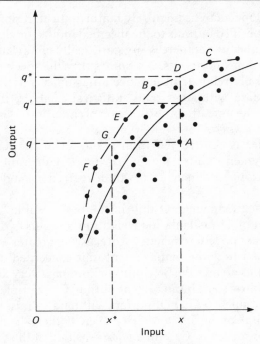

Chart 9.6 *Frontier analysis*

By joining up observations such as B and C, those on the frontier nearest to A, it calculates that with resources Ox the management of A should be capable of reaching point D with output Oq^*. The output efficiency score for A is Oq/Oq^*; likewise the input efficiency score for A is $Ox^*/O\dot{x}$.

In practice more than one output and more than one input may be involved and the mix of outputs and of inputs may vary between management units. Data envelope analysis weights inputs, and outputs, so as to produce a single summary measure of input and output for each management unit. Weights are calculated so as to maximise the efficiency score for each management unit (subject to the constraint that they do not exceed 100 per cent); Appendix 2 provides a summary of the method.

In Chapter 12 below we summarise a statistical model of police authority performance where the relative performance of each authority is assessed according to average expected output, as estimated from regression models, which gives the best fit to all the data; we then provide a summary of a data envelope analysis treatment of the police and briefly compare the two procedures.

Data envelope analysis can be related to microeconomic theory along the lines outlined earlier. But it has a number of important features which need to be borne in mind:

(a)   Data envelope analysis is entirely mathematical; it simply calculates the ratio of the specified outputs to the specified inputs (or vice versa) but it does not test whether or not there is any statistically significant relationship between the outputs and inputs: it assumes that the specified inputs and outputs are causally related. In practice an assumed relationship can be difficult to validate without careful statistical analysis, if at all. Data envelope analysis assumes that the direction of causation is known, which is not always clear *a priori*.

(b)   The frontier is constructed from a sub-set of the data (the most efficient management units) making it more vulnerable to extreme observations and measurement errors than regression models of average behaviour.

(c)   It shows each management unit in the best possible light, given its output and input mix by calculating weights for outputs and inputs which produce the highest possible efficiency score, giving greater weight to those inputs or outputs where the management unit concerned does relatively well. However, this creates the possibility of finding a very favourable but inappropriate ratio of some input to some output; for example, a favourable ratio of tonsillectomies to kitchen porters will tend to raise the efficiency score of a hospital or health authority even if there is a low ratio of tonsillectomies to surgeons. Careful *a priori* selection of the variables to be included is clearly essential.

A number of further theoretical issues concerning this method of analysis need to be resolved which are discussed in Appendix 2; alternative assumptions about the relationship between inputs and outputs discussed there are taken into account in the alternative results for police forces shown in Chapter 12. A general introduction to frontier models, of which data envelope analysis is one example, is provided in Appendix 3.

10

EDUCATION

EDUCATION OUTPUT

The main aim of education might be summarised in rather general terms as the development of the full potential of pupils. It involves the development of basic cognitive skills such as literacy and numeracy, of a wide range of knowledge and of non-cognitive personal and social attributes. The latter will embrace attitudes, behaviour, self-confidence, self-awareness, social integration and so on. The relative priorities among the various cognitive skills and among the various non-cognitive attributes, and between cognitive and non-cognitive development are matters for debate (Department of Education and Science, 1981b, 1985). The main quantitative indicator of educational output or performance has traditionally been examination results, although there are methodologies for evaluating non-cognitive development. As for the assessment of the contribution of education services to pupil attainment, the traditional focus has been on professional standards and on the curriculum. HM Inspectorate was established in the last century to monitor and improve professional teaching standards. The evaluation of the school curriculum has also been a major focus of attention with emphasis on the suitability of what is taught in relation to educational objectives and pupils' needs. In the past twenty years or so increasing attention has been paid to the effect of variations in family circumstances, parents' education, and resources on pupil performance. Most studies, whether comparisons of education authorities, schools, or individual pupils, have emphasised the importance of socio-economic factors, and the educational qualifications of parents, which most studies have found considerably to outweigh the impact of education resources or differences in schools; such studies include those by Jencks *et al* (1973), Marks *et al* (1983), the Department of Education and Science (1984) and Darlington and Cullen (1984). The precise contribution of socio-economic factors to differences in education attainment vary between the studies cited although all attribute a major weight to such factors.

The emphasis on the importance of socio-economic and parental influences on educational attainment, reported by United States studies and by the Plowden Report (1967) in the 1960s and early 1970s, created a pessimistic impression of the contribution of schools to educational attainment; and the more recent studies noted above might be thought to confirm this view. However, studies by Marks *et al* and by the Department of Education and Science itself show that there are wide variations in attainment even among education authorities and schools with similar socio-economic characteristics. This creates a presumption that differences among schools and authorities themselves must have an impact. Rutter (1979) investigated what it is that happens within schools which creates differences in academic and non-cognitive attainment among pupils; broadly he emphasised the importance of the 'ethos' of the school including such factors as the leadership offered by the headmaster, the involvement of teachers in the development of the curriculum, the structured school day, teacher continuity, high expectations by teachers of pupils, a work-oriented environment, regular pupil assessment and record keeping, and so on. Work in the United States by Sizer (1984) and Lerner (1982) reached broadly comparable conclusions. A recent report by the Inner London Education Authority (1986) reiterated and emphasised such factors: it notes that the ethos of the school may be indicated by such things as examination results, absenteeism, classroom behaviour, pupils' attitudes towards learning and towards continuing in education, their employment, delinquency, and so on. There can be little doubt that the influences noted by Rutter and others make an important contribution to educational attainment; but no nationwide indicators of their values exist by school or by local authority. Nevertheless, the work being done in this field by the Inner London Education Authority shows that at the level of the individual authority there is scope for the development of a more systematic approach towards the evaluation of these influences.

The only readily available indicators of educational output or performance on a national basis are examination results at GCE and CSE levels. These indicators tell us nothing about cognitive performance in the lower half of the ability range, for which these examinations were not designed, nor about non-cognitive achievement. These deficiencies were emphasised at a 1984 Royal Statistical Society Conference on the measure of educational achievement (Royal Statistical Society, 1984) and at a 1984 Economic and Social Research Council Conference sponsored by the Society of Education Officers (ESRC, 1985).

No United Kingdom data are available on a national basis for cognitive achievement by the lower half of the school ability range. In the United States a number of tests exist such as the scholastic aptitude test, the national assessment of educational progress (which is particularly intended to allow states to compare themselves with one another), and other tests are being developed by the Council of Chief State School Officers of the newly established Centre for the Coordination of Educational Assessment and Evaluation. The Royal Statistical Society and Economic and Social

Research Council conferences heard criticisms of the use of GCE/CSE results but they did not propose tests of cognitive attainment by the less academically gifted children. Some criticism of the use of GCE/CSE may reflect a rejection of any tests of academic attainment as measures of educational performance.

The use of GCE/CSE results also raises the question of the relative weight to be assigned to academic and non-academic education activities and performance. In practice examination performance is regarded as important by parents, employers and pupils. Work at the National Institute by Prais and colleagues has demonstrated that the level of achievement in mathematics in England by average and below average schoolchildren is considerably below that in major competitor countries with serious implications for the country's economic performance and for the employability of the children themselves. Prais and Wagner (1985) have noted that in an arithmetic test involving the addition of fractions the correct answer was attained by 4 per cent of the lower half of the English ability range, by 25 per cent of English children as a whole, but by 67 per cent of the *bottom* half of the German ability range; Prais has also noted that in a comparison between English and Japanese children, the Japanese children got scores in addition and subtraction tests which were approximately double those scored by the English children, although the Japanese children were younger and had started school at a later age. These differences in mathematics attainment are reflected in differences in the rigour of the technical and apprentice training schemes in the United Kingdom on the one hand and Germany and Japan on the other.

This is not to say that non-cognitive personal and social skills are unimportant. But questions arise as to what precisely is meant by personal and social skills and how they are to be measured. In the late 1970s the Department of Education and Science initiated an inquiry into the possibility of assessing personal and social development; such factors as self-awareness, self-confidence, self-knowledge, behaviour, knowledge and understanding of social values and institutions and so on were included as relevant considerations. A survey of the literature in this area revealed 40,000 references to studies along these lines: various psychometric and other approaches to the assessment of personal and social development among schoolchildren were revealed, including self-completion questionnaires distributed to children and questionnaires for completion by teachers; the use of this kind of approach to educational development seems to be more common in the United States than elsewhere (Department of Education and Science, 1981a). However, the Department of Education and Science concluded that there were considerable practical difficulties facing the introduction of such assessment in the United Kingdom on a nationwide basis (partly because of the existence of differences in opinion among the population as a whole about political and moral issues). The possibility of non-cognitive assessment somewhat along these lines in one education authority at least is suggested by the Inner London Education Authority Junior Schools Project.

COMPARING LOCAL EDUCATION AUTHORITIES

The methods of analysing performance, which have been described in Chapter 9, can be applied to secondary education. First we consider the variation in secondary education spending amongst the 96 English local education authorities, then the relationship between expenditure and examination results, and finally we consider the relative performance of authorities.

Education expenditure

Differences in spending between local education authorities may be regarded as reflecting differences in the number of pupils, differences in socio-economic characteristics taken into account by the government in assessing special needs, and differences in practices between, and within, authorities with respect to education policies and efficiency.

We allow for differences in numbers of pupils by concentrating on average expenditure per pupil. Pupils in senior years need to be taught in smaller classes than younger children and, because teaching costs are the most important element of cost, we make use of an age-weighted pupil–teacher ratio $(APTR)$ as a variable to be taken into account in examining differences among authorities. Where pupil numbers are falling (especially because of demographic factors) there is a lag in the adjustment in the number of teachers (and in the capital stock, which continues to need heating, lighting, maintenance, and so on) so that spending per pupil is relatively high. We allow for this by making use of a variable which measures the change in rolls (mean pupil numbers) (CHR).

The government makes extra provision for additional educational need (AEN) by a formula which takes into account the proportion of households with heads in certain occupations (for example, unskilled, farm workers), with only one parent, with large numbers of children, in poor housing, dependent on social assistance (supplementary benefit), and from certain ethnic backgrounds. We also take into account the possibility that expenditure may respond to pressures from higher social groups: HSG indicates the proportion of households in this category.

The remainder of the variation in expenditure will reflect differences in efficiency and in policies as well as measurement problems and variables we have not included in the analysis. Efficiency in this case means securing the lowest cost per unit of input and the lowest cost combination of inputs at a given level of output. A difference in priorities might reflect differences in the weights to be attached to different educational outputs, for example, differences in teaching provision for the less able (or most able) pupils, or for the range of subjects available; it might reflect differences in attitudes to teacher morale – an input – in the form of provision of free periods, training. But when differences in staffing are *not* associated with differences in output, or the precise output intended is not defined or monitored, the borderline between questions of priorities and efficiency is obscure. We are not able by statistical analysis to throw light on these matters, which require school-based research (Taylor, 1985).

Our regression model of the determinants of expenditure takes the form of an equation:

$$TEXP \text{ or } NTEX \text{ or } EXP = a + b.HSG + c.AEN + d.APTR + e.CHR + u$$

where $TEXP$ is teaching expenditure per pupil, $NTEX$ is non-teaching expenditure, EXP is total spending and u is a disturbance term to capture the unexplained variation in spending. Our results are in table 10.1.

The statistic $\bar{R}^2$ indicates the proportion of the variation in the left-hand (expenditure) variable explained by the equation. Thus in the case of teaching expenditure per pupil ($TEXP$), 80.9 per cent of the differences among authorities is explained by the equation. The slope coefficient for

Table 10.1 *Education expenditure per pupil*

	$\bar{R}^2$	C	HSG	AEN	APTR	CHR
TEXP	0.809	1150.0	1.391	0.498	−35.692	−2.131
		(21.0)	(4.1)	(3.3)	(11.3)	(4.8)
NTEX	0.604	616.0	4.214	1.175	−30.848	−3.733
		(5.2)	(5.7)	(3.7)	(4.7)	(4.0)
EXP	0.729	1769.0	5.597	1.668	−66.654	−5.870
		(11.2)	(5.8)	(3.9)	(7.6)	(4.7)

Source: Data are based on the statistics published by the Department of Education and Science (1984), that is, examination results for 1983/4, socio-economic variables derived from the 1981 Census, and school-based variables are averages for three years 1979/80–1981/2.
t values in parenthesis.
Definition of variables in tables 10.1 to 10.4:
TEXP = teaching expenditure per pupil.
NTEX = non-teaching expenditure.
EXP = total spending.
HSG = proportion of households in higher social groups.
AEN = additional educational need.
APTR = age-weighted pupil-teacher ratio.
CHR = change in rolls (mean pupil numbers).
POV = dependent on social assistance.
ETH = high proportion of non-white population.
TTUR = teacher turnover.

each variable shows the change in spending associated with a unit change in each variable *alone*, that is, holding all the others constant. Thus an increase in AEN alone raises total spending (EXP) per pupil by £1.67. Falling rolls raise spending per pupil (because there are fewer of them over which to spread the cost of premises, and there is a lag in the adjustment of teacher numbers to pupil numbers).

The results show that expenditure per pupil rises both with HSG and with AEN. This implies that local education authorities with populations which are neither especially well-off nor deprived tend to spend least (Economic and Social Research Council, 1985). We also show that expenditure per pupil moves inversely with differences in the pupil–teacher ratio.

Performance: examination results

Examination performance is not a comprehensive indicator of the output of the education service. Neither, unless we can take into account the initial abilities of pupils, is it a very good indicator of academic achievement attributable to secondary education alone. However, for good reasons outlined above, examination results are used here.

The measurement of examination performance presents a problem. There are two nationwide examinations for which results are available by each authority; the Certificate of Secondary Education (CSE), and the General Certificate of Education (GCE) for a somewhat higher ability range; pupils may take no examinations at all, or separate examinations in up to over twelve subjects, their results are classified by subject and each may be in any one of several grades.

The most comprehensive analysis of the results available to date which was carried out by Department of Education and Science officials (1984), sought to explain six examination performance indicators (ranging from no graded results at all up to Advanced Level GCE). Fifteen socio-economic variables, seven school-based variables (including pupil–teacher ratios and teacher turnover), and three resource variables ($TEXP$, $NTEX$, EXP) were all examined as possible statistically significant explanatory variables in a step-wise regression analysis. $TEXP$ was statistically significant for only three of the six examination performance indicators; the other explanatory variables included in the regression equations were different (and different in number). Broadly speaking, a negative relationship with indicators of deprivation emerged, but the particular social indicators found to be the most statistically significant differed according to the particular examination indicator being explained. The reasons for this are obscure in the absence of any specified model of the social processes at work. (For instance, the variables in the Department's equations to explain differences in the proportion of school leavers gaining five or more grade GCE/CSE passes differed from those explaining differences in the proportion gaining six or more passes, for no clear reason.) The commonsense interpretation is that the social indicators in question all capture similar, but not identical, aspects of deprivation. In our own work we have made use of principal components analysis in the search for more robust results. As explained in Chapter 9 above, this technique is designed to extract the relevant information from a set of variables (such as social deprivation indices) which are highly collinear.

For examination results we have tried two approaches: one is to generate a new, general, indicator (EX) by principal component analysis of the six official indicators of examination results. The other is to classify CSE/GCE examination results into three groups. These groups are a high group (proportion of school leavers with five or more higher grades, (Xh)), a low group (two or fewer of any grade (Xl)); and, by inference in accordance with the linear probability model, a middle range (Xm), given that

$$Xh + Xl + Xm = 1.$$

For the socio-economic variables we have also adopted two approaches to reduce the number of collinear variables. One is simply to take AEN, the sum of the individual needs variables, and HSG. The other is to generate new uncorrelated variables POV and ETH by principal component analysis (table 10.2); both reflect poor housing, unemployment, large or one-parent families; but POV especially reflects dependence on social assistance whereas a high score on ETH is associated with a high proportion of non-whites but not especially great dependence on assistance or high unemployment. Liverpool and Knowsley, for example, feature as being very deprived according to the indicator POV but they have low scores in terms of ETH; on the other hand none of the authorities with high ETH scores have high POV scores.

Results in table 10.3 for our general performance indicator EX show, unsurprisingly, a positive association with high social groups, and a negative relationship with AEN. A small, but statistically significant, association with $TEXP$ emerges, but there is a negative relation with non-teaching expenditure.

In both equations in table 10.3 teacher turnover $(TTUR)$ has a deleterious effect on examination performance. However, in the first equation, using principal components, ETH is not statistically significant. If $TTUR$ is dropped the coefficient on ETH doubles and the t values rises to 1.44. This probably reflects the relatively high correlation between the ethnic variable incorporated in ETH and $TTUR$ (as demonstrated in the Department's analysis). On the other hand, dropping $TTUR$ has no significant impact on the equation incorporating AEN.

Turning to results by range, we estimated

$$Xh = ah + bh.HSG + ch.AEN + dh.TEXP + eh.NTEX + fh.T\,TUR$$
$$and\ Xl = al + bl.HSG + ce.AEN + dl.TEXP + el.NTEX + fl.T\,TUR$$

(where $TTUR$ = teacher turnover).

Table 10.2 *Principal component analyses of certain socio-economic variables*

	$PC_1 = POV$	$PC_2 = ETH$
Cumulative fraction of variance explained	0.65	0.87
Factor loadings:		
Poor housing	0.89	0.30
Unemployment	0.78	−0.59
Large families	0.91	0.04
Supplementary benefit	0.87	−0.45
One-parent families	0.81	0.15
Non-white children	0.51	0.83

Extreme values: mean percentage of households with poor housing and so on nationally and LEAs with extreme[a] principal component scores

		POV		ETH	
	all 96 LEAs	highest 6	lowest 6	highest 6	lowest 6
Poor housing	4.3	9.1	1.9	8.9	4.7
Unemployment	9.8	15.2	5.5	9.2	17.7
Large families	9.2	15.3	6.5	11.4	10.6
Supplementary benefit	12.7	26.1	6.2	13.2	24.0
One-parent families	13.0	19.1	10.7	16.5	15.1
Non-white children	10.9	18.2	7.0	41.2	2.8
Identity of LEAs with		ILEA	Havering	Brent	Knowsley
highest or lowest		Birmingham	Sutton	Ealing	Liverpool
percentage scores		Wolverhampton	Herts	Haringey	Sunderland
		Knowsley	N. Yorks	Newham	Cleveland
		Liverpool	Surrey	Barnet	S. Tyne
		Manchester	W. Sussex	Hounslow	Wirral

[a]Mean percentages are unweighted.
For definition of variables see table 10.1.

Table 10.3 *Regressions using principal component exam indicator EX*

	$\bar{R}^2$	C	TEXP	NTEX	HSG	POV	ETH	TTUR
EX	0.809	−4.008	0.005	−0.003	0.080	−0.381	−0.040	−0.043
		(4.15)	(2.92)	(2.56)	(8.61)	(4.68)	(0.62)	(2.05)

	$\bar{R}^2$	C	TEXP	NTEX	HSG	AEN	TTUR	
EX	0.800	−2.962	0.005	−0.003	0.084	−0.015	−0.035	
		(3.09)	(2.61)	(2.39)	(10.06)	(4.36)	(1.76)	

Note: t values in parenthesis.
For definition of variables see table 10.1.

Table 10.4 *'Low' and 'high' results*

	$\bar{R}^2$	C	HSG	AEN	TEXP	NTEX	TTUR
Xh	0.792	−1.21	0.534	−0.033	0.029	−0.016	−0.177
		(0.2)	(12.2)	(1.8)	(3.0)	(2.4)	(1.7)
Xl	0.667	22.21	−0.295	0.115	−0.019	0.018	0.198
		(3.3)	(5.0)	(4.8)	(1.5)	(1.9)	(1.4)

Note: Xh = percentage of children with five or more higher grade GCE/CSE passes; Xl = percentage of children with less than two GCE/CSE passes. t values in parenthesis. For definition of variables see table 10.1.

Because $(Xh + Xl + Xm) = 1$, a new equation can be inferred for the middle result range:

$$Xm = am + bm.HSG \ldots + fm.T\,TUR$$

given that the intercepts $(ah + am + al)$ sum to unity and the slope coefficients $(bh + bm + bl) \ldots (fh + fm + fl)$ in each case sum to zero. Regression results are set out in table 10.4. The results confirm the positive impact of *HSG* and the negative impact of *AEN*, the small positive impact of *TEXP* on performance (that is, positive in relation to high results and inverse with respect to low results); the deleterious negative effect of teacher turnover is confirmed; again there is the curious negative relationship with non-teaching expenditure.

Non-teaching expenditure

The negative relationship between non-teaching expenditure and examination performance was examined further by breaking down *NTEX* into its main parts: spending on premises, non-teaching staff, books and equipment. Variables for each were substituted for *NTEX* alone in the equations for *EX*, *Xn* and *Xl*. The change in the fit of the equations as measured by $\bar{R}^2$ was very small, as were the changes in *C*, *TTUR*, *TEXP*, *HSG* and *AEN*. The signs for the coefficient on premises were negative (as for *NTEX*) in the case of *EX* and *Xh* and statistically significant; the coefficient on the non-teaching staff variable was negative but not significant for *EX* and positive but not significant for *Xh*. The coefficient for books was non-significant in every case. Therefore for *EX* and *Eh* disaggregation did not seriously alter the picture shown in tables 10.3 and 10.4. In the case of *Xl* (low performance) a positive coefficient appeared for non-teaching staff with a t value of 1.6 (significant at about the 90 per cent level), which is analagous to a negative relationship between changes in performance and higher spending.

In case the inner and outer London boroughs, with above national average non-teaching spending of each type, were distorting the overall national picture, they were then excluded from the regressions: exclusion made little difference although the fit of the model tended to decline.

In short, greater non-teaching spending tends to be associated with worse performance. It might be argued that some increased $NTEX$ – especially on non-teaching staff – might be intended to prevent the even worse performance which would otherwise arise but, provided that the regression model has correctly allowed for the socio-economic factors which tend to impede educational performance, this has been allowed for and this line of reasoning is without substance. However, *spending* on premises and on books tells us nothing about the available *stock* of buildings or books. High spending on premises might be on the maintenance of buildings still seriously below standard, or it might be on new or modernised building intended to boost pupil and teacher morale. High spending on books might be to make good past deficiencies or it might reflect above-average provision. The available data do not help to identify what the spending is on or what it means in terms of the stock and quality of premises or books.

Teaching expenditure

Spending on teaching staff is a very incomplete measure of the quantity or quality of teaching. Different schools with similar total teaching resources are likely to produce different levels of achievement (whether academic or other) if their policies, management and morale differ. It is sometimes suggested that differences in teaching inputs have little impact on educational outputs. For example, there is said to be low, or perverse correlation between class size and performance. But the reason for these findings may be that the most backward children are taught in the smallest classes. There can be little doubt *a priori* that a well-run school (in Rutter's terms) can sometimes achieve more than a badly run school which has more resources; but it is also very probable *a priori* that schools of similar quality would all achieve more with more resources. We have no data on such inputs as head teachers' leadership, management, teachers' morale, or pupil motivation: the only data we have is on the volume of resources. Teaching, measured in this way, might have a significant effect on examination results, although at first sight it may appear to be a very small one. In the Department of Education and Science analysis the coefficients in the equation explaining Xh are 0.3 for teaching expenditure but 0.56 for the proportion of higher social groups (see Department of Education and Science, 1984). But, as the Department warns, 'the relative sizes of coefficients is not indicative of the relative importance of variables' since they depend on the units in which the variables are measured. In our equations below we use the original variables transformed into logarithms.

Table 10.5 *Elasticities of examination performance with respect to input and social variables*

	L.Xh	L.Xl	L.Xh (DES)
$\bar{R}^2$	0.79	0.63	0.84
C	−2.02	5.25	−1.24
	(1.41)	(2.16)	(0.91)
L.HSG	0.64	−0.45	0.70
	(11.77)	(4.48)	(10.97)
L.AEN	−0.12	0.44	
	(2.01)	(4.26)	
L.TEXP	0.83	−0.77	0.53
	(2.88)	(1.58)	(1.94)
L.NTEX	−0.26	.28	−0.12
	(2.33)	(1.53)	(1.11)
L.TTUR	−0.14	0.22	−0.10
	(1.97)	(1.80)	(1.36)
L.PAR1			−0.34
			(4.18)
L.UNEM			0.18
			(2.69)
L.DENS			0.03
			(3.06)
L.PHOU			0.05
			(1.63) − 17
L.PGRA			0.68
			(3.00)

Note: $PAR1$ = proportion of single parent households; $UNEM$ = unemployment rate; $DENS$ = population density; $PHOU$ = proportion of children in poor housing; $PGRA$ = proportion in grammar schools (this variable appeared as significant in some but not all DES results; for example, for 'five or more' higher graded GCE/CSE results but not for 'six or more' graded results, for 'no results' but not for 'two or less' – which *includes* no results; it was much debated at the RSS Conference (1984)).

The coefficients which emerge are therefore elasticities, which are pure numbers and less dependent on the units of measurement used.

Results are shown in table 10.5 for *Xh* and *Xl* using a log-transformation of the variables previously shown in table 10.3 above, and for *Xh* using the same variables previously used by the Department officials in their step-wise regression analyses. The results suggest that, on average, a one percentage difference in teaching spending is associated with differences in examination performance of broadly 0.5 to 0.8 percentage points (other things being equal). Given that in the average education authority 23 per cent of pupils gain at least five higher grade GCE/CSE passes, the first equation means that a 10 per cent difference in *TEXP* is associated with 8.32 percentage points difference in *Xh*. Thus the effect of extra resources on exam results may be quite considerable in scale as well as statistically significant.

RELATIVE PERFORMANCE OF INDIVIDUAL LOCAL EDUCATION AUTHORITIES

The regression models described earlier estimate first how much, on average, we would expect an education authority to spend per pupil, given the social characteristics of the authority, the change in pupils rolls, and the age composition of its pupils, and secondly, what GCE/CSE performance we would expect, given the authority's social composition, and its spending per pupil, and teacher turnover. The regression approach indicates the average impact, for the country as a whole, of those influences, on either spending or performance, which are individually statistically significant and which together give the best statistical explanation of differences in the variable to be explained. On average we would expect deprived areas to spend more than better off areas, other things being equal; we would also expect the more socially deprived areas to achieve less, for a given level of pupil spending, more than affluent districts. That being said, we may still need to consider whether a particular authority is spending more or less than we would expect, given its social circumstances, and whether its pupils are achieving more or less than we would expect, given its social circumstances and spending. In the discussion below we concentrate on the second question, concerning examination performance.

We take as a criterion for identifying authorities with especially good or weak performance a range on either side of expected performance of one standard error. With a normal distribution of residuals – the difference between actual and expected performance – we would expect 95 per cent of authorities to have actual performance within twice the standard error of the regression equation.

Three indicators of performance have been used: EX, Xh and Xl. No single indicator is ideal and we have no unambiguous, widely acceptable and non-arbitrary way of weighting them. Table 10.6 shows those authorities with actual performance more than one standard deviation beyond that predicted for at least two of the indicators. Table 10.7 shows characteristics of those authorities with high and low scores – in terms of the difference between actual and predicted performance – on all three indicators.

The authorities with relatively high performance include not only affluent authorities A and D but also the relatively deprived B and E; the lower group includes relatively deprived M and N but also relatively middle class L and O (where social deprivation or affluence are indicated by AEN and HSG). On average the upper group have more relative deprivation (AEN) than the national average and the lower group. In terms of HSG the upper group as a whole is as middle class as the lower, and both are slightly more middle class than the national average.

Table 10.6 *Relative performance – authorities with residuals more than one-standard error for at least two indicators[a]*

Percentages

	EX	Xh	Xl
National average[b]	0	22.61	17.88
Standard error of regression	0.45	2.34	3.12
	Positive residuals		*Negative residuals[c]*
Authority: A	1.02	7.52	−5.10
B	0.95	4.06	−6.65
C	0.57	(1.87)	−3.85
D	0.54	3.16	−3.31
E	0.81	4.49	−3.69
F	0.62	5.73	(−0.66)
G	0.55	3.39	(−1.65)
H	0.61	(0.24)	−4.80
I	0.59	(−0.03)	−6.20
J	0.73	(0.87)	5.59
K	0.75	(2.26)	−4.15
	Negative residuals		*Positive residuals[c]*
L	−0.97	−3.80	4.00
M	−0.81	−4.75	4.10
N	−0.68	−2.51	3.39
O	−0.73	−2.93	5.10
P	−0.70	−2.58	4.59
Q	−0.47	−2.89	(2.24)
R	−0.56	−2.42	(2.30)
S	−0.70	(−1.33)	5.08
T	−0.68	(0)	6.28
U	−0.62	(−2.17)	4.01
V	−0.59	(−1.70)	4.05
W	−0.54	−2.41	4.03

[a] Brackets indicate residuals *within* one-standard error.
[b] The principal component *EX* has been normalised, that is it is an index with a mean of zero.
[c] In the case of *Xl positive* residuals means more pupils than expected get *low* GCE/CSE results; negative residuals mean fewer than expected get low results.

In terms of expenditure the upper group as a whole spends more per pupil than the lower group and more than the national average; in any case the prediction of expected performance allows for their actual (above average) spending; two deprived areas in the upper group B and E spend less than the national average. The lower group includes two authorities which spend more than the national average, one of which is also relatively affluent.

We have defined relative performance not in terms of a comparison between actual performance and the national average, but in terms of

Table 10.7 *Authorities with residuals beyond one standard error on three indicators: actual Xh and Xl scores, social and expenditure variables*

	Xh %	Xl %	AEN %	HSG %	EXP £	$TEXP$ £
A	37.2	9.8	60.6	41.4	1275	760
B	21.7	16.3	93.1	19.9	948	639
D	33.2	9.4	48.6	42.9	1025	652
E	22.7	17.1	26.7	19.9	926	629
Average	*28.7*	*13.1*	*69.8*	*31.0*	*1043*	*670*
L	28.8	15.0	43.7	48.4	1036	650
M	12.8	26.1	81.7	21.6	878	589
N	18.0	24.4	85.5	23.9	1017	686
O	26.9	16.6	46.6	40.1	895	617
P	16.9	22.2	56.5	20.6	826	590
Average	*20.7*	*20.9*	*62.8*	*30.9*	*930*	*626*
National average	*22.6*	*17.9*	*66.5*	*28.2*	*972*	*646*

Note: Unweighted averages.
For definition of variables see table 10.1.

actual performance compared to that predicted. Even so it is noticeable that the upper group in table 10.7 has, on average, better actual scores than the lower; B does better in terms of avoiding low GCE/CSE scores (Xl) than more affluent O and almost as well as affluent L which also spends more. B and E have better actual results in terms of Xh and Xl than less deprived M, N (which spends more) and P.

The regression model standardises for the differences in social composition and in spending per pupil. These differences have already been taken into account in computing the differences between actual and expected results. We would expect to find some residuals because of statistical noise (measurement errors, omitted variables, random influences, factors peculiar to a specific authority). The level of aggregation may also be a limitation (although the use of school based data does not seem to alter the general picture, see Darlington and Cullen, 1984). Therefore the existence of residuals does not demonstrate relative efficiency or inefficiency. However, the residuals might reflect not only factors beyond the control of local management but also the effect of local practices and priorities which differ from the average and which warrant close examination.

Differences in the way in which pupils are taught, which presumably at least partly reflect local policies, and in their motivation, might offer explanations of differences in performance. An analysis of the kind we have carried out may help to identify areas and authorities where examples of good practice might be found. Spending more for the same kind of education which produces poor results in some areas may be less effective than spending on a different approach, perhaps along the lines practised in some of the authorities in the upper half of table 10.7.

Finally, it needs to be recalled that the examination indicators used tell us nothing directly about cognitive developement among the least academically gifted who do not take GCE/CSE examinations; it is possible that authorities which do not do well in GCE/CSE terms nonetheless produce better cognitive development with respect to such children than authorities which demonstrate good GCE/CSE performance. However, table 10.6 suggests that those authorities which have the best performance in terms of high GCE/CSE results (at least five graded GCE/CSE passes, Xh) also tend to do well in terms of the numbers gaining at least two graded GCE/CSE passes (Xl) and include those which do best in this respect. Conversely, those which have weak performance in terms of the larger than expected proportion of pupils failing to get at least two graded passes include those which also do worst in terms of the proportion getting at least five passes. In these circumstances it seems unlikely that those which have weak results for high numbers of passes and a high proportion failing to get at least two passes will demonstrate good performance still further down the cognitive range. But it is not impossible.

Considerable differences in examination performance between local education authorities remain after we have standardised for differences in their social composition and their spending. These differences warrant closer examination 'on the ground' to identify good practice. However, education in the United Kingdom is bedevilled by a remarkable degree of difference in opinion (not found among our competitors) as to what education is for and, in consequence of this, as to the value of cognitive tests and examination results as measures of performance.

As for the average contribution of teaching and non-teaching resources to performance, our results suggest, in contrast to common opinion, that differences in teaching inputs do have a significant positive impact on performance. Non-teaching inputs present more of a problem, their relationship with performance looks perverse, for the available data tells us nothing about differences in the stock of buildings, books and equipment, only annual spending. It is conceivable that high spending might be associated with, and intended to correct, a poor stock of 'capital'; alternatively the spending might be inefficiently used: we do not know.

11

HEALTH

The primary aim of the health service is to treat ill health and to prevent its recurrence. Health care has a long history of the evaluation of output and performance; summaries of this history are provided by Goldacre and Griffin (1983) and by Rosser (1983). Medical practitioners have a tradition of assessing the output and effectiveness of their procedures and publishing their results in medical journals. But there is also a long history of management concern with health care outcomes: according to Rosser, in ancient Babylon mistreatment carried penalties for the doctors concerned on a scale according to the severity of the damage done and the status of the patient. Florence Nightingale proposed the systematic analysis of hospitals' resources and outputs (Goldacre and Griffin, 1983 and Rosser, 1983). More recently the Guillebaud Committee (Guillebaud, 1957) advocated the regular evaluation of health service performance; since 1984 performance indicators have been available, covering every district health authority (DHA) as a conscious attempt to focus attention on relative performance (see DHSS, 1984; Gibbs, 1985; Goldacre and Griffin, 1983; Rosser, 1983; Yates, 1985 and Meara and Gossman, 1986).

In practice the performance indicators are largely concerned with activities or processes, such as patients treated, hospital throughput, patient turnover, day-case surgery, and detailed costs by district health authority, by hospital type and department, per case (actual and expected) and by input type; there is much less information on health outcomes except for standardised mortality rates. Outcomes involve the impact on 'avoidable' deaths from conditions amenable to treatment, and on ill-health short of actual death, that is morbidity, such as hip failure. Morbidity data are notably scarce on a comprehensive basis for the population as a whole and by district health authority, although the incidence of many diseases is known when patients come forward for treatment; but the severity of their incapacity or distress is not systematically recorded and it is difficult to aggregate separate morbidity indicators for different conditions. Output or performance indicators in these circumstances tend to be of three types: population-based indicators such as standardised mortality rates where many influences other than health services have an impact; patient-based indicators such as death rates for those who undertook a particular treatment; controlled trials where the effectiveness or output of a treatment is assessed by providing it for some patients but not others in matched samples. A number of cost–benefit analyses of particular sorts of health care have attempted to place values on the outputs where lives have been saved. This involves imputing a value to human life based on estimates of foregone earnings, but such an approach cannot cope with improvements in morbidity where earnings are not lost, quite apart from all the inherent statistical and ethical problems associated with the approach.

The performance indicators are not based on new data and a consideration in their development was that they should draw on available statistics. However, performance indicators do represent an important step in the systematic and consistent assessment of relative performance: they make data available for the first time by district health authority for a wide range of indicators. Every authority has access to the data and it is intended to be used by authority managers to assess their own performance in relation to others, by regional managers in assessing relative performance at regional level and among their district authorities, and at ministerial level in the annual reviews of regions. But interpretation of some of the indicators is felt, by some health authority officials, to be difficult, and ambiguities can arise. For instance, an important indicator is 'length of stay'; average national length of stay has fallen for several years and is believed to have reduced in-patient costs. Variations in average length of stay among hospitals or authorities however, may reflect not relative efficiency, but differences in the mix of patients, the severity of their condition, the availability of non-hospital care opportunities such as community health services and personal social services, whether the patients live alone, the availability of hospital beds, waiting lists, and clinical and management practices. Moreover, a district health authority with a shorter average length of stay than another might be one where patients are more frequently readmitted. Length of stay refers to a patient's admission and not a complete treatment, in which readmission might be involved; a recent analysis has shown that when readmissions are included even large differences in length of stay can be substantially reduced.[1]

Another intermediate output indicator where difficulties can arise concerns day attendances for the elderly. A high attendance per head of the elderly population may indicate the existence of either good day-care facilities or poor in-patient facilities. Similarly, a short turnover interval, that is a measure of unused in-patient capacity between the departure of one patient and the arrival of the next, may be low because admission procedures are efficiently planned or because patients are kept in unnecessarily in order to improve this performance indicator. A particularly difficult proxy indicator of service effectiveness or output is the length of the waiting list, where differences in list sizes may reflect differences in the pressure of unmet needs or differences in consultants' policies with respect to the admission of patients onto the list in the first place. Differences in rates of surgery may reflect differences in surgical policies, in the availability of resources including beds, or in morbidity; evidence on the latter is relatively rare (see McPherson, Strong, Epstein and Jones, 1981 and McPherson, Strong, Jones and Britton, 1985). Another example of the need for care in interpreting the data concerns day-case surgery, where a high rate of day cases is often thought to reflect a more efficient use of resources. But it is also possible that some of those treated would not have been admitted as in-patients so that an increase in day cases might be associated with an increase rather than a reduction in costs.

A psychometric approach: QUALYs

We have commented in an earlier chapter on the problems of defining and measuring final outputs and of aggregating together the individual outputs of the separate parts of any service provided by the public sector. In the measurement of private sector output, changes in the volume of output of different goods can be aggregated using their prices as relative weights, but this procedure is not available for free public services. An approach to health output, which could perhaps be applied in other services, has been explored by Rosser and King (1978) and its implications for NHS resource allocation have been examined by Williams (Kind, Rosser and Williams, 1982). Rosser has attempted to devise a composite index for health output where good health scores 100, death 0. Ill-health is defined according to two dimensions: an eight-point scale of physical incapacity/immobility and a four-point scale of pain or distress. (Toothache would have a worse score on the pain index than the absence of a limb but the latter will have a worse score on the incapacity scale.) Each point on the two-dimensional matrix has an index or score derived from a detailed psychometric analysis of the responses of a sample of doctors, nurses and patients. The score is called a 'quality adjusted life year' (QUALY) where one year of healthy life scores 100. The impact of a treatment for a given condition is measured by the change in the QUALY which it induces. No statistically significant differences in scores obtained from Rosser's sample seem to be associated with differences in the socio-economic status of respondents, although there seem to be differences between health professionals and ex-patients.

On the whole the scores demonstrate diminishing marginal utility as health status improves: the less severe the initial degree of pain or incapacity the lower the impact on the QUALY of a further reduction in pain or incapacity. They also show, on the whole, that the greater the incapacity the greater the marginal impact on the QUALY of the relief of pain and the greater the initial degree of pain the greater the marginal impact on the QUALY for a given reduction in incapacity. But although at certain points in the matrix of QUALY scores the marginal changes seem perverse or inconsistent, they are not discussed by the authors. Williams has proposed that the QUALY approach should be used to compare alternative health service resource allocations; for example, to suggest that a given sum spent on renal dialysis has a smaller impact on QUALYs than the same amount devoted to hip replacement.

The implications of this approach are clearly controversial not least because they exclude the distress of patients' families. However, the approach has three major merits. It focusses attention on final output (relief of incapacity and pain); it enables the relative values of a wide range of different activities to be imputed and compared; and it provides a basis for aggregating the overall output of the service.

Estimating the relationship between resources and outputs

The methods of measurement and of analysis, which have been described in Chapter 9 and applied to education in Chapter 10, cannot so readily be applied to the National Health Service. Data limitations restrict the definition of 'outcomes' since there are no aggregate, comprehensive, nationwide indicators of morbidity or ill-health of all types or of changes in QUALYs. However, nationwide data do exist for 'avoidable deaths', that is, deaths from conditions usually amenable to treatment if it is sought in good time; we have used these data as our indicator of health outcomes, although they account for fewer than 10 per cent of all deaths. Information on the health service resources devoted to treating these deaths is not readily available, so we have taken spending on all acute in-patient services, by District Health Authorities (DHAs). However, some of the patients treated in a given DHA are patients from other DHAs while some of the residents of a given DHA are treated outside the district. This problem of cross boundary flows has been tackled by relating avoidable deaths of residents of a DHA to spending by the DHA on its own residents *wherever* they are treated. The expenditure data therefore do not necessarily indicate the resources available within the District. Further, the information available for arriving at expenditure by DHAs on their own residents is subject to a number of problems, in particular the quality of the data on costs and on patient 'imports' and 'exports' appears to be mixed and it seems likely that DHAs use a degree of judgement in arriving at the estimates they provide.

The Family Practitioner Services (FPS) are organised into Committee Areas which differ from DHAs and it is not possible at present to examine FPS and hospital resources or patient treatment on a fully consistent basis. FPS expenditure has been imputed to DHA areas on the basis of their relative population sizes and is clearly subject to error. London DHAs have been excluded from this analysis because the complexity of the boundaries there is particularly difficult to handle.

Another problem is that DHAs with teaching hospitals differ from others with respect to the mix and severity of the cases they treat, and the resources which they have available. The London Districts tend to differ from most others in housing, for historical reasons, more general hospitals and associated resources, but they also provide care for treating severe or rare conditions from far afield.

All these considerations make attempts to compare health spending and outcomes across the country more difficult and prone to error than the analogous analyses we have undertaken for education and the police, services where, although no formal performance indicator programmes have been developed, the data present fewer problems.

Finally, a topic, which we do not explore below, is the performance of the National Health Service in terms of improving the health status of the less well-off, both absolutely and relative to the better-off: an important element in the original *raison d'être* of the NHS (and an important consideration in any discussion of alternative financing arrangements). Discussions of this theme can be found in Atkinson, Hills and LeGrand (1986) and in the further references therein.

THE GEOGRAPHICAL DISTRIBUTION OF SPENDING

Before considering the relationship between resources and outcomes it may be of interest to examine the relationship between some elements of spending by area and the social characteristics of those areas.

The socio-economic and demographic factors we have taken into account as possible influences include: the proportion of over 65s in the population, the proportion of elderly living alone (and hence possibly more dependent on health services than those with families); indicators of deprivation or stress such as the proportion of the population with poor household amenities, in overcrowded accommodation, with unskilled heads or with single parents; ethnic minorities; and the proportion moving house (an indicator of weak local roots). We also have examined a number of summary, composite social indicators. The demographic and socio-economic indicators are listed in table 11.1. Because these indicators are closely correlated with one another, a principal component analysis was undertaken (see Chapter 9 above) from which two variables were obtained, one an indicator of relative affluence, the other of age structure. As can be seen from table 11.2, two components together explain 70 per cent of the total variation of the full set of ten variables. It is possible to provide a simple interpretation of each of these components.

The first component, relative affluence (AFF), is strongly *negatively* related to measures of social deprivation and disadvantage, such as overcrowding, lack of amenities, one parent families, low social class, the presence of ethnic minorities and unemployment. We can therefore

Table 11.1 *District health authority data*

Variable name	Definition
NHS	Total NHS revenue expenditure per head.
CHSPC	CHS spending per head.
FPSPC	FPS spending per head (for derivation see text).
PHCPC	Total primary health care spending per head.
HREPC	Total hospital spending per head.
OV65	People aged 65 or more as a percentage of all residents in private households.
ELDA	Pensioners living alone as a percentage of all residents in private households.
UN5	Children under 5 as a percentage of all residents in private households.
OPAR	People in households consisting of one person over 16 and one or more children under 16 as a percentage of all residents in private households.
UNSK	People in households headed by a person in socio-economic group 11 as a percentage of all residents in private households.
UNEM	People aged 16 or more seeking work or temporarily sick as a percentage of the total economically active population.
NOAM	People in households lacking exclusive use of a bath and inside WC as a percentage of all residents in private households.
OVER	People in households living at more than one person per room as a percentage of all residents in private households.
MOHO	People aged 1 or over with a usual address one year before the census different from present usual address as a percentage of total residents.
ETH	People in households headed by a person born in the New Commonwealth or Pakistan as a percentage of all residents in private households.
J10	Index based on social variables above using weights from Jarman (1983).
J8	Derived as *J10* excluding *OV65* and *NOAM*.
DOES	Based on weights given for social index of deprivation in Department of the Environment (1983).
SFR	Standardised fertility ratio.
SMR	Standardised mortality ratio.
CDR	Crude death rate.
AIP	Spending on acute in-patient treatment of the district's resident population, wherever they are treated.
SAD	Summary of avoidable deaths.
PERI	Perinatal death rate.
HYST	Hypertensive/cerebrovascular diseases.
CERV	Malignant neoplasm of cervix uterus.

Note: The data used in the analyses refer to the 192 district health authorities in England and come from a variety of sources. Information on current expenditure is based on the 1984/5 costing returns. The demographic and socio-economic data were derived from the 1981 census and made available to us by the inter-authority comparisons consultancy. The data on *SFR*, *SMR*, and *CDR* refer to 1983 and were taken from Vital Statistics (OPCS, 1985). Avoidable deaths indicators were taken from a recent paper by Charlton and Lakhani (1986) and refer to 1979–83.

interpret AFF as being *positively* related to the level of general affluence among the population. The second component, *AGE*, seems to reflect the age composition of the population, being positively related to the proportion of pensioners and of elderly people living alone and negatively related to the proportion of young children. We would therefore expect this component to be positively associated with *per capita* health spending.

Table 11.2 *A principal component analysis of ten social and demographic indicators by district health authority*

	Principal component 1 (Affluence)	Principal component 2 (Elderly)
Cumulative fraction of variance explained	0.43	0.70
Factor loadings:		
OV65	0.08	0.91
ELDA	−0.29	0.90
UN5	−0.16	−0.86
OPAR	−0.88	0.02
UNSK	−0.79	−0.19
UNEM	−0.73	−0.17
NOAM	−0.82	0.24
OVER	−0.94	−0.13
MOHO	−0.32	0.45
ETH	−0.76	−0.03

In attempting to explain the differences in spending among districts it was clearly necessary to make special allowance for the Thames area. London weighting and the concentration of teaching hospitals in the capital would lead us to expect spending to be greater here than elsewhere. This is borne out by table 11.3 which shows that *per capita* spending on the National Health Service by Thames districts is about 20 per cent above the average for the rest of England, although this will include the effect of patients living outside the Thames districts coming in for treatment. For this reason we decided to treat the Thames districts separately in our analysis. Even excluding them we still observe a ten-fold variation in hospital spending *per capita* (table 11.3) part of which is accounted for by cross-boundary flows. It is also necessary to distinguish between teaching and non-teaching areas because of the special circumstances of the former.

Table 11.4 sets out the results of multiple regression analyses of spending *per capita* on resident acute in-patients (*AIP*), the community health services (*CHS*), and (outside the Thames districts) the family practitioner service (*FPS*), in relation to our principal components of relative affluence (*AFF*) and *AGE*. We would expect, or hope, that spending would be negatively associated with *AFF*, that is, poorer areas would attract more resources per head, given the link between morbidity and socio-economic circumstances. This is indeed confirmed in every case: the relationship is also statistically significant except in the case of the family practitioner service. The relationship of spending with *AGE* is, as one might expect, positive (apart from the non-significant result for teaching districts).

Comparing the results for the different types of spending, the proportion of spending explained by the regression equations (measured by $\bar{R}^2$) is

Table 11.3 *The distribution of 1984/5 per capita NHS spending by Thames and non-Thames area DHAs*

£

	Minimum	Maximum	Mean	Coefficient of variation[a]
England excluding Thames area				
Hospitals	48	490	166	42.1
Community health	13	31	18	15.8
Family practitioner[b]	43	75	65	9.0
Total NHS	135	588	249	29.4
Thames area only				
Hospitals	85	897	218	66.2
Community health	12	41	20	29.7
Family practitioner[b]	62	78	66	3.8
Total NHS	163	1003	303	49.1

[a] The coefficient of variation expresses the standard deviation as a percentage of the mean.
[b] The figures for FPS are likely to be inaccurate (see section on data).

greatest for acute in-patients and lowest for family practitioner services in the case of each geographical grouping.

Turning to the different sets of results by area, the strongest relationship with social factors, and the highest $\bar{R}^2$, are found for the Thames districts and for (all) teaching districts, with around 80 per cent of spending explained. These results may be, in part, a result of the historical accident that large teaching hospitals were built in what are now socially deprived districts. However, community health service spending is also more strongly negatively related to affluence in Thames (and teaching districts) than elsewhere. Although the overall explanatory power of the regressions is lower in non-Thames and non-teaching areas, there is still a statistically significant negative relationship between spending on acute in-patient and community health service on the one hand and *AFF* on the other.

HEALTH SERVICE PROVISION AND AVOIDABLE DEATHS

Avoidable deaths, as estimated by Charlton and Lakhani (1986), refer to deaths resulting from those disease groups where 'medical and health interventions are sufficiently effective to prevent or cure almost all cases in the more resilient age groups, provided attention is sought in good time'. These deaths provide an indicator of 'the outcome of primary prevention, secondary prevention and curative aspects of the health services on the residents of defined geographical areas'.

As noted above, avoidable deaths account for a minority of all deaths and, by implication, of health resources. There are also problems associated

Table 11.4 *Multiple regression analysis explaining variations in per capita health expenditures across DHAs*

		Constant	AFF	AGE	R^2	$\bar{R}^2$	n
Thames:	AIP	92.63 (59.85)	−16.75 (15.39)	4.19 (3.54)	0.827	0.821	59
	CHSPC	19.13 (41.55)	−3.22 (9.94	1.41 (4.01)	0.694	0.683	59
Non-Thames:	AIP	83.91 (96.61)	−9.49 (8.52)	6.92 (6.56)	0.422	0.414	133
	CHSPC	18.08 (81.61)	−1.81 (6.22)	0.46 (1.67)	0.230	0.218	133
	FPSPC	65.73 (131.35)	−1.44 (2.20)	2.27 (3.66)	0.106	0.092	133
Teaching:	AIP	91.01 (25.49)	−15.58 (8.09)	8.54 (3.60)	0.793	0.775	26
	CHSPC	17.63 (17.70)	−3.48 (6.48)	3.13 (4.74)	0.764	0.743	26
	FPSPC	67.16 (54.86)	−0.06 (0.09)	−0.55 (0.68)	0.020	−0.065	26
Non-teaching:	AIP	84.70 (100.90)	−10.25 (9.67)	5.33 (6.21)	0.407	0.400	166
	CHSPC	18.20 (89.04)	−1.87 (7.25)	0.56 (.2.70)	0.249	0.240	166
	FPSPC	65.31 (163.83)	−0.42 (0.83)	1.73 (4.23)	0.099	0.088	166
Thames non-teaching:	AIP	91.81 (57.75)	−15.61 (9.79)	2.99 (2.32)	0.686	0.672	48
	CHSPC	18.75 (48.27)	−2.61 (6.70)	0.68 (2.17)	0.514	0.492	48
Non-Thames non-teaching:							
	AIP	82.15 (97.19)	−6.75 (5.65)	5.58 (5.65)	0.301	0.289	118
	CHSPC	17.91 (73.98)	−1.26 (3.71)	0.29 (1.04)	0.107	0.091	118
	FPSPC	65.34 (116.73)	−0.71 (0.90)	1.96 (2.99)	0.072	0.056	118
Thames excl.inner London:							
	AIP	91.39 (54.02)	−14.51 (8.31)	2.84 (2.13)	0.620	0.602	46
	CHSPC	18.44 (47.64)	−2.15 (5.24)	0.55 (1.80)	0.400	0.372	46

Table 11.5 *The association between avoidable deaths indicators and social indicators across non-Thames area DHAs (simple correlation coefficients)*

Social indicators[a]	Summary avoidable deaths	Perinatal death rate	Hypertensive/ cerebrovascular diseases	Malignant neoplasm of cervix uterus
$OV65$	−0.13	−0.26	−0.08	−0.09
$ELDA$	0.17	—	0.24	0.16
$UN5$	0.18	0.22	0.04	0.10
$OPAR$	0.45	0.34	0.35	0.30
$UNSK$	0.59	0.46	0.60	0.51
$UNEM$	0.63	0.49	0.58	0.53
$NOAM$	0.50	0.29	0.39	0.30
$OVER$	0.70	0.56	0.58	0.37
$MOHO$	−0.29	−0.32	−0.46	−0.30
ETH	0.45	0.35	0.25	0.05
$J10$	0.51	0.29	0.42	0.32
$J8$	0.59	0.43	0.48	0.37
$DOES$	0.60	0.41	0.52	0.35

[a] For definitions see table 11.1.

with the cross boundary flows adjustments to the expenditure data which we use to indicate health service inputs. As noted earlier, the data used by us refer to the *average* for the five year period 1979–83 and so do not exactly coincide with our expenditure data, but given the considerable (and necessary) inertia which exists in the allocation of health spending this may not be too serious a problem. With all these caveats in mind it is clear that only a very tentative analysis is possible.

The Charlton and Lakhani data on avoidable deaths refer to district level indicators based on mortality from eight disease groups for the years 1974–83. All the indicators were standardised for age, and in addition age limits were set for each disease group: death becomes increasingly unavoidable as age rises. In our analysis we have focused on the three disease groups which resulted in the largest number of avoidable deaths, together with a summary measure derived by Charlton and Lakhani which placed equal weight on each of the eight individual disease groups.

The first column of table 11.5 shows the simple correlations across non-Thames districts between the 'summary indicator of avoidable deaths' and various social and expenditure variables. Among the social variables, particularly high positive correlations emerge between avoidable deaths and overcrowding, low social class and unemployment.

Table 11.6 shows the simple correlations between four avoidable deaths indicators and various social and expenditure measures across the Thames area. As in the case of the rest of England sample, we observe particularly

Table 11.6 *The association between avoidable deaths indicators and social indicators across Thames area DHAs (simple correlation coefficients)*

Social indicators[a]	Summary avoidable deaths	Perinatal death rate	Hypertensive/ cerebrovascular diseases	Malignant neoplasm of cervix uterus
OV65	0.01	−0.01	0.004	0.22
ELDA	0.36	0.07	0.31	0.40
UN5	—	0.33	0.03	−0.05
OPAR	0.78	0.36	0.75	0.36
UNSK	0.81	0.57	0.69	0.40
UNEM	0.78	0.52	0.78	0.49
NOAM	0.67	0.35	0.66	0.43
OVER	0.78	0.46	0.73	0.36
MOHO	0.50	—	0.47	0.31
ETH	0.63	0.36	0.64	0.22
J10	0.77	0.41	0.73	0.52
J8	0.84	0.46	0.79	0.49
DOES	0.79	0.37	0.76	0.46

[a] For definitions see table 11.1.

high positive correlations between avoidable deaths and indicators of social deprivation or disadvantage such as low social class, unemployment and overcrowding.

Regression analysis of avoidable deaths

Although only part of health spending is devoted to the conditions covered by the avoidable deaths indicators it is of interest to see whether differences in avoidable deaths among districts are negatively related to spending, after allowing for social factors. In other words, are avoidable deaths likely to be lower when spending is higher, *ceteris paribus*? Given the special circumstances of teaching hospitals the analysis concentrates on non-teaching districts.

The results show a negative statistically significant effect for spending on acute in-patients, but not for expenditure on the community health services or the family practitioner service, and the explanatory power of the equations is low. Furthermore, the effect of excluding Thames non-teaching districts from the sample (not shown here) is to render most of the expenditure variables statistically insignificant. So while these results provide some evidence for the contribution of resources to outcomes in non-teaching districts as a whole, they are far from conclusive (the importance of social factors does seem to emerge clearly – AFF is strongly statistically significant throughout). However, there are a number of problems with the analysis. The data are very aggregative, and there is a mismatch between

Table 11.7 *Multiple regression analysis explaining variations in avoidable deaths across non-teaching DHAs*

	SAD	PERI	HYST	CERV
Constant	10.88	16.28	111.83	104.15
	(2.64)	(8.89)	(5.02)	(2.98)
PCI(AFF)	−4.49	−1.59	−19.27	−17.90
	(9.80)	(7.81)	(7.78)	(4.60)
AIP	−0.10	−0.03	−0.32	−0.39
	(3.69)	(2.86)	(2.25)	(1.73)
CHSPC	0.15	−0.05	0.40	1.14
	(1.32)	(0.90)	(0.64)	(1.15)
FPSPC	0.003	−0.001	0.15	0.16
	(0.05)	(0.03)	(0.48)	(0.33)
R^2	0.436	0.290	0.326	0.160
$\bar{R}^2$	0.422	0.272	0.309	0.140
n	166	166	166	166

the period to which the resources and outcome data refer. More importantly, avoidable deaths represent a small proportion of all deaths, and expenditure on acute in-patients covers many types of health service activity, so that there are difficulties in attempts to relate the two. Nevertheless, the analysis suggests that there is some tentative evidence that differences in acute in-patient resources do have an impact on health outcomes.

POLICE

The principal aims of the police are to deter crime and to maintain public order. We concentrate on the former. The contribution of the police to the deterrence of crime includes their crime prevention activities such as patrols, as well as the deterrent effects of their apprehension of criminals. The latter is an intermediate output with respect to final output defined as the reduction in the (true) crime rate. Further, the deterrent effect of the whole criminal justice system depends partly on the probability of being caught (to which the police contribute) and partly on the law, sentencing policy, the courts and prisons. However, here we shall concentrate on the police alone. Apart from the activities of the police directly related to deterring crime, they also have traffic, court, ceremonial and various other duties, the outputs of which we do not consider.

The precise definition and measurement of the crime rate is problematical. The recorded crime rate will not necessarily reflect the true crime rate if the public do not report some crimes; this can arise because they do not want to waste police time over trivial offences, or where the prospects for successful detection seem remote, unless an insurance claim requires reporting, or through fear of reprisals from the offenders and their friends, unwillingness to face publicity, or through feelings of intimidation by police or court procedures. Responses by the victims of crime to the General Household Survey suggest that there is considerable under-reporting of crime to the police. The police themselves have some discretion as to whether or not to record incidents reported to them as crimes, for example, if they are doubtful as to whether an incident really occurred and (if it did) whether it was a crime. For all these reasons the relationship between the true crime rate and the recorded crime rate might vary over time and between police forces, but the recorded crime rate is all that is available.

Another problem concerning the recorded crime rate is that increases in police manpower might induce the public to report more crime, perhaps because the public feels there is a greater chance that the offenders will be caught (in much the same way that increases in the number of hospital consultants can induce an increase in the number of patients on waiting lists); the additional police themselves may notice and record more crime. For these reasons increases in police numbers can be associated with increases in measured crime, although to a greater or lesser extent this effect might be offset by a reduction in the true crime rate as a result of the deterrent effects of increased policing.

The main intermediate output of the police – indicating what they actually do towards deterring crime – is the apprehension of offenders, measured by recorded crimes cleared up. Its deterrent effect is indicated by the clear-up rate which gives a measure of the probability of being caught. However, the clear-up of crimes depends to a considerable extent on the information made available by the public, which is probably more important than the detecting efforts of the police alone according to several studies (Burrows and Tarling, 1982). Differences in the ways in which clear-ups arise are important: the contribution of 'crimes taken into consideration' offered by those charged with other offences is particularly suspect, for example if offenders hope to obtain better treatment by the police or lighter sentences through confessing to crimes they did not commit and which might never have occurred. Again some discretion is open to the police with respect to crimes taken into consideration. In view of the possible flaws in the data both for criminal activity and for clear-ups, it is clear that the ratio of the two, the clear-up rate, needs to be treated with caution. Nonetheless, a Home Office study concluded that the clear-up rate is reasonably robust and, in common with several other studies, we use it below (Burrows and Tarling, *op.cit.*)

Some studies of police output have proposed aggregate measures based on the imputation of money values to reductions in the 'cost' of crime. However, there are serious practical difficulties in assigning monetary values to personal injuries and to the loss of and damage to property involving crime, which involves personal distress and the sentimental value of stolen or damaged goods (Pyle, 1983 and Becker, 1968).

Survey or psychometric techniques might be used to establish the relative seriousness of different types of crime to provide weights in an appropriate index. This approach (akin to QUALYs) offers the possibility, at least in theory, of deriving an aggregate measure of overall crime seriousness, and of improving allocative efficiency within the police service by indicating the sorts of crime the public dislikes most. One study has asked police officers to rank the seriousness of various offences in relation to a £10 larceny (Bryant, Chambers and Falcon, 1968). A different study (Kinsey, 1984) reveals a mismatch between the priorities of the police and the public with respect to policing activities.

A complex interaction exists between the provision of police manpower, the recorded crime rate, and the recorded clear-up rate. In order to estimate the relationships a simultaneous equation procedure was employed, based on the pioneering work of Carr-Hill and Stern (1979), involving three linked regression equations, to explain differences in the size of the police force per head of population, variations in the recorded crime rate, and in the clear-up rate. The econometric results can be used in two ways. The average relationship between police resources and the crime clear-up rates contains information about the effectiveness of spending at a national level. The results also permit comparisons between the actual performance or costs of individual police authorities and those predicted by the model, after taking into account the differences in local circumstances facing police forces and differences in their resources. The results on relative performance differ from those which emerge from simple comparisons of costs per head or clear-up rates with respect to the average of all the police authorities (the authority with the *highest* excess of actual over expected clear-up rate has a clear-up rate which is in fact *below* average); they also differ from those obtained from simpler regression models which give biased results because they do not take into acount the interactions between the main variables.

Further analysis of police force areas involved the use of data envelope analysis. Alternative assumptions were used with respect to the possibility of non-constant returns to scale. Efficiency scores (which measure the ratio of actual to best possible performance) were computed with respect to both output efficiency and input efficiency. As might be expected the efficiency scores and the number of inefficient authorities vary according to the model chosen and it is a matter for judgement which set of assumptions and restrictions most closely approximates to the real world in which police forces operate.

AN ECONOMETRIC MODEL OF POLICE MANPOWER, RECORDED CRIME AND CLEAR-UP RATES

We have estimated a simultaneous-equations model which attempts to explain differences in recorded crime *per capita*, clear-up rates and police strength *per capita* – taking into account their interactions upon one another – across police force areas in England and Wales (excluding London and three neighbouring forces).[1] In what will of necessity be a rather terse account, we shall concentrate on two main aspects of the work: firstly, the implications for the average relationship between police resources or inputs (police officers *per capita*, spending per officer) and output broadly defined (the recorded crime rate and the clear-up rate); and, secondly, the light our analysis sheds on the relative performance of different police forces. We first describe the specification of the model including the nature of the three equations, and the estimation procedure employed; then we discuss the results, including their general statistical properties, the estimated relationship between police resources, recorded crime and clear-up rates, and the relative performance of individual police authorities.

The specification and estimation of the model

Our estimated model was based on earlier work by Carr-Hill and Stern (1979), although our precise choice of explanatory variables differed from theirs in several respects. The model consists of three simultaneous equations which can be thought of as explaining the recorded crime rate (that is, recorded crime *per capita*), the clear-up rate, (that is, the proportion of recorded crimes cleared up) and the number of police officers *per capita*. The model incorporates, *inter alia*, a number of demographic and socio-economic variables (such as age structure, population density, social class and unemployment) as explanatory variables to allow us to standardise for the different conditions faced by individual authorities. It also explicitly allows for the interactive, or simultaneous nature of the relationship between police manpower and recorded crime and clear-up rates (in other words, for the fact that each of these variables influences and is influenced by the other two) and for this reason the model was estimated using a simultaneous-equations technique. (Failure to allow for simultaneity would lead to inconsistent parameter estimates, see Chapter 9.) A brief discussion of the form of each of the equations in the model is given below; a fuller account is contained in Joyce (1985). Variables are listed in table 12.1.

The crime rate equation (Equation (1))

The first equation is intended to explain the recorded offence or crime rate in each area, measured by the total number of notifiable offences per 100 thousand of the population. It is important to stress at the outset that we are modelling the number of *recorded* offences *per capita* rather than the *true* number of offences and in interpreting our results this distinction is crucial (see below). For convenience in what follows, by 'crime rate' we refer to the recorded crime rate, unless the contrary is indicated.

Theoretical reasoning suggests the inclusion of a number of explanatory variables in the crime rate equation (for the implications of economic theory see Becker, 1968). Most obviously we might expect the crime rate to be negatively associated with both the probability of detection – proxied here by the clear-up rate – and the (perceived) severity of punishment, but positively associated with the opportunity for offending. To measure severity we included a variable which measures the percentage of those sentenced at magistrates' and crown courts who receive custodial sentences (SEV); 'swag' was proxied by the average domestic rateable value (RV).

Deterrence theory suggests the inclusion of the number of policemen *per capita*, POL, (here measured per thousand population) and the amount of

Table 12.1 *Definitions of variables*

Endogenous variables	
TNO	Total notifiable offences per 100 thousand population (crime rate)
CUR	Clear-up rate (%)
POL	Police officers per thousand population
Exogenous variables	
DIV	Percentage of police officers deployed in the divisions
SEV	Custodial sentences as a % of all sentences in magistrates' and crown courts
EXP	Net police expenditure per officer
MIX	Offences of violence against the person as % of total notifiable offences
ACC	Fatal and other road casualties per thousand population
M1524	Males aged 15 to 24 as % of total population
WKC	% of population in households with head in socio-economic groups IV and V
RV	Domestic average rateable values
DEN	Population density
OVC	Percentage of households with one or more persons per room
POP	Population (night-time home population)
MIDC	% of population in households with head in socio-economic groups I and II
MU	Male unemployment rate (%)

Sources: Census 1981, Key statistics for local authorities, Great Britain, OPCS (1984). Census 1981, Sex, age and marital status, Great Britain, OPCS (1983). Police Statistics, 1983–4 Actuals, CIPFA (1984). Police Statistics, 1983–4 Estimates, CIPFA (1983). Regional Trends, 1983 Edition, CSO. Criminal statistics, England and Wales 1983, *Cmnd* 9349. Criminal statistics, England and Wales, Supplementary Tables, 1983 Volume 3.

equipment per officer, EXP, (proxied by net expenditure per police officer) as additional explanatory variables in this equation. Moreover to allow for the fact that total police strength *per capita* may not be a good measure of the effective police manpower devoted to crime fighting, we have also included the percentage of police officers deployed in the divisions $(DIV)^2$ as an additional explanatory variable, as this may give an indication of the proportion of officers deployed on the beat. We would expect these variables to be negatively associated with the true crime rate but their relationship with the recorded crime rate cannot be determined *a priori*. This is because the police are engaged in both crime prevention and crime detection, and additionally, the mere presence of more police officers may lead to the reporting of more offences. Thus the net effect of more police officers/resources on recorded crime will depend on the relative strengths of these factors.

Some of the other explanatory variables in the crime rate equation owe their inclusion mainly to criminological and sociological theories which suggest that different groups in society are differentially prone either to offending behaviour or to be labelled as offenders. The variables used are the percentage of male youths $(M1524)$ and working class composition (WKC). Population density (DEN) was included to allow for differences in criminal behaviour between urban and rural areas; overcrowding (OVC) because of its association with delinquency and criminal activity.

The clear-up rate equation (Equation (2))

The second equation essentially models the proportion of cases solved, which is proxied by the percentage clear-up rate (CUR). This can be thought of as an output[3] which depends positively on inputs such as the number of policemen *per capita*, *POL*, and the resources available to them (here net expenditure per police officer, *EXP*). The sign of the relationship, however, is not self-evident, *a priori*, because while more police should generate more clear-ups, they could equally increase recorded crime (through their effect on detection and reporting), thereby making their effect on the clear-up rate ambiguous. (The meaning and measurement of offences that are cleared up itself is subject to a number of difficulties, as indicated above).

However, total police manpower *per capita* may be a misleading measure of effective police manpower inputs because of activities not related to clearing up crime; for this reason the clear-up rate equation also includes the percentage of divisional police officers as an additional explanatory variable. The argument is that it will be those forces which deploy a greater proportion of their manpower at the sharp end, outside police headquarters, who will record the highest clear-up rates, other things being equal. To measure the workload faced by the police we have included the crime rate (*TNO*), the number of fatal and other road casualties per thousand population (*ACC*) and the size of the night-time population (*POP*). Since some crimes are easier to solve than others we have also included a crime mix variable (*MIX*) which measures the percentage of total notifiable offences which involve violence against the person (these typically have higher clear-up rates because there is a witness and because the offender might be known to the victim).

The equation also includes a number of additional socio-economic variables which might be thought important: the percentage of youths (*M1524*), working class composition (*WKC*) and population density (*DEN*).

Police manpower per capita equation (Equation (3))

The third equation is intended to explain the determination of the number of police officers (*POL*) 'as an interaction between demand for police set by the authorities and supply in terms of average daily strength of the existing force' (Carr-Hill and Stern, 1979). If we consider this equation as modelling the allocation of police officers across police authorities then this suggests the inclusion of the crime rate (*TNO*) and population density (*DEN*) as explanatory variables, since they are factors in the grant-related expenditure (*GRE*) assessment.[4] Road length also enters the *GRE* formula and to allow for the impact of traffic duties on the demand for police manpower we have included the number of fatal and other road casualties per thousand population (ACC) as an additional explanatory variable. Also on the demand side, local pressures for more law and order are likely to come from those with most to lose from crime, and for this reason we have also included a measure of the proportion of the population who are middle class $(MIDC)$.

A priori, it is unclear what sign the coefficient on the crime rate will have in this equation because the amount of recorded crime will not only affect the demand for police protection but may also affect the supply side by influencing how readily individuals come forward to join up. The clear-up rate may also be important as a determinant of manpower because it is likely to affect the level of morale and influence decisions on whether to stay in the force or not. Another factor likely to influence supply is the amount of violent crime, and so we have included the MIX variable as another explanatory variable. The final explanatory variable in equation (3) is the rate of male unemployment (MU) which is included as a measure of the state of the labour market. It indicates the relative ease of recruitment and may be expected to be positively associated with the dependent variable.

The basic model has the following form:

Crime rate equation:
$$TNO = f(CUR, POL, DIV, SEV, M1524, WKC, RV, EXP, DEN, OVC, u_1) \tag{1}$$

Clear-up rate equation:
$$CUR = g(TNO, POL, DIV, M1524, WKC, EXP, MIX, ACC, POP, DEN, u_2 \tag{2}$$

Police manpower equation:
$$POL = h(TNO, CUR, MIDC, DEN, MIX, MU, u_3) \tag{3}$$

All the variables were expressed in logarithmic form and are defined in table 12.1. TNO, CUR and POL are endogenous variables, that is, variables which are determined within the system described by the model; the rest are exogenous, and u_i (where $i = 1, 2, 3$) are random errors with the normal statistical properties.

Estimation and results

The model set out above was estimated by three-stage least squares using 1983/4 data for a cross-section of 38 police authorities in England and Wales (excluding London and three surrounding police force areas).[5] Since the model was explicitly set up as a simultaneous system (that is, on the assumption that the crime rate, the clear-up rate and the number of police officers *per capita* are all simultaneously determined) it would have been inappropriate to employ ordinary least squares which in a simultaneous system is biased and inconsistent. We have chosen three stage least squares in preference to two stage least squares because, although both yield

Table 12.2 *Estimates of the 3SLS models*

	Full model			Restricted model		
	TNO (1)	*CUR* (2)	*POL* (3)	*TNO* (1)	*CUR* (2)	*POL* (3)
CONST	−6.45 (0.70)	−6.97 (1.15)	1.89 (0.71)	−6.39 (0.70)	−6.55 (1.21)	−1.36 (0.71)
TNO		−0.41 (1.98)	0.15 (0.75)		−0.45 (2.63)	0.19 (1.36)
CUR	−0.97 (2.07)		0.35 (1.25)	−1.02 (2.35)		0.38 (1.42)
POL	0.72 (1.19)	1.32 (3.72)		0.73 (1.23)	1.34 (4.60)	
DIV	0.39 (1.02)	0.52 (2.05)		0.40 (1.05)	0.46 (2.09)	
SEV	−0.13 (0.70)			−0.14 (0.82)		
M1524	0.19 (0.41)	0.01 (0.02)				
WKC	0.43 (1.40)	−0.06 (0.25)		0.50 (2.03)		
MIDC			−0.04 (0.19)			
RV	−0.22 (1.16)			−0.23 (1.15)		
EXP	1.19 (2.05)	0.64 (1.35)		1.21 (2.08)	0.62 (1.43)	
DEN	0.04 (0.80)	−0.06 (1.84)	0.04 (1.35)	0.04 (0.80)	−0.06 (1.94)	0.04 (1.35)
OVC	0.51 (2.25)			0.50 (2.44)		
MIX		0.20 (2.61)	−0.12 (1.35)		0.19 (2.73)	−0.11 (1.47)
ACC		−0.28 (1.84)	0.14 (0.91)		−0.26 (1.85)	0.13 (0.89)
POP		−0.01 (0.24)				
MU			0.13 (1.34)			0.13 (1.42)
S	0.12	0.11	0.08	0.12	0.11	0.08
Mean of dependent variable	8.62	3.77	5.35	8.62	3.77	5.35

Note: Sources and definitions as table 12.1. 't'-values are in parenthesis.

consistent parameter estimates, only the former allows for cross-equation correlation and for this reason it is more efficient.[6]

Before discussing the findings of the analysis in terms of the relationship between police resources and output or in terms of the relative performance of individual police authorities, some general remarks on the estimates are in order. The results from estimating the full model are presented in table 12.2 (equations (1), (2), and (3)). In general, the model may be judged to fit the data reasonably well, although the performance of equation (2) is perhaps disappointing. Our difficulty in explaining the variation in clear-up rates is probably in part due to differences in recording practices between police force areas; this problem was also encountered in earlier work by Carr-Hill and Stern. However, on the whole, the results accord with our prior expectations as to the signs on the coefficients[7] and, given the uncertain nature of much of the underlying theory and the problem of multicollinearity (between the socio-economic variables), a reasonable number of the parameters are statistically significant.

Since not all the coefficients in the full model were found to be statistically significant, we also estimated a restricted version of the model so as to improve the efficiency of the parameter estimates and these results are also shown in table 12.2. In selecting a more parsimonious specification, we excluded the variables which were least statistically significant in the full model, whilst retaining the variables of most theoretical interest. This resulted in the exclusion of $M1524$ from equation (1); $M1524$, WKC and POP from equation (2); and $MIDC$ from equation (3). In general the significance levels of the coefficients in the restricted model are higher than in the full model, but the parameter estimates themselves are virtually unchanged.[8] In the discussion which follows we shall focus on the results from the restricted model. We shall concentrate on the implications which emerge for the relationship between police inputs and performance, as measured by the recorded crime and clear-up rates.

Police resources and recorded crime and clear-up rates

If we consider the estimated crime rate equation, perhaps the most striking feature is that the coefficients on both police manpower and police expenditure are positive, although only EXP is statistically significant at the 5 per cent level. The implication is that increased police resources do not in themselves lead to lower recorded crime rates. In fact, the opposite seems to be the case, presumably because of the effect of increased resources on the detection and reporting of crime. This may well be consistent with a reduction in the 'true' crime rate. This finding is consistent with the earlier work of Carr-Hill and Stern (as well as with more recent work by Willis (1983) using a slightly different simultaneous-equations model with data for 1979), although we found the coefficient on the police manpower variable to be only weakly significant in contrast to some of their results.

Another feature of the crime rate equation which also echoes previous work in this area is the negative and significant coefficient on the clear-up rate variable (Pyle, 1983). Like many other researchers, our findings also suggest that the crime rate is more responsive to improvements in the clear-up rate than to increases in the severity of punishment.

Where our results do appear to diverge somewhat from the findings of other studies is with regard to the clear-up rate equation. The coefficient on the police manpower variable is positive and strongly significant in our estimated clear-up rate equation: more police clear up a greater proportion of crimes. The expenditure variable is also positive although only weakly significant. This contrasts markedly with the finding of Carr-Hill and Stern (1979) that the effect of more police officers on the clear-up rate was 'broadly speaking negative'. There is little consensus in the literature regarding this. For example, Burrows and Tarling, using data for 1977, found that in some of their regressions the variable 'police *per capita*' was significantly and positively related to the clear-up rate, but their results consistently indicated 'that a 1 per cent increase in police would not increase the clear-up rate by the same amount' (Burrows and Tarling, 1982). On the other hand, our results suggest that a 1 per cent increase in police manpower *per capita* leads to a 1.3 per cent improvement in the clear-up rate. Given the relatively small size of our sample we would not want to put too much weight on our precise parameter estimate on police *per capita* as opposed to theirs: the important point is that both results suggest that the relationship between police manpower and the clear-up rate is now broadly positive in contrast to the period of the 1960s up the the early 1970s.

Other factors which appear from our results to be important in explaining the clear-up rate are the proportion of police officers deployed in the divisions (presumably this picks up other pressures on police time) and the crime mix. The size of the workload facing the police also seems to have a bearing on their success in solving crime: the variable measuring road accidents *per capita* and the crime rate both have negative coefficients and both are statistically significant.

We can summarise our main results as follows: while the direct impact of increased police resources seems to be to increase the recorded crime rate, police numbers may also indirectly lead to reductions in recorded crime rate through their impact on clear-up rates. The *net* effect of increased police numbers on the crime rate is not something that emerges straightforwardly from our results because we have specified the relationship between police manpower, clear-up rates and recorded crime as a *simultaneous* system. However, by following through all the interactions in the model it is possible to show that increased police numbers do seem to be associated with reductions in the recorded crime rate once allowance is made for both direct and indirect effects. But it should be stressed that this finding remains rather tentative given the complexity of the interactions in the model.

The relative performance of individual police authorities

Our results can also be used to make comparisons across different police authorities. We can do this by comparing the predictions of the model with the actual performance of each police force, in terms of the magnitude of the residuals from the regression equations. However it perhaps needs to be stressed at the outset that although this procedure is useful for identifying those authorities where outcomes differ significantly from that expected, this need not necessarily be indicative of either good performance or inefficiency. Such a conclusion would require a more detailed study at the level of individual police forces; our procedures simply indicate outliers which may be worth examining further.

In what follows we shall concentrate on the results from the restricted form of the clear-up rate equation since this equation probably gives the best indication of comparative police effectiveness. The question of effectiveness was excluded from the 1983 audit inspectorate report on police force manpower which suggested that some forces appeared to have more resources than criminal activity in their areas appeared to warrant, but it did not consider whether such forces were relatively effective at clearing up crimes (Department of the Environment Audit Inspectorate, 1983). In section (b) of table 12.3 we set out those authorities which fall outside one standard error of the clear-up rate equation in the restricted model estimated by three-stage least squares. It is interesting to compare these results with section (a) in the same table, which ranks police force areas according to their clear-up rates, without taking into account in any way the different circumstances they face. Casual inspection reveals a number of important differences between the two sets of rankings. For example, of the seven police force areas which have negative residuals greater than one standard error under (b), that is, those authorities with an apparently poor record on crime detection taking into account their circumstances (namely, forces coded as 25, 38, 2, 3, 17, 13 and 10), not one appears as an outlier on the basis of the simple overall clear-up rate comparisons set out under (a). (However we may note that all but one have overall clear-up rates below the sample average.) At the other end of the scale, of the seven authorities with positive residuals greater than one standard error in the clear-up rate equation (section (b)), that is, those authorities with relatively high clear-up rates allowing for other factors, only three (19, 20 and 32) also appear as outliers on the basis of the simple comparisons presented in section (a). Force number 31, which appears to have the best record on crime detection allowing for the other factors contained in the model, has an overall clear-up rate which is actually *below* the sample average.

To the extent that the rankings under (a) and (b) differ, our results emphasise the importance of comparing police authorities only after making allowance for local circumstances. But as has already been pointed out, it is not appropriate to interpret the ranking in table 12.3 as a league table of police efficiency. One of the reasons for this is that some of the variation observed between areas will be due to differences in the recording practices of different police forces with respect to crime and differences in

Table 12.3 *Police authority outliers based on clear-up rates for total notifiable offences*[a]

Ranking using unadjusted clear-up rate			Ranking using 3SLS model		
Rank[b]	Code no. (a)	Deviation from mean	Rank[b]	Code no. (b)	Residual from equation[c]
Low values					
1	30	− 10.84	1	25	− 0.19
2	40	− 7.84	2	38	− 0.18
3	41	− 7.84	3	2	− 0.14
4	1	− 5.84	4	3	− 0.13
5	11	− 5.84	5	17	− 0.12
6	21	− 5.84	6	13	− 0.11
			7	10	− 0.11
7	4	− 4.84			
8	25	− 4.84	8	1	− 0.11
High values					
			31	14	0.11
32	7	5.16	32	32	0.11
33	36	5.16	33	23	0.12
34	19	5.16	34	20	0.13
35	34	7.16	35	37	0.17
36	20	7.16	36	19	0.17
37	32	11.16	37	6	0.22
38	33	13.16	38	31	0.24
Mean	43.84		Mean of dependent variable		3.77
Standard deviation	5.30		Standard error		0.11

[a] Sample excludes London, Essex, Herts and Surrey.
[b] Ascending order.
[c] A positive/negative residual indicates that the equation under/over predicts the value of the dependent variable for that particular police force.

the importance of alternative methods of clearing up crime: the role of 'crimes taken into account' is particularly suspect (criminals might confess to crimes they never committed or which never even occurred in the hope of more lenient treatment over the crime for which they have been arrested). More generally, in using regression analysis to assess relative performance in this way there is always the problem of distinguishing any systematic efficiency component from the statistical noise always present in any estimated relationship (the result of misspecification and/or measurement error). Nevertheless, it seems reasonable to attribute part of the unexplained variation in clear-up rates to differences in efficiency which are worth following up on the ground.

A DATA ENVELOPE ANALYSIS OF THE POLICE

The work using data envelope analysis fell into two main parts. The first part compared the results of the analysis with those of the more conventional regression analysis approach described above. The initial specification was chosen to replicate as closely as possible the restricted version of the clear-up rate equation, including only those inputs and outputs present in the restricted regression model. The second part sought to exploit more fully the potential of the method itself, and involved investigating the implications of including additional inputs and multiple outputs.[9]

A comparison with conventional regression analysis

As in the econometric analysis of 38 English and Welsh police authorities, reported above, output was defined as the clear-up rate, that is the proportion of recorded crimes cleared up. Data envelope analysis enables a distinction to be made between variables within management control and those not within their control. Variables specified as non-controllable were the road accident rate, population density, the recorded crime rate (all of which tend to reduce the clear-up rate) and the proportion of crimes of violence against the person in total recorded crimes, which tends to raise the clear-up rate (see above).

For direct comparison with the earlier econometric work, controllable inputs included the number of police officers per head of population, the proportion of officers deployed in divisions (outside HQ) and net expenditure per officer. (Variants were also examined by which one or two of these inputs were defined as non-controllable to examine the effect of varying the number of controllables.)

Three main forms of data envelope analysis were used; their general properties are summarised below (for a more detailed exposition see Appendix 2):

(a) Constant returns to scale are imposed.
(b) Diminishing returns are allowed; both input and output lie on a frontier starting from the origin, referred to as the 'Farrell' case (a specification due to Cubbin and Wriglesworth).
(c) Diminishing returns are allowed; input must be above a certain level before any output is possible, referred to as the 'Banker' case (Banker, 1984).

As noted in Chapter 9, data envelope analysis permits a comparison to be made of relative efficiency in terms of both output efficiency (the ratio of actual to potential maximum output given input) and input efficiency (the ratio of potential minimum to actual inputs for given output).

Table 12.4 sets out the technical efficiency scores under input

Table 12.4 *Technical efficiency scores, DEA methods: police authorities (identified by code numbers)*

Percentages

DEA method	Output maximisation[a]		Input minimisation[b]	
	Code no.	Score	Code no.	Score
'Farrell'[c]	25	78.8	25	74.9
(diminishing	30	80.5	24	81.7
returns possible)	24	84.7	10	84.4
	10	85.0	17	87.0
	17	88.6	9	88.1
	1	88.6	1	90.6
	27	90.0	27	91.3
	4	91.2	12	94.2
	9	91.4	35	97.1
	12	91.6	30	97.5
	36	99.1	4	98.3
	35	99.4	36	99.3
	22	99.6	22	99.4
Constant returns	25	78.8	25	74.9
imposed	30	80.5	24	81.7
	24	84.7	10	84.4
	10	85.0	17	87.0
	17	87.5	9	88.1
	1	88.6	1	90.6
	27	90.0	27	91.3
	4	91.2	12	94.2
	9	91.4	35	96.9
	12	91.6	30	97.5
	36	98.8	4	98.3
	35	99.4	36	99.1
	22	99.6	22	99.4
'Banker'[d]	25	79.3	25	86.0
(diminishing returns	10	86.8	10	87.7
possible; origin not	17	88.6	17	91.7
feasible)	1	89.8	27	92.7
	27	90.0	1	94.4
	24	92.4	12	96.8
	12	94.4	35	97.1
	36	99.1	24	97.9
	35	99.5	36	99.3

[a] The score expresses the actual clear-up rate as a percentage of the maximum feasible clear-up rate, given inputs.
[b] The score shows the percentage of actual controllable inputs with which the actual clear-up rate is still feasible.
[c] A specification due to Cubbin and Wriglesworth.
[d] Banker (1984).

minimisation and output maximisation for those forces identified as inefficient authorities (all others score 100). The series are presented as percentages: on output maximisation the clear-up rate as a percentage of the maximum feasible clear-up rate; on input minimisation the percentage of inputs actually used with which the given clear-up rate could be achieved.

The majority of authorities are efficient; fewer are inefficient under 'Banker', as expected, which also produces the highest scores. It so happens that with the data used here, the 'constant returns' and 'Farrell' models, give identical rankings and virtually identical scores. The rankings are not the same (given the model) for output and input efficiency (although the sets of inefficient authorities tend to be the same). A reduction in the number of controllables (re-defining one or two as uncontrollable) had no effect on output efficiency because output maximisation treats all inputs, however defined, as given; but for input efficiency the effect was to reduce the score, because a reduction in the number of controllables reduces the probability of finding a high ratio of output to any controllable input (see Appendix 2).

Police authorities are more likely to be managed so as to improve their clear-up rates with given resources, rather than in a way which would reduce the resources while aiming at some specific clear-up rates. Therefore, the output efficiency scores seem more relevant to judging their performance.

Table 12.5 sets out the *negative* residuals, (that is lower than expected clear-up rates) obtained from the restricted econometric model described above. Table 12.6 compares the rankings obtained under the six data envelope analysis models, and three-stage least squares. Although the results produced by both approaches are not identical there is a good deal of overlap between the sets of authorities identified as less efficient in each case.

Some additional results from alternative data envelope analysis specifications

The results described above were deliberately based on model specifications which were as comparable as possible with our earlier regression analysis. However, the variable definitions employed for the regression model (which tend to be in terms of ratios, for example, the number of police officers *per capita* (POL), the percentage of recorded crime cleared up (CUR)) are not entirely appropriate in the context of data envelope analysis, which is more closely related to production theory (described in Chapter 9) and therefore defines the relationship between inputs and outputs in terms of their absolute levels. Therefore further analysis examined the effect of re-specifying the data envelope analysis in terms of absolute values (thus output becomes the 'number of recorded crimes cleared up' rather than the 'clear-up rate', and so-on). We also wanted to

Table 12.5 *Police authorities with farthest below expected clear-up rates,
restricted model[a]*

Rank[b]	Code no.	Score[c]
1	25	83.1
2	38	83.5
3	2	86.8
4	3	87.7
5	17	88.4
6	13	89.4
7	10	89.5
8	1	90.0
9	30	90.7
10	24	91.0

[a] Negative residuals larger than one standard error.
[b] Ascending order.
[c] Actual clear-up rate as percentage of predicted.
Note: Seven authorities had clear-up rates more than one standard error *above* predicted.

Table 12.6 *Comparison of rankings for inefficient police authorities[a]*

Code no.	DEA Output maximisation			DEA Input minimisation			3SLS[b]
	Farrell	CRS	Banker	Farrell	CRS	Banker	
1	6	6	4	6	6	5	8
2	—	—	—	—	—	—	3
3	—	—	—	—	—	—	4
4	8	8	—	11	11	—	—
9	9	9	—	5	—	—	—
10	4	4	2	3	3	2	7
12	10	10	7	8	8	6	—
13	—	—	—	—	—	—	6
17	5	5	3	4	4	3	5
22	13	13	—	13	13	—	—
24	3	3	6	2	2	8	10
25	1	1	1	1	1	1	1
27	7	7	5	7	7	4	—
30	2	2	—	10	10	—	9
35	12	12	9	9	9	7	—
36	11	11	8	12	12	9	—
38	—	—	—	—	—	—	2

[a] Police authorities which are inefficient under at least one method. The remaining 21 are efficient for all methods. The highest ranking (that is, 1) indicates the lowest efficiency for each model. A dash indicates the authority was efficient for that model.
[b] In terms of clear-up-rate residuals (which are more analogous to DEA output maximisation than to input minimisation).

Table 12.7 *Summary of the revised DEA specifications*

	Model A	Model B	Model C
Output measures	CUPS	CUPS	CUSAV
			CUPROP
Controllable inputs	DIVO	DIVO	DIVO
	NDIVO	NDIVO	NDIVO
	CIV	CIV	CIV
	KAP	VEH	
Non-controllable inputs: positive	SAV	SAV	SAV
	PROP	PROP	PROP
Non-controllable inputs: negative	P_1	P_1	P_1
	H_2	H_2	H_2
	TACC	TACC	TACC

Definitions: CUPS = the number of recorded crimes cleared up (1) (4); *CUSAV* = the number of violent and sexual offences cleared up (1) (4); *CUPROP* = the number of non-violent and non-sexual offences cleared up (1) (4); *DIVO* = divisional police officers (2) (3); *NDIVO* = non-divisional police officers (2) (3); *CIV* = police civilians (2); *VEH* = total number of vehicles (3); *KAP* = non-employee spending (2); *SAV* = violent and sexual recorded offences (4); *PROP* = non-violent and non-sexual recorded offences (4); P_1 = population (2); H_2 = area (hectares) (2); *TACC* = fatal and other road casualties (2) (5).
Sources: (1) Home Office; (2) 'Police Statistics, 1983–4 Actuals', CIPFA (1984); (3) 'Police Statistics, 1983–4 Estimates', CIPFA (1983); (4) 'Criminal Statistics, England and Wales 1983', *Cmnd* 9349; (5) 'Regional Trends', 1983 edition, CSO.

exploit more fully the ability of this method of the analysis to handle not only multiple inputs but also multiple outputs and, with this in mind, a number of extensions to the basic model were investigated.

Three different models summarised in table 12.7, all defined in levels, were used to generate further results. Models A and B incorporate a single output measure, the number of recorded crimes cleared up (*CUPS*). In contrast, model C has two outputs since it distinguishes the number of clear-ups according to whether they refer to crimes against the person (*CUSAV*), that is, violent and sexual offences, or against property (*CUPROP*), that is, all other crimes. By making this distinction we are able to allow for the possibility that forces may have different priorities towards the solution of one sort of crime as opposed to the other.

The set of controllable inputs used in all the models includes three different types of manpower. In addition to the divisional/non-divisional manpower distinction used in the initial analysis, the revised specifications also incorporate the number of police civilians as an input. Models A and B also include an additional controllable input which can be thought of as proxying the effect of capital for which there was no readily available direct measure. In A, non-employee related expenditure (*KAP*) was included as an input, while in B the total number of vehicles (*VEH*) was used instead.

The non-controllable (NCR) inputs included in all of the specifications were based on the variables TNO, ACC, MIX and DEN employed in the initial analysis. The two positive NCRs shown in table 12.7 are both measures of recorded crime: the number of violent and sexual offences (SAV) and the number of non-violent and non-sexual offences ($PROP$). Offences are distinguished in this way because crimes against the person typically have higher clear-up rates than other offences. Both SAV and $PROP$ are assumed to have a positive relationship with the specified output(s) because in the case of some crimes 'the observance of the offence identifies the offender' (Home Office, 1984). Each specification also includes three non-controllable inputs with a negative impact on output: population size ($P1$), area ($H2$), and a proxy for the scale of police traffic duties, the number of fatal and other road casualties ($FORC$). It seems plausible to argue that increases in any of these variables will tend to make the solution of crime more difficult, other things being equal.

Results: technical efficiency and scale effects

Results were produced for each of the three specifications described above, for output maximisation only, table 12.8. It is clear that there is a good deal of similarity between the approaches in terms of which authorities are identified as technically inefficient. The main differences arise from different assumptions about returns to scale and the feasibility of the origin.

As might have been expected, the imposition of constant returns to scale produced the largest number of technically inefficient authorities (between thirteen and fifteen) whereas the less demanding Banker method produced the smallest number (between five and seven) (see Appendix 2). This discrepancy tends to suggest that scale effects are present in policing. Table 12.9 shows how many forces are identified as technically inefficient under the constant returns hypothesis, distinguishing between those operating above and below optimal scale. It is clear from this that most 'inefficient' authorities appear to be operating at *above* optimal scale (although this is rather less marked in model A) and this implies that diminishing returns are present.

CONCLUSIONS

It is well known that a positive correlation exists between police resources and the recorded crime rate, possibly because more resources induce increases in the proportion of crimes which are reported and recorded. The econometric results reported above suggest, however, that increased resources are associated with improvements in the clear-up rate and the deterrent effect of this is, indirectly, to reduce the crime rate.

Looking at relative performance in clearing up crime across police

Table 12.8 *Police authorities identified as technically inefficient, using the output maximisation approach, listed in rank order*

Percentages

Method	Rank	Model A Code no.	Model A Score	Model B Code no.	Model B Score	Model C Code no.	Model C Score
Farrell	1	10	84.8	10	84.8	38	89.7
	2	25	88.5	25	85.1	3	89.8
	3	38	89.1	17	85.5	10	91.4
	4	3	89.6	3	88.8	24	93.2
	5	17	90.6	38	89.1	25	97.7
	6	24	91.0	24	91.0		
	7	4	98.7	35	99.2		
	8	11	99.7				
Constant	1	30	78.3	30	74.7	41	79.2
returns	2	25	79.2	25	79.2	30	84.0
	3	41	81.7	41	79.3	24	85.0
	4	24	84.7	17	83.5	38	86.7
	5	10	84.8	24	84.7	3	89.8
	6	40	85.5	10	84.8	10	91.3
	7	38	86.1	40	85.5	40	91.4
	8	3	89.6	38	86.1	25	91.5
	9	27	90.4	3	88.8	36	92.4
	10	17	90.6	27	91.0	27	95.3
	11	36	92.4	36	92.4	39	99.1
	12	4	98.7	39	95.8	17	99.6
	13	11	99.7	22	96.6		
				21	97.4		
				35	99.2		
Banker	1	10	84.9	10	84.9	38	89.7
	2	25	88.5	25	85.1	10	91.4
	3	38	89.1	17	85.5	24	93.2
	4	17	90.7	38	89.0	3	93.7
	5	24	91.0	24	91.0	25	97.7
				3	93.3		
				35	99.2		

Note: For model definitions see table 12.7.

authorities, the results reveal significant differences between police forces, after allowing for differences in their resource inputs and socio-economic factors beyond their control; these differences are not the same as those which emerge from simple comparisons between each police force's clear-up rate and the sample average: such comparisons cannot take account of the effects of differences in resources and local circumstances.

A comparison between data envelope analysis rankings of output efficiency (defined in terms of clear-up rates) and those obtained from the econometric analysis suggest that the results, while not identical, have a good deal in common. The data envelope analysis was also extended to take

Table 12.9 *Number of authorities found technically inefficient, based on output maximisation*

Method	Model A	Model B	Model C
Farrell	8	7	5
Constant returns	13	15	12
of which:			
below efficient scale	5	2	1
above efficient scale	8	13	11
Banker	5	7	5

into account the possibility of multiple outputs, in this instance the clearing up of crimes against the person and crimes against property; the number of inputs was varied (to distinguish between police officers in headquarters, on divisional duties, civilians, and expenditure on vehicles and other equipment). In the future this kind of analysis might even permit an examination of the trade-offs between different outputs and the scope for substituting one input for another. Work in this area is currently in progress.

Part IV

CONCLUSIONS

13

CONCLUSIONS

ASPECTS OF GROWTH IN EXPENDITURE

Spending since 1969

Between 1969 and 1974 total general government expenditure rose by 33 per cent in real terms; over the comparable period 1979–84 it grew by only 8 per cent. In the meantime something of a sea change occurred in attitudes towards public spending and its financing. The change was triggered by the clash between previously held aspirations and macroeconomic constraints, which was made brutally explicit in 1976 when 'crisis' cuts in spending plans were negotiated with the IMF in return for credit (while the alternative was an uncontrollable collapse in the value of the pound). The large unplanned cuts, coming soon after rapid increases in spending, the steepest increase in income tax progressivity in peacetime, and the highest peacetime income tax burden on the low paid, all induced a more receptive popular audience for those who challenged the growth of the state, the value of its output, its costs and the quality of its management. Following the 1979 general election, tight constraints on spending were retained as a matter of deliberate policy intended to reduce the role of the state and to reinforce efforts to strengthen its management, as well as for reasons of macroeconomic policy. Nonetheless, despite plans to hold spending broadly constant in real terms (after allowing for general inflation) after 1979, total spending has grown, although for reasons different from those of the early 1970s and clearly much more slowly. On the other hand, changes in the pattern of spending by programme do not seem to have corresponded to party political priorities in the way that is often assumed.

The growth of public spending in the early 1970s reflected several factors: efforts to stimulate demand in the face of rising unemployment in 1973, the cost of large public sector pay settlements following lengthy strikes; increases in subsidies to alleviate rapidly rising inflation; increases in social spending and increases in industrial support.

The stimulation of domestic demand more or less coincided with, and aggravated, the deterioration in the balance of payments produced by the OPEC oil price rise, and the current account balance of payments deficit reached £4 billion in 1974. To avert a possible collapse in the external value of the pound, spending plans were cut and by 1979 real spending was 1 per cent lower than in 1975, with cuts of as much as 30 to 40 per cent in some categories (see Appendix 1 for details). In 1979 a new, Conservative, administration took office; it did not raise total spending to stimulate demand in the recession which began shortly after it took office; after honouring the previous administration's commitment to paying a number of major catching-up awards public sector pay was tightly controlled; the social wage concept was abandoned; total spending (after allowing for the proceeds of privatisation) was planned to remain broadly flat in real terms. In practice total departmental spending grew and the 1986 Autumn Statement abandoned the aim of holding the total broadly level, although the plan was still to reduce the share in GDP.

Politics and doctrine 1970–86

Over the period since 1970 as a whole it is not possible to identify as clear a distinction between the actual spending by governments of different political parties in office as might be imagined. The Conservatives started out in 1970 with the intention of tight constraint but the total grew rapidly from 1973, accelerated under Labour in 1974, was cut by Labour in 1976 and 1977 after which it grew more slowly than prior to 1976, albeit still more slowly under the Conservatives in 1979-85. Spending on education and health including personal social services grew most rapidly in the early 1970s, under a Conservative administration. Defence spending grew rapidly in 1979/80–1985/6 in line with a NATO commitment undertaken by the previous Labour administration, which the 1979 Conservative government extended for a time, but later ended. Spending on housing grew rapidly under the Conservative and Labour administrations of the early to mid-1970s, but was reduced by Labour and Conservative governments after 1975. Industrial support was rapidly expanded then cut by Labour in the mid-1970s. Since 1979, as well as defence and law and order (which one might expect to have grown under a Conservative administration), spending has grown on education, health and personal social services, social security and employment.

This picture suggests that there was continuing support for many of the aims and institutions of public spending which emerged during and after the 1939–45 war as instruments of social cohesion but more widespread scepticism about the case for spending on industrial support and housing. This is confirmed by regular surveys showing public support for spending economies on social services. There may also be inertia within the institutions of the public sector, which defy government attempts to restrict their activities, and less effective lobbying by those affected by cuts in housing and industrial support because fewer people have been involved. A further factor, which has been important in recent years, is the tension between central and local government, where the discretion available to the latter reduced the ability of the former to determine the size and pattern of spending on many services.

Some would argue that widespread popular support for public spending on services which might otherwise be provided by the private sector (or for the use of which charges could be levied or increased) merely reflects ignorance of other possibilities, refusal to take greater personal responsibility for meeting one's needs, or the effective lobbying of special-interest groups which favour the status quo and which frighten the general public about the alternatives.

Opinions clearly differ on where to draw the boundary between the needy and those not in need, and what are essential services or benefits. In both respects one must not exaggerate the similarity between the different administrations responsible for public spending over the past decade and a half. In particular between 1980 and 1985 important changes in social security arrangements were made, for example, to restrict the eligibility to benefit of the young unemployed, with the implication that they are less deserving of support than some other claimants. The link between benefits upratings and the increase in average earnings was ended, implying a concept of need defined in absolute terms rather than related to the growth in average living standards. The changes announced for the state earnings related pension scheme in 1986 were explicitly intended to stimulate the growth of private occupational pension arrangements.

The rapid growth in the number of social security beneficiaries after 1979 (especially the old and the unemployed, but also newly important groups such as the disabled and single parents) imposed constraints on the amount available for real upratings, within the overall spending constraint set by the government, so that it is difficult to identify doctrinal factors as the only cause of the change in practice towards eligibility and upratings. Local authority ownership and building of houses were considerably curtailed and home ownership encouraged after 1979 (although the reduction in spending on council houses started in 1976, that was the result of external constraints on spending).

There were no major moves between 1979 and 1986 towards the substitution of private provision of education or health, nor, apart from an aborted attempt to impose tuition fees on undergraduates in 1984,[1] to introduce charges for those deemed able to pay them. There may be scope for increased charging of those deemed able to pay for services which they currently obtain free, and for encouraging greater private provision of services. But in practice the principle of access for the poor and ill-informed was not seriously challenged. And the preference of many people for obtaining services collectively through the state, and of a quality which does not depend on ability to pay, did not change.

Pay

Another concern which emerged in the later 1970s, after some years of debate among economists, was over the implications of Baumol's analysis for public service pay. He had shown that, in theory, if public service pay grows in line with pay in the rest of the economy the relative cost of government services will rise because, unlike the private sector, there are no offsetting productivity increases. This implies that the financing of a given volume of spending on manpower inputs (at constant prices) will create a rising financial burden after allowing for general inflation, so that an attempt to maintain a constant volume share of government services will mean that the financing burden will take a rising share of GDP. We have noted that in practice, over the two decades after 1962, the growth of the share of total general government in GDP was made up of the growth in the volume of transfer payments and the RPE on government services (where the latter accounted for a constant share of GDP at constant prices). However the picture of zero productivity growth is a national accounting convention, which some might take for reality and as a justification for smaller pay rises than in the private sector where measured productivity growth is faster, if relative pay changes are intended to reflect relative productivity trends. In any event (but not necessarily for that reason) much of public service pay was broadly frozen in real terms after 1980 and comparability with the movement in private earnings was largely dropped. Exceptions were made for groups unable to strike (armed forces, the police), those deemed to be in short supply (top officials), and those able to command wide popular support (nurses); and in late 1986, following lengthy disruptions in schools, large pay increases were proposed for teachers, although in exchange for more stringent conditions of service. For the rest, relativities tended to fall vis-à-vis private earnings (apart from those public service groups with comparability arrangements). Trinder (1987) examines these pay arrangements and their effects in some detail. Current expenditure plans and our long-term projections imply little scope for real pay increases for most public servants.

If a policy of no automatic real increases were to be adhered to, disparities between public service pay and pay in the rest of the economy would continually widen, with potentially serious implications for the recruitment and the retention of staff and the risk of industrial disputes. On the other hand expensive catching-up awards to restore some past relativity, when economic conditions were different, seem unlikely. One way ahead might be to relate pay to performance or productivity (perhaps for particular individuals by discretionary performance-related increments or one-off special payments, possibly for entire groups). So far such developments have not found much favour: unions and some of the management are concerned about the risks of arbitrariness and unfairness in the discretionary element, unless clear criteria and measures of performance are agreed, while those charged with controlling spending are concerned about the risk of purely cosmetic productivity deals – again unless clear criteria can be established.

The pressures

The increase in real spending after 1979, despite an initial intention to cut it, subsequently revised to maintaining it broadly flat, is testimony to the pressures on programmes. Moreover, although spending in fact rose, there were complaints of actual or threatened deterioration in the quality or effectiveness of public services. When spending rises less than the amount the pressures on programmes imply, the quality of service may be perceived to deteriorate or fall short of expectations. This can be the case when the public expects the quality of provision to rise faster than plans permit, so there is a gap between expected and actual provision even where the latter improves.

Quality falls when resources grow by less than the number of 'clients' using the resources, so that resources per client are cut, unless there are offsetting productivity increases. However it is often difficult to dem-onstrate unambiguous productivity increases or to guarantee that they will materialise over the forward planning period; this difficulty underlies much of the concern about the adequacy of health and defence spending. On the other hand old-style volume planning, which guaranteed resources to meet agreed pressures, weakened the incentive to raise productivity and to contain costs. The public expenditure plans published in the first half of the 1980s placed considerable emphasis on the need to raise productivity if the effectiveness of services was to be maintained or improved. This need was not removed by the 1986 Autumn Statement even though it announced increases in planned spending above those previously published for the rest of the 1980s. All programmes remained tightly constrained relative to the pressures upon them.

Pressures exist to raise spending on virtually every programme: for new and better defence equipment; to reduce hospital waiting times and to improve community care; to rebuild and re-equip schools, restore past purchasing power of student awards, to replenish university finances and research funds; to increase the purchasing power of social security benefits and to extend entitlement to them; to repair and increase the council housing stock; to repair roads and sewers and build new ones; to support many declining industries and regions; to provide more resources to fight crime; to restore public service pay to some past relativity vis-à-vis private earnings. (We leave aside the case for expanding public spending to stimulate demand and employment.) The Treasury's 1984 Green Paper on long-term spending prospects acknowledged the extent of such pressures and argued that the way to approach them was first to decide what could be afforded in total and then to establish priorities between competing claims.

This view contains some echo of the approach of the late 1960s and early 1970s when plans took into account the likely growth of total resources, the 'prior' claims of the balance of payments and the investment needed to support growth, and judgements about the political implications of the possible balance between public spending and 'privately financed consumption'. That is to say, both approaches address themselves to the question of what can be afforded, although the 1984 view was dominated by the objectives of reducing taxes and government borrowing. The issue of affordability is unavoidable, the question is how to approach it.

Several commentators argued that the Green Paper view was excessively restrictive: affordability seemed to involve no real growth in spending at all even when GDP is expected to grow, so that the financing constraint was felt by some to be artificial and self-imposed.

There are two sorts of financing constraint: one is set by any *targets* the government might have towards the burden of taxation and government borrowing; the other is set by judgements about the public's *maximum tolerance* of taxation (which is only tested at election times) and the maximum scope for financing debt at tolerable interest rates – which can be tested very abruptly and sometimes disastrously. The 1984 Green Paper was framed within the first set of constraints whereas spending plans in much of the 1960s and 1970s were based on the second sort.

Clearly if the second approach is adopted in a growing economy one might judge that public spending can also grow, possibly in line with GDP or even faster, and still be affordable; although one's precise judgements might turn out to be wrong. Zero growth is not necessarily the maximum affordable spending, unless the government chooses to adopt tighter targets for taxation and borrowing. But *either* way the constraints are self-imposed in the sense that they are consciously chosen. The government might choose targets below the maximum possible tax and debt financing tolerance of the public. However, in that case one must accept that the public might wish for and be prepared to pay for at least some more public spending than it plans to provide: again, this is only infrequently tested (and only imperfectly, given all the other issues involved in elections).

The choice of a target for taxation, especially for income tax, implies an *a priori* view about what the level and possibly the structure of taxation ought to be. As such it leaves aside the possibility of a trade-off at the margin between higher spending and lower taxation. Whereas acceptance of the possibility of a trade-off implies no overriding priority for one over the other, the Green Paper approach implied that lower taxes were preferred to higher spending, and policies in much of the 1960s and 1970s often implied the opposite. Possibly the Green Paper approach was tactical and intended to strengthen the establishment of relative priorities between spending programmes before relaxation in the financing constraint could be considered; in any event public opinion surveys have revealed that the public recognises a trade-off and that some increases in spending are desired, some of which were conceded in the 1987 Expenditure White Paper, after spending had increased in practice anyway.

Our examination of the possibilities for spending to the mid- and late-1990s suggests that if GNP were to grow no faster than productive potential and if financing targets were adopted which permit non-North Sea taxes and budget deficits to grow no faster than GNP, then public spending would need to grow more slowly than GNP and more slowly than in the period since 1980; a period when expenditure plans were very tightly constrained. However, the discussion so far has been entirely in terms of spending on inputs, whereas the purpose of spending is to achieve outputs in terms of policy goals. Outputs will grow at the same rate as volume inputs only if government productivity does not rise. This is a national accounting convention but, as earlier chapters indicate, it does not reflect reality. The definition, measurement and achievement of increased productivity and efficiency in public services involve difficult conceptual, statistical and management problems respectively. But the outlook is such that without substantial increases in tax revenues it will be difficult to maintain or improve effectiveness of public services unless productivity is improved, given the existing structure of services provided by the state.

OUTPUT AND PERFORMANCE

Our examination of a variety of public services suggests that there is much greater scope for the quantification of output and performance in government than has been common hitherto. Genuine conceptual and statistical problems face any attempt to undertake such quantification, but the lack of priority attached to such work in the past is probably the main explanation for the dearth of quantification.

The analyses presented in earlier chapters offer evidence of significant productivity growth in government. The differences in performance between the managements of the locally-administered education, health and police services suggest scope for improvements in efficiency in future. The analysis of relative performance among industries with varying dependence on defence contracts suggests scope for significant improvements in the industries most dependent on defence procurement, and in the value for money of defence spending.

Considerable efforts have been made in recent years to improve the management, and the measurement, of performance in government. The extent of the external scrutiny of government and of the information it produces (about budgets, plans and outturn and, increasingly, about the quantity and quality of its services) have no close private sector parallels. Government has had a great deal to learn from the examples of resource (and personnel) management from the best-run firms, which provided the models for the Financial Management Initiative, but it is appropriate to acknowledge that not all private firms are as well run as the best, and that lessons may be learned by each sector from the other.

The analyses of performance in locally-administered services have illustrated the use of a number of quantitative techniques (regression analysis, data envelope analysis) the applications of which have much wider scope, in both the public and private sectors than at present.

These analyses do not tell us whether we should aim to improve efficiency by raising output, given inputs, or to minimise inputs for a given output. Efficiency is intrinsically a politically neutral concept, concerned with making the best use of limited resources. Politics inevitably enters the scene because political judgements determine which of the two routes to improved efficiency should be chosen. Anyone can cut taxes by destroying the quality of public services, just as anyone can increase their output (perhaps by not very much) by lavishing resources on them. Reducing tax burdens on the one hand or increasing the provision of public services on the other are legitimate political aims. The art is in achieving either aim efficiently.

Table A1.1. *General government expenditure, economic categories, shares in total, per cent*

	1969	1970	1971	1972	1973	1974	1975	1976	1977	1978	1979	1980	1981	1982	1983	1984
Current expenditure on goods and services	40.8	42.0	42.7	42.9	42.3	41.0	43.3	44.5	46.0	44.7	43.9	45.3	45.7	45.4	45.9	46.1
Current grants to personal sector	20.8	20.9	20.6	22.2	21.0	20.1	19.9	21.7	24.4	24.9	24.6	24.6	26.7	28.3	28.5	29.2
GDFC	11.8	11.8	11.0	10.4	12.0	11.2	9.7	9.3	7.8	6.5	6.1	5.3	4.0	3.4	4.1	4.4
Subsidies	4.4	4.2	4.0	4.4	4.7	7.6	7.1	5.9	5.2	5.0	5.3	5.4	5.4	4.6	4.7	5.3
Capital grants and net lending to: private sector	4.2	4.1	4.2	3.4	4.1	4.7	2.8	2.1	1.9	2.1	2.1	2.1	1.9	2.3	2.1	2.3
public corps.	5.0	4.4	5.2	4.5	2.7	2.2	3.9	2.4	0.5	1.7	2.4	2.3	1.4	1.6	1.1	0.1
Debt interest	10.2	9.8	9.0	8.8	9.0	9.2	8.2	9.2	10.2	9.8	10.2	10.5	10.9	10.9	10.3	10.7
Other	2.8	2.8	3.3	3.4	4.2	4.0	5.2	4.9	4.0	5.3	5.4	4.5	4.0	3.5	3.3	1.9
Total expenditure	100.0	100.0	100.0	100.0	100.0	100.0	100.0	100.0	100.0	100.0	100.0	100.0	100.0	100.0	100.0	100.0

Table A1.2. *General government expenditure, economic categories, growth in real terms (1983 GDP prices)*

	1969	1970	1971	1972	1973	1974	1975	1976	1977	1978	1979	1980	1981	1982	1983	1984
Current expenditure on goods and services	100.0	105.1	109.5	115.3	123.4	133.9	145.8	148.4	141.8	144.5	146.9	154.1	155.9	158.6	164.5	167.2
Current grants to personal sector	100.0	102.9	103.8	117.3	120.3	128.6	131.9	142.4	147.4	157.8	161.3	163.8	178.4	193.7	200.2	207.8
GDFC	100.0	101.2	97.5	96.2	120.7	125.8	112.5	106.3	82.7	71.8	69.9	62.5	46.5	40.4	51.0	55.5
Subsidies	100.0	97.6	94.9	107.8	126.4	229.8	221.5	181.2	146.7	149.3	162.0	168.2	171.0	147.8	154.3	178.0
Capital grants and net lending to: private sector	100.0	99.7	104.6	87.9	115.7	148.4	90.5	68.3	57.6	65.7	69.6	70.5	64.7	79.5	74.1	80.7
public corps.	100.0	90.2	108.4	98.4	65.4	58.1	106.0	66.1	13.2	44.4	66.9	63.3	39.4	46.6	30.8	2.6
Debt interest	100.0	98.2	92.6	94.5	104.7	120.2	110.3	122.9	125.6	127.5	136.4	142.6	148.7	152.3	147.3	155.5
Other	100.0	102.5	121.3	131.7	179.1	190.1	251.3	235.6	176.5	250.5	260.7	220.5	196.7	174.4	171.2	97.9
Total expenditure	100.0	102.1	104.6	109.5	119.0	133.1	137.4	136.0	125.5	132.0	136.5	138.6	139.1	142.3	146.0	147.9

Table A1.3. *General government expenditure, growth 1969–84, economic categories, growth in volume terms at constant own prices*

	1969	1970	1971	1972	1973	1974	1975	1976	1977	1978	1979	1980	1981	1982	1983	1984
Current expenditure on on goods and services	100.0	102.68	103.49	109.42	113.28	115.07	121.24	122.20	120.74	123.31	125.65	128.14	128.39	128.88	131.88	133.80
Current grants to personal sector	100.0	103.97	105.81	121.25	123.21	128.89	136.04	145.87	149.87	163.59	168.56	176.41	192.84	207.09	213.77	220.51
GDFC	100.0	103.77	97.21	96.48	110.68	109.69	100.48	95.89	75.92	65.30	63.18	56.90	43.07	39.18	50.10	54.65
Subsidies	100.0	98.61	96.73	111.35	129.40	230.28	228.46	185.64	149.17	154.78	169.24	181.20	184.76	157.99	164.73	188.88
Capital grants and net lending to: private sector	100.0	102.23	104.29	88.21	106.08	129.43	80.82	61.65	52.87	59.73	62.89	64.25	59.94	77.03	72.80	79.43
public sector	100.0	92.49	108.05	98.76	59.93	50.64	94.68	59.64	12.08	40.41	60.44	57.70	36.52	45.17	30.29	2.60
Debt interest	100.0	98.03	92.19	94.17	104.59	119.90	110.02	122.52	125.38	127.17	136.04	142.34	148.33	152.02	146.95	155.21
Other	100.0	102.40	120.77	131.14	178.76	189.50	250.78	234.86	176.17	249.88	259.92	220.02	196.18	174.00	170.80	97.69
Total expenditure	100.0	101.91	102.56	107.74	113.23	120.99	124.71	122.90	115.14	121.49	125.96	127.65	127.85	130.6	132.67	133.95

Table A1.4. General government expenditure, shares by function

	1969	1970	1971	1972	1973	1974	1975	1976	1977	1978	1979	1980	1981	1982	1983
Defence	12.1	11.9	11.9	11.8	11.3	10.4	10.0	10.6	11.1	10.5	10.5	11.0	10.8	11.3	11.5
Public order & safety	2.7	2.9	3.1	3.1	3.1	3.1	3.1	3.4	3.4	3.4	3.4	3.6	3.8	3.9	4.0
Education (incl. meals)	12.7	13.1	13.2	13.6	13.7	12.5	13.6	13.2	13.5	12.7	12.0	12.1	12.1	11.8	11.7
Health	9.1	9.6	9.7	9.9	9.7	9.9	10.1	10.5	10.9	10.7	10.6	11.2	11.5	11.0	11.6
Personal social services	1.1	1.2	1.3	1.4	1.7	1.8	2.0	2.0	2.0	2.0	2.1	2.2	2.2	2.2	2.2
Social security	18.8	18.9	18.5	19.5	18.1	17.4	17.3	19.2	21.3	21.9	21.6	21.3	23.5	24.9	24.4
Housing	6.4	6.3	5.6	5.7	7.6	10.7	8.6	8.7	8.2	7.3	7.3	7.0	4.8	4.2	4.8
Employment services	0.6	0.6	0.8	0.8	0.7	0.7	0.9	1.2	1.6	1.6	1.4	1.6	2.0	1.8	2.1
Other industry & trade	8.3	7.0	7.9	6.6	5.8	4.4	6.8	4.7	1.5	3.5	4.2	4.0	3.1	2.8	2.2
Debt interest	10.2	9.8	9.0	8.8	9.0	9.2	8.2	9.2	10.3	10.0	10.5	10.9	11.3	11.3	10.6
Transport and roads	5.9	6.2	6.0	6.2	5.8	6.6	5.8	4.6	4.0	3.9	4.0	3.4	3.9	3.9	3.7
Other	12.1	12.5	13.0	12.6	13.5	13.3	13.6	12.7	12.2	12.5	12.4	11.7	11.0	10.9	11.2
Total	100.0	100.0	100.0	100.0	100.0	100.0	100.0	100.0	100.0	100.0	100.0	100.0	100.0	100.0	100.0

Table A1.5. *General government expenditure in real terms (1969 GDP prices), by function*

	1969	1970	1971	1972	1973	1974	1975	1976	1977	1978	1979	1980	1981	1982	1983
Defence	100.0	100.5	103.2	106.9	112.0	114.8	114.1	119.4	115.5	114.9	118.9	126.1	124.9	133.5	139.1
Law and order	100.0	108.7	117.1	122.6	135.6	151.8	157.6	168.4	157.8	163.4	170.8	181.4	195.3	203.9	213.6
Education (incl. meals)	100.0	104.7	108.4	117.3	128.3	131.2	146.6	141.6	133.8	131.5	129.3	132.1	132.1	131.8	133.9
Health	100.0	106.8	110.9	118.5	125.9	143.4	151.2	156.0	150.8	155.7	157.7	169.3	174.8	171.3	184.8
Personal social services	100.0	117.7	129.9	143.7	184.5	217.5	249.3	258.1	234.0	251.0	262.2	278.9	282.9	287.5	296.9
Social security	100.0	102.6	103.1	113.1	114.4	123.1	125.9	138.3	142.4	153.4	156.9	157.0	173.8	188.5	189.0
Housing	100.0	101.7	92.5	98.0	141.7	224.1	185.8	186.1	162.5	150.9	157.3	152.4	105.4	94.4	110.3
Employment services	100.0	103.1	130.3	141.7	134.3	146.4	207.2	264.1	321.2	338.6	321.0	363.1	452.6	413.4	502.9
Other industry & trade	100.0	85.7	99.0	87.3	83.5	71.3	113.2	77.4	22.1	55.3	68.8	66.9	51.5	47.4	39.2
Transport and roads	100.0	107.4	106.6	114.4	118.0	147.9	136.0	105.3	86.2	88.0	92.2	80.5	91.6	95.6	92.6
Other	100.0	105.8	112.7	115.3	133.2	146.8	154.7	143.1	127.1	137.2	140.7	135.0	127.1	128.8	135.1
Debt interest	100.0	98.2	92.6	94.5	104.7	120.2	110.3	122.9	127.7	129.5	140.6	148.8	155.5	157.6	152.0
Total expenditure	100.0	102.1	104.6	109.5	119.0	133.1	137.4	136.0	126.0	132.0	136.7	138.7	139.3	142.4	146.0

Table A1.6. *Expenditure on goods and services at constant own prices*

1969 = 100

	1969	1970	1971	1972	1973	1974	1975	1976	1977	1978	1979	1980	1981	1982	1983
Defence	100.0	94.3	94.2	93.8	95.2	92.6	94.6	95.0	94.0	93.1	94.6	101.3	101.3	103.8	106.4
Education	100.0	105.4	110.3	118.6	127.2	130.2	134.6	135.4	132.6	135.8	138.7	136.5	134.7	134.8	136.5
Health	100.0	103.6	106.0	110.1	113.2	118.2	128.2	131.7	136.9	141.0	142.6	145.4	144.3	148.0	150.2

Source: National Income Blue Books, NIESR estimates.

DATA ENVELOPE ANALYSIS[1]

Data envelopment (or envelope) analysis (DEA) is a non-statistical technique based on linear programming which provides a way of measuring the relative technical efficiency[2] of different decision-making units of whatever kind (be they private firms or public sector agencies such as social security offices or district health authorities) performing the same or similar tasks. The technique owes its origins to Farrell (1957) (whose work is discussed in Chapter 9 and Appendix 3) but its name and recent popularity is due to Charnes, Cooper and Rhodes (1978). The main merits of DEA are that it can deal with the case of multiple inputs and outputs, as well as factors outside the control of individual managements (treating them effectively as fixed inputs), and this means that it is potentially well suited to the task of measuring relative efficiency in the public sector. Below we provide a brief sketch of some of the main features of this form of analysis; a general introduction to other frontier models is provided in Appendix 3.

To simplify somewhat, we can think of DEA as measuring the technical efficiency of a given organisation through the calculation of an efficiency ratio equal to a weighted sum of outputs over a weighted sum of inputs. For each decision-making unit (DMU) in turn these weights are selected by solving an optimisation problem, which involves maximising the efficiency ratio for that DMU subject to the condition that the equivalent ratios for every DMU in the set are less than or equal to unity. More formally, we can express this algebraically as

$$\text{maximise } h_o = \sum_{r=1}^{s} u_r y_{ro} / \sum_{i=1}^{m} v_i x_{io} \tag{1}$$

$$\text{subject to } \sum_{r=1}^{s} u_r y_{rj} / \sum_{i=1}^{m} v_i x_{ij} \leqq 1; \qquad j = 1,...,n$$

$$\text{and } u_r, v_i \geqq 0; \qquad r = 1,...,s, \quad i = 1,...,m$$

where y_{rj} and x_{ij} are respectively the observed outputs and inputs of the jth DMU; u_r, v_i are the weights to be determined from the solution of the maximisation problem; and there are s outputs, m inputs and n DMUs (Charnes, Cooper and Rhodes, op.cit).

From the formulation above a number of important features of DEA become apparent. One of the most fundamental is the fact that the technical efficiency score of each DMU will depend on the performance of the sample of which it forms a part. In other words, DEA produces *relative* (rather than absolute) measures of technical efficiency for each DMU being considered. Furthermore, these measures are solely dependent on observed best practice in the sample, those DMUs whose performance may be said to be best and who thus may be described as 'enveloping' the other DMUs being considered. This follows from the fact that the weights for each DMU are calculated so as to maximise its efficiency ratio subject to the proviso that they will not produce efficiency ratios which exceed one for any of the other DMUs in the sample. The effect of this is that it is the best DMUs which are used to measure the efficiency of the others and for each inefficient DMU there will be at least one other which is technically efficient (has a score of unity) using the same set of weights. One of the consequences of measuring efficiency relative to observed best practice is that DEA is very sensitive to extreme outliers and measurement errors.

One other feature of DEA brought out by the formulation in (1) is the fact that the weights for each DMU are chosen so as to give the most favourable efficiency ratio possible subject to the specified constraints. In this sense DEA shows each DMU in the *best possible light*; in effect, giving greater weight to those inputs or outputs where each DMU does relatively well. One well established property of the technique is that efficiency scores will tend to improve as the number of inputs or outputs included in the analysis rises since there is then more chance of finding a more favourable comparison with the rest of the sample. It is worth noting that DEA will evaluate a DMU as technically efficient if it has the best ratio of *any* output to any input and this clearly emphasises the importance of taking great care when initially specifying which inputs and outputs are to be included in the analysis.

The formulation in (1) shows the basic concept behind DEA but in its present form it is a 'nonconvex nonlinear fractional mathematical programming problem' and therefore not readily soluble. In practice a linear programming dual is solved instead, involving the assumption of either output maximisation or input minimisation (a distinction discussed in Chapter 9). The algebra involved in actual DEA programmes is too complicated to be discussed here (see Charnes, Cooper and Rhodes, *op.cit*), but it is nevertheless important to gain some insight into the economic logic which lies behind most DEA programmes. The remaining part of this section therefore returns to the production frontier framework used in Chapter 9 to clarify some of the issues involved.

Chart A2.1a gives an example of DEA for the simple case of one output and one input (see also Chapter 9). DEA constructs an efficient frontier from the sample of observations by constructing a piece-wise linear locus

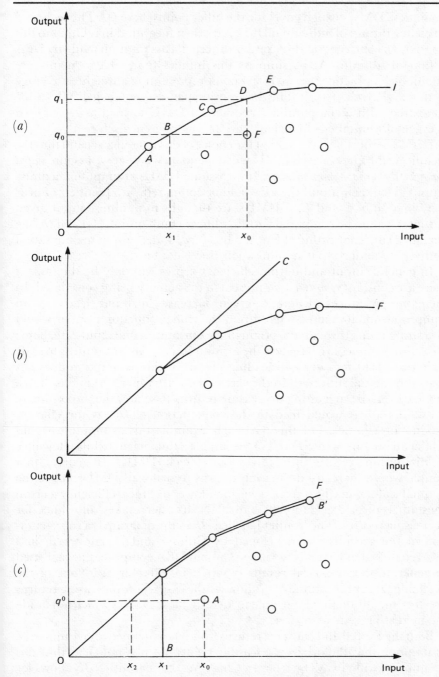

Chart A2.1 *Data envelope analysis illustrated for the case of one input and one output*

from those DMUs which envelope the other points, here OI. The technical efficiency ratings of individual DMUs are then measured in relation to this frontier. In constructing this frontier the crucial assumption made by DEA is that of *convexity*. At its simplest this implies that, 'if two points are attainable in practice then so is any point representing a weighted average of them' (Farrell, 1957). This basic principle enables each DMU to be compared with a comparable hypothetical DMU formed as a weighted average of a number of efficient DMUs, the reference set.

It is clear from chart A2.1a that the choice of this reference set and thus the technical efficiency of each DMU will depend on whether we assume *output maximisation or input minimisation*. If we assume DMUs attempt to maximise output given their input, then F would be compared with point D, a linear combination of C and E; if DMUs are thought to minimise input given output, F would be compared with B, a linear combination of A and C. The technical efficiency rating of F would be oq_0/oq_1 under output maximisation and ox_1/ox_0 under input minimisation (see Chapter 9).

In general, input and output efficiency scores will only be the same if there are constant *returns to scale* present in the activity being considered. In these circumstances, where a given increase in input leads to an equiproportionate increase in output, the true production frontier would be a straight line through the origin in the one output one input case. Some DEA programmes are based on the assumption of constant returns to scale which can lead to a very misleading picture *if* this assumption does not reflect the actual situation. In the case of the scatter of observations shown in Chart A2.1b (suggesting decreasing returns to scale), the imposition of constant returns would lead to the construction of OC as the efficient production frontier. For this particular example this assumption would render all but one of the DMUs in the sample as inefficient, while allowance for diminishing returns in OF gives four efficient DMUs. In general, in a sample where there are decreasing returns to scale, all DMUs above the optimal scale (x_0 in Chart A2.1b) will have lower technical efficiency scores if constant returns are imposed than if the frontier makes allowance for decreasing returns. The frontier labelled OF in the diagram is a representation of the specification developed by Cubbin and Wriglesworth and referred to as the 'Farrell' case in the Cubbin DEA computer package used to generate the empirical results reported in Chapter 12. None of the available DEA programmes can allow for the case where increasing returns are present, although it is possible to identify those DMUs which fall inside the increasing returns region.

Both the Farrell and constant returns frontiers as defined above make the assumption that the origin is a feasible point, but it is not clear that this assumption will always be true. In Chart A2.1c the frontier BB allows for diminishing returns like the Farrell method but is constructed so that only interior solutions are feasible, and hence the origin does not form part of the frontier. If this frontier is used as our basis for calculating technical efficiency, then point A has an input efficiency score of ox_1/ox_0 compared with only ox_2/ox_0 if the Farrell frontier, OF, is used. As this example illustrates, the assumption that the origin is not a feasible point will tend to improve the technical efficiency scores of the sample. The frontier $B\acute{B}$ is a representation of a DEA specification proposed by Banker (1984), referred to as the Banker case in Chapter 12.

AN INTRODUCTION TO PRODUCTION FRONTIER MODELS

A production *frontier* is a technological relationship which describes the *maximum* output that an efficient firm can produce from any given combination of inputs over a given time period. However, in much of the empirical literature on the subject standard regression techniques are used to estimate what are, in effect, *average* production functions (where observations on actual outputs will lie both above and below the predictions of the model). This distinction is particularly important if we are concerned with measuring efficiency because to do this we need to relate actual output to the maximum output that is potentially achievable. Thus from the point of view of efficiency measurement it is the concept of the frontier which is most relevant.[1] Since the publication of Farrell's seminal paper in 1957 a large literature has grown up around the theme of the estimation of frontier models (See Førsund *et al.*, 1980, and Schmidt, 1985–6). Below we provide a short sketch of some of the main approaches.

The natural starting point for any discussion of frontier models is provided by the highly influential work of Farrell (1957). Before we proceed to examine his proposed method of frontier estimation, it will be useful to begin by setting out the conceptual framework for measuring efficiency which is also described in his paper.

Consider the simple case of a firm producing a single output, y, from two inputs, x_1 and x_2. Suppose the firm's production function/frontier may be written as $y = f(x_1, x_2)$. If we also assume that the firm produces under conditions of constant returns to scale then the production function will be homogeneous of degree 1 and can be written as $1 = f(x_1/y, x_2/y)$. This means that we can represent the technical possibilities open to the firm in terms of a unit isoquant such as II' shown in chart A3.1. From the definition of a production function/frontier it is clear that no firm could produce at a point such as A below II' because this would not be technically feasible. On the other hand, a firm producing at, say, point C, or indeed at any other point above II' will be technically inefficient because at B the same output can be produced using the same factor ratio, but with lower quantities of each factor. Farrell proposed the ratio OB/OC as an obvious measure of the technical inefficiency of a firm at point C. It gives the ratio of the inputs technically necessary to the inputs actually used to produce one unit of output, given the actual input mix. Allocative efficiency occurs if, for a

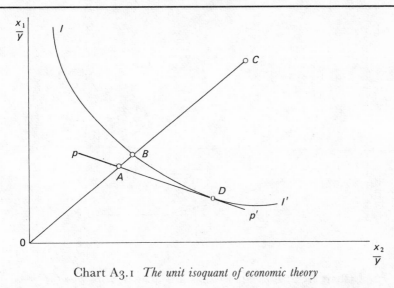

Chart A3.1 *The unit isoquant of economic theory*

given level of output, the firm combines its factors of production so that costs are minimised. If we let the line PP′ denote the ratio of factor prices, then point D will now be more efficient than B because the cost of producing one unit of *y* at D will be lower. Farrell proposed the ratio OA/OB as the best measure of allocative (what he called price) efficiency at point B because at point D the cost of producing one unit of *y* will be this fraction of the costs at B. Overall efficiency at C is then defined as OA/OC, which is the ratio of costs at the most efficient point at D to their actual level at C. This is equal to the product of Farrell's measures of allocative and technical efficiency.[2]

In his 1957 paper Farrell proposed the use of linear programming techniques to estimate the efficient unit isoquant in piece-wise linear fashion from the observed sample of unit input–output ratios. In the context of the simple one output two input example given above this involves constructing the south-west convex envelope around the sample of points, II′ in chart A3.2. More generally, we can think of Farrell's efficient unit isoquant as a series of connected hyperplanes in input space.

From this description of the Farrell method it should be clear that the technique involves constructing a frontier from the observed best practice in the sample. Thus the efficient unit isoquant will only depend on a subset of the full sample of observations. In this sense the technique may be described as inefficient because it does not make full use of all the information available, the main consequence of this being that it will be sensitive to measurement errors and extreme observations.

It should also be apparent from this account that the method is entirely non-statistical. Deviations from the efficient unit isoquant arise solely due

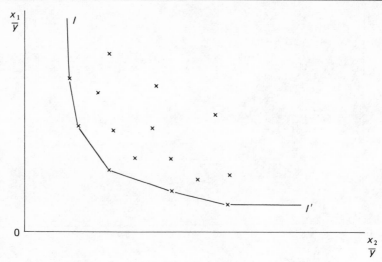

Chart A3.2 *The unit isoquant estimated by the Farrell method*

to technical differences in efficiency with no allowance for statistical noise of any form (the result of misspecification or measurement error). Thus we cannot perform any statistical tests on the frontier nor on the resulting efficiency measures.

Another important feature of Farrell's method is its non-parametric nature. In arriving at the efficient unit isoquant it is not necessary to impose a functional form on the data. This is potentially important because otherwise we run the risk of imposing overly restrictive assumptions such as those associated with the well-behaved production function of neo-classical theory (strong disposability of inputs, differentiability and monotonicity). It can be shown that the more restrictive our assumptions about the technology of the sample the lower our estimates of efficiency will be for a given sample (see Grosskopf, 1986).

One of the limitations of Farrell's approach in his 1957 paper was that it was based on an assumption of constant returns to scale which is itself very restrictive. In fact in a subsequent paper Farrell and Fieldhouse (1962) were able to extend the approach to non-constant returns to scale technologies. More recent work based on Farrell's non-parametric approach, sometimes also referred to as data envelopment analysis (see Appendix 2), has shown that the assumptions made about the reference technology can vary widely and need not be restrictive. According to a recent paper by Grosskopf (1986), 'the least restrictive reference technology used in this [non-parametric] literature allows for increasing, decreasing, or constant returns to scale and relaxes the assumption of strong disposability of inputs'.

Farrell's paper also suggested a parametric approach to the estimation of the frontier using the Cobb-Douglas functional form. This idea was taken up subsequently in a paper by Aigner and Chu (1968). Their basic model may be written in simplified form as

$$y = f(x) - u, \quad u \gtreqless 0$$

$$= a_0 + \sum_{i=1}^{n} a_i \ln x_i - u, \quad u \gtreqless 0 \tag{1}$$

where y is output, x_i are inputs, u is a disturbance term and a_i are parameters to be estimated (x_i and y are in logarithmic form). On the assumption that all variation from the frontier in (1) is due to technical inefficiency the residuals are constrained to be one-sided and thus output is bounded from above, that is $y \leqslant f(x)$. This sort of frontier can be described as deterministic (as opposed to stochastic – see below) in that it is assumed that all firms, or DMUs, face the same frontier and no allowance is made for exogenous shocks outside the control of the firm which may affect performance, nor indeed for the effects of measurement error or omitted variables. Estimation of the parameters of the frontier in (1) is possible using mathematical programming techniques and the residuals can be used to generate measures of technical efficiency for each of the observations in the sample.

The main advantage of this sort of parametric approach is that it enables the frontier technology to be described in a relatively simple functional form, reducing the amount of computational complexity involved.[3] The disadvantage is that the structure imposed on the data may be unwarranted. As in the case of Farrell's non-parametric approach there is the same sensitivity to outliers and measurement errors/misspecification and, as before, the absence of any statistical assumptions about the residuals means that we cannot conduct statistical tests.

An obvious extension to the model in (1) is to make some statistical assumptions about u and this has often been the approach adopted in the empirical literature. It is typically assumed that observations on u are independently and identically distributed and that x is independent of u. Estimation of the frontier is usually by either corrected ordinary least squares (which will not be described here, see Richmond, 1974) or by maximum likelihood (*ML*). To derive the likelihood function it is necessary to specify a particular one-sided distribution for the disturbance term. There are a large number of possible choices but the difficulty is that the *ML* estimates will be sensitive to which distributional assumptions are made and theoretical grounds provide little guidance for preferring any particular assumption. However, in practice, the importance of this problem can be evaluated by examining the effects of alternative assumptions about u. A more serious problem with this approach, first pointed out by Schmidt (1976) is that the range of the dependent variable will depend on the parameters to be estimated. This means that one of the conditions for ML to be consistent and asymptotically efficient no longer holds, making the statistical properties of ML uncertain. Nevertheless it has been shown that the normal desirable properties of ML can still be retained if the distribution of technical inefficiency satisfies certain fairly restrictive conditions. However, as Førsund et al. (1980) have pointed out, 'it is a little troubling that one's assumptions about the distribution of technical inefficiency should be governed by statistical convenience'.

A feature common to both statistical and non-statistical deterministic frontiers is that all variations in performance from the frontier are attributed to inefficiency. In contrast, the stochastic frontier, or composed error model, of Aigner et al. (1977) and Meeusen and van den Broeck (1977) gets round this problem by decomposing the error term into two parts. One symmetric component, v, is intended to capture random effects or statistical noise factors outside the control of the individual firm. The second one-sided component, u, is intended to capture the effects of inefficiency relative to the stochastic frontier. The stochastic frontier model can be written as

$$y = f(x) + v - u \qquad (2)$$

where $u \gtreqless 0$ so that all points lie on or below the stochastic frontier (that is, $y_i \lessgtr f(x_i) + v_i$). Unfortunately, this approach does not enable us to obtain measures of technical efficiency by observation, but it can provide measures of average inefficiency over the sample. Estimation of the frontier is possible using either corrected least squares or maximum likelihood. The asymptotic properties of ML now hold because of the presence of the symmetric error component (Førsund et al., 1980).

A possible weakness with the approach is that in order to be able to distinguish the two error components it is also necessary to make some strong distributional assumptions. In most stochastic frontier models the symmetric error, v, has been assumed to be iid normal but a variety of different assumptions have been made about the distribution of technical inefficiency. However, a number of studies have shown that the choice of different distributional assumptions can lead to different results in terms of estimated efficiencies. This does not of course imply that the problem is avoided by assuming the frontier to be deterministic because, to quote Schmidt (1986), 'assuming statistical noise not to exist is itself a strong distributional assumption'.

Given the heterogeneity of the group of frontier models described above, it is difficult to draw any overall conclusions about the approach. While on theoretical grounds there are clear reasons for preferring frontier models to regression models which predict average expected performance, doubts still remain over their usefulness in practice, particularly regarding the plausibility and robustness of their results. But, as Førsund et al. have pointed out, the evidence is still coming in.

EXAMPLES OF ACTIVITIES AND OUTPUT INDICATORS, UNITED STATES FEDERAL PRODUCTIVITY MEASUREMENT SYSTEM

FUNCTION	ACTIVITY	INDICATOR
1. Audit	e.g. perform audit.	Audits completed
2. Buildings and grounds	– paint, clean, repair, renovate buildings – construction of new buildings	– square feet maintained – $ value of work
3. Communications	– send and receive messages – provide security	– number of messages – establishments protected
4. Education & training	– train pilots – provide professional military training – evaluate instructors	– number trained – student-years – number evaluated
5. Electric power	– produce and market power	– kilowatt hours
6. Equipment maintenance	– routine vehicle maintenance – vehicle repairs – overhaul aero-engines	– vehicle miles – vehicles repaired – engines overhauled
7. Finance & accounting	– issue pay checks – conduct audits – prepare, submit and administer budgets – process supplies bills – process grants and loans – scrutinise travel claims	– pay checks issued – audits completed – budgets submitted – invoices paid – number processed – claims inspected
8. General Support Services	– postroom, receipt, transmission and sorting of mail – provide legal advice	– items handled – opinions provided

	– provide warehouse services	– items handled
	– clean buildings	– square feet cleaned
	– operate ADP equipment	– operator hours
	– punch data cards	– cards punched
	– notify Congress of navy contracts over £50 million	– contracts notified
	– answer Congressional inquiries	– inquiries answered
9. Information services	– respond to media requests	– requests answered
	– provide statistics on (prices, construction, etc.)	– monthly reports
	– prepare weather forecasts	– forecasts made
	– undertake topographic mapping	– square miles
	– prepare speeches	– speeches prepared
10. Legal & judicial	– process and adjudicate civil service appeals	– appeals adjudicated
	– conduct court-martials	– trials conducted
	– investigate violations of competition regulations	– investigations
	– prepare briefs	– briefs prepared
	– investigate possible fraud	– investigations considered
	– litigation under child labor, equal opportunities, etc. Acts	– litigation conducted
11. Library services	– loan materials	– materials loaned
	– provide documentary references	– inquiries answered
	– order books	– books ordered
12. Loans & grants	– issue rural housing loans	– loans issued
	– issue grants to minority businesses	– grants made
	– provide education	– grants made

	grants to areas with high concentration of low-income families/non-English speaking/etc. families* *(there are *many* such grants)	
	– support student loan funds	– loans made
	– support nursing schools	– awards made
	– support research on infectious diseases	– grants made
13. Medical services	– treat airforce patients (ditto army and navy)	– a *weighted* indicator, with weights for in- and out-patients, and hospital procedures
	– reduce morbidity from venereal diseases	– persons followed-up and treated
	– laboratory tests to reduce illness from chronic diseases	– *weighted* composite indicator
	– develop methods for measuring exposure to occupational hazards	– methods developed
	– provide training in industrial safety	– number trained
	– support research into occupational safety	– grants supported
	– maintain national surveillance of infectious diseases	– *composite* output (of investigations made, field studies, reports published)
	– provide health services to Indian Americans	– patients discharged and out-patient visits
	– veterans' hospital care	– in-patients treated
	– veterans' surgical treatment	– surgical in-patients
	– veterans' dialysis treatment	– dialysis treatments
	– train blind veterans	– blind patients trained
14. Military base services	– service meals	– meals served
	– clean clothing	– items processed

15. Natural resources and environment management	– timber production	– thousand board-feet sold
	– improve forest stands to sustain yield	– acres treated
	– improve access to timber areas	– miles of road constructed
	– make resource surveys and inventories	– reports completed
	– issue snow warnings	– snow forecasts made
	– investigate and map flood hazard areas	– analyses completed
	– dredge rivers and harbours	– cubic yards of silt removed
	– operate environmental centres	– visitor days
16. Personnel investigations	– investigate suitability for security sensitive posts	– investigations made
	– review material for security classification	– pages reviewed
17. Personnel management	– improve knowledge and capabilities of government employees	– participants trained
	– adjudicate performance rating appeals	– cases processed
	– investigate employee grievances	– number of cases
	– fill vacancies	– vacancies filled
	– review post gradings	– number reviewed
	– advise employees on retirement policies	– applications completed
	– changes in pay	– pay changes completed
	– make performance awards	– awards made
18. Postal services	– process mail (by category)	– items processed
19. Printing & duplicating	– print items	– pages/items printed
20. Procurement	– various activities relating to equipment procurement	– purchase orders completed
		– items purchased

		– security clearances granted to contractors and personnel
21. Records management	– search census records on request of individuals needing documentation of age, citizenship, etc.	– cases completed
	– produce special studies	– studies completed
	– search fingerprint records	– searches made
22. Regulations – compliance and enforcement	– ensure warehouses for storing agricultural commodity stocks are secure	– warehouses examined
	– inspect and grade cotton samples	– samples classified
	– inspect possible carriers (vessels, luggage, etc.) for foreign pests and prohibited materials	– vessels, items of luggage etc. inspected
	– inspect cattle herds	– herds tested
	– proceed against firms violating Commodity Exchange Acts	– cases closed
	– undertake laboratory tests to ensure product compliance with standards	– sample analyses made
	– inspect oil etc. pollutant spills	– inspections made
	– direct removal of spills	– directions made
	– prepare Federal regulations	– regulations published
	– investigate Anti-dumping Act breaches	– investigations completed
	– training to upgrade anti-drug capabilities of foreign police forces	– student hours
	– reduce distribution of illicit drugs	– arrests made* (* several indicators for several drugs)
	– prevent illegal immigration	– illegal immigrants apprehended

	– arrest violators of Federal laws for whom warrants have been issued	– arrests made
	– protect endangered Federal witnesses	– witnesses protected
	– train Federal prisoners	– inmates completing vocational training
23. Regulations – rulemaking and licensing	– supervise Federal use of airways	– frequencies assigned
	– examine patent applications	– patents disposed
	– licence gas/electricity etc. production	– licenses processed
	– examine applications for television channels	– applications processed
	– inspect animal food/drug manufacture	– establishments inspected
	– remove unsafe animal drugs from market	– seizures
	– issue passports	– passports issued
24. Social services & benefits	– process Medicare/Medicaid insurance claims	– claims processed
	– process requests for reconsideration of retirement insurance claims	– decisions made
	– collect premiums for supplementary medical insurance	– premiums collected
	– receive and redetermine claims referred back by a US Court	– decisions made
	– maintain employer tax identification records	– number processed
	– make grants to Indian students	– students assessed
	– assist Indian tribes to manage land resources	– cases completed

		– pay veteran beneficiaries, maintain records and administer system	– weighted composite indicator
25.	Specialised manufacturing	– produce munitions	– equivalent units produced
		– produce special clothing	– (deflated) $ value
		– produce ammonia for fertilizer (T.V.A.)	– tons produced
		– produce, store, distribute new coins	– number of coins
26.	Supply & inventory control	– receive and store forms	– units received
		– issue and transport Air Force/Army/Navy stocks*	– issues and shipments made* *(some indicators also by weight and volume)
27.	Traffic management	– operate Navy freighters	– cargo-ship days
		– provide automobiles to government agencies	– fleet miles operated
		– assist in obtaining equitable transport facilities for agricultural products	– actions taken
28.	Transportation	– manage motor fleet	– miles driven
		– break ice to maintain navigation	– ice-breakers' operating hours

NOTES

NOTE TO CHAPTER 1

1 When government services and the components of GDP as a whole are measured at common international prices (Levitt, 1984).

NOTE TO CHAPTER 2

1 The reports of the House of Commons Treasury and Civil Service Committee on the annual Public Expenditure White Papers prefer the latter approach.

NOTES TO CHAPTER 5

1 The 'Social Indicator' studies of the 1960s and 1970s represented an attempt to supplement conventional national accounts with indicators bearing more directly on social welfare.
2 Based on discussion with relevant United States officials.

NOTES TO CHAPTER 6

1 Civil Service numbers refer to April 1986.
2 However, relatively poor performance might indicate existing low morale. Some firms regard the refusal of others to circulate internal performance comparisons as indicative of low morale at the top.
3 In this context the efforts of CIPFA to develop public indicators of performance in, for example, education, health and local government authorities should be noted.
4 *Common activities*: indicators of work done, costs and manpower involved could cover such common activities as: payment of staff; staff recruitment; staff training; staff movements; staff catering; secretarial services; payment of invoices; internal audit; travel and subsistence; office security; use of space; building maintenance; heating and lighting; messenger services; post and telephones; ADP installations; stationery. *Departmental specific activities*: indicators of certain activities which are more specific to departments – but which nonetheless can have private sector analogues – include the determination of tax liability; the collection of taxes; the collection of fees and charges; the issue of permits, licences and passports; the payment of cash benefits to individuals; the payment of grants to firms (including farms); the production of military equipment; the repair and maintenance of vessels, vehicles, aircraft and their components (measured separately); staff medical services; the maintenance and distribution of stores; the use of vehicles.

NOTES TO CHAPTER 7

1 The Gramm-Rudman Act put a ceiling on the Federal deficit; any excesses require equal percentage across-the-board cuts in all agency programmes.
2 Statement of C.W. Ardolini to United States Senate Committee on Government Affairs, 19 September 1984, reviews the basis of FPMS.
3 Statement by the Comptroller General, C.A. Bowsher, 'Management Improvement in Federal Government', Senate Committee on Government Affairs, 26 February 1986.
4 Statement by Dr Alice Rivlin, House Budget Committee, 14 February, 1978.

NOTE TO CHAPTER 8

1 This convention appears to be broadly consistent, under conditions of difficult or changing specifications, cost-plus pricing and the relative rarity of competition with the reality of low productivity growth.

NOTE TO CHAPTER 11

1 Goldacre in 'Implications of record linkage for health services management' in Baldwin (1985) cites two hospitals where length of stay per episode was 29 days in one hospital and 120 in the other, with throughput of 11.9 and 2.9 episodes per bed per year. Once patients' records for readmission were linked, average LOS per individual became 126 and 156 days respectively and individuals treated per bed were 2.8 and 3.8.

NOTES TO CHAPTER 12

1 Parts of Essex, Hertfordshire and Surrey are part of the Metropolitan Police area and it was not possible to allocate demographic and socio-economic indicators based on local authority boundaries to the parts of these counties outside the 'Met'. At the same time the Metropolitan Police have ceremonial, anti-terrorist, public order, etc. duties which differ in extent from those facing other police forces but for which useful variables to include in the analysis are not readily available. For these reasons the Metropolitan Police area and the three county forces named above were *excluded* from the econometric (and DEA) analyses.
2 Divisional staff excludes all headquarters staff (which includes headquarters, CID, communications, traffic, administration, training and district support) as well as officers deployed in traffic divisions.
3 The question of how useful the clear-up rate is as a measure of police output is discussed below; see also Chapter 4.
4 The GRE formula is used to assess the expenditure needs of local authorities for the purpose of allocating the block grant.
5 The socio-economic variables were derived from the last census and therefore refer to 1981. See also note 1 to this chapter.
6 In econometric theory there are strong grounds for preferring full-information maximum likelihood (FIML) to other simultaneous-equations techniques but we encountered serious convergence problems with this technique and conse-

quently only the 3SLS results are reported here. This may have been due to a degrees of freedom problem because our sample size (38 observations) is relatively small.

7 Notice that since all the variables are expressed in logarithmic form the estimated coefficients can be interpreted as elasticities.

8 To test that these restrictions were correct we computed the 3SLS minimands under the null and alternative hypotheses, using the same estimate of the residual covariance matrix. The difference between the two minimands was 0.33 (23.42–23.09) which is a great deal less than the critical value for χ^2 with 5 degrees of freedom at the 5 per cent level of significance (that is, 11.07) and so we may accept the restricted model.

9 The programme used was developed by John Cubbin, of Queen Mary College, London, following on from earlier work with John Wriglesworth. We are grateful to John Cubbin for assistance in interpreting the results.

NOTE TO CHAPTER 13

1 The plan was to impose tuition fees on a sliding scale related to parental income up to a ceiling; charges would have started at around $1\frac{1}{2}$ times average earnings which, given the tendency for many wives to work, is not an especially high middle-class income, while the ceiling at around three times average earnings would have introduced a regressive element at top incomes; the dropping of the proposal in the face of intense opposition was misleadingly attributed in a press comment to the efforts of the most well-off.

NOTES TO APPENDIX 2

1 For a much fuller discussion of DEA and an evaluation of its comparative advantages and disadvantages see Joyce (1987).

2 The distinction between technical and allocative efficiency is discussed in Chapter 9.

NOTES TO APPENDIX 3

1 Here our focus is on the production frontier but the point applies equally to other representations of a firm's efficient production technology such as cost or profit *frontiers*. Notice, however, that if the object is to measure *technical* efficiency then it is necessary to estimate the production frontier.

2 The precise efficiency measures adopted have not, typically, been the same as Farrell's. See Kopp (1981) on this point. Since our focus here is on production frontiers, we shall have nothing further to say about the measurement of *allocative* efficiency.

3 Of course, there is no necessity for adopting the relatively restrictive Cobb-Douglas functional form; more flexible functional forms such as the CES or translog could equally well be used.

REFERENCES

Aigner, D.J. and Chu, S.F. (1968), 'On estimating the industry production function', *American Economic Review*, vol. 58, pp. 226–39.

Aigner, D.J., Lovell, C.A.K. and Schmidt, P. (1977), 'Formulation and estimation of stochastic frontier production function models', *Journal of Econometrics*, vol. 6, pp. 21–37.

Atkinson, A.B., Hills, J. and Le Grand, J. (1986), The welfare state in Britain 1970–1985: extent and effectiveness, Discussion paper no. 9, Welfare State Programme, Suntory-Toyota International Centre for Economics and Related Disciplines, London School of Economics, July.

Bacon, R. and Eltis, W. (1976), *Britain's Economic Problems: Too Few Producers*, London, Macmillan.

Baldwin, J.A. (Ed.) (1985), *Textbook of Medical Record Linkage*, Oxford University Press.

Banker, R.D. (1984), 'Estimating most productive scale size using data envelope analysis', *European Journal of Operations Research*, 8, pp. 35–44.

Baumol, W.J. (1967), 'Macroeconomics of unbalanced growth: the anatomy of the urban crisis', *American Economic Review*, vol. 57, no. 3, June, pp. 415–26.

Beales, R.E. (1967), *Estimates of expenditure, income and product at constant prices*, IARIW Conference, Maynooth, mimeo.

Becker, G.S. (1968), 'Crime and punishment: an economic approach', *Journal of Political Economy*, vol. 76, no. 2, pp. 169–217.

Bradford, D.F., Malt, R.A. and Oates, W.E. (1969), 'The rising cost of local public services', *National Tax Journal*, June.

Bryant, J.W., Chambers, M.L. and Falcon, D. (1968), *Patrol effectiveness and patrol development*, University of Lancaster Operations Research Department.

Buchanan, J.M. and Tullock, G. (1962), *The Calculus of Consent*, University of Michigan.

Bureau of Labor Statistics (1985), *Federal government productivity summary data fiscal years 1967–1984*.

Burkhead, J. and Ross, J.P. (1974), *Productivity in the Local Government Sector*, Lexington, D.C. Heath.

Burrows, J. and Tarling, R. (1982), *Clearing up Crime*, Home Office Research Study 73.

Carr-Hill, R.A. and Stern, N.H. (1979), *Crime, the Police and Criminal Statistics*, London, Academic Press.

Caves, R. and Krause, L.B. (Eds.) (1980), *Britain's Economic Performance*, Washington D.C., Brookings.

Central Statistical Office (1956), *National Income Statistics: Sources and Methods*, London, HMSO.

Charlton, J.C. and Lakhani, A. (1986), *Avoidable death indicators for DHAs (1974–83)*, Department of Community Medicine, St. Thomas's Hospital, April, mimeo.

Charnes, A., Cooper, W.W. and Rhodes, E. (1978), 'Measuring the efficiency of decision making units', *European Journal of Operational Research*, no. 2, part 6, pp. 429–44.

Darlington, J.K. and Cullen, P.D. (1984), *Pilot study of school examination performance and associated factors*, Government Economic Service Working Paper 75.

Department of Education and Science (1981a), *Personal and social development*, Assessment of Performance Unit.

Department of Education and Science (1981b), *The School Curriculum*, London, HMSO.

Department of Education and Science (1984), 'School standards and spending', *Statistical Bulletins* 13/84 and 16/83.

Department of Education and Science (1985), *Better Schools, Cmnd 9469*, London, HMSO.

Department of the Environment, Audit Inspectorate (1983), 'Police service: civilianisation and related matters, Summary', London, HMSO.

Department of the Environment (1983), Inner Cities Directorate, Census Information Note no. 2: Urban deprivation, London, HMSO.

Department of Health and Social Security (1985), *Reform of Social Security*, Background papers, vol. 3, *Cmnd* 9519, London, HMSO.

Dunne, J.P., Pashardes, P. and Smith, R.P. (1984), 'Needs, costs and bureaucracy: the allocation of public consumption in the UK', *Economic Journal*, vol. 94, March.

Economic and Social Research Council (1985), *Can education account for itself?* Report of ESRC Conference on Understanding and Managing the Performance of Educational Systems, sponsored by the Society of Education Officers, May, Ref. no. C03260001.

Ewing, B. (1986), *The productivity challenge in Federal Government*, Office of Management and Budget, mimeo.

Executive Order (1986), *Productivity improvement program for the Federal Government*, EO 12552, 25 February.

Fanning, D. (1982), 'Banking productivity: an improving performance', *The Banker*, July.

Farrell, M.J. (1957), 'The measurement of productive efficiency', *Journal of the Royal Statistical Society*, vol. 120, Series A, General, pp. 253–90.

Farrell, M.J. and Fieldhouse, M. (1962), 'Estimating efficient production functions under increasing returns to scale', *Journal of the Royal Statistical Society*, vol. 125, Series A, part 2, pp. 252–67.

Fisk, D.M. (1983), 'Modest productivity gains in state unemployment insurance service', *Monthly Labour Review*, January, pp. 24–7.

Fisk, D.M. (1985), 'Productivity trends in the Federal government', *Monthly Labour Review*, October, pp. 3–9.

Førsund, F.R., Lovell, C.A.K. and Schmidt, P. (1980), 'A survey of frontier production functions and of their relationship to efficiency measurement', *Journal of Econometrics*, vol. 13, pp. 5–25.

Frazer, P. (1982), 'How not to measure bank productivity', *The Banker*, August.

Geehan, R. (1977), 'Returns to scale in life insurance', *Bell Journal of Economics*, Autumn.

General Accounting Office (1983), *Increased use of productivity management can help control government costs*, Report by the Comptroller General of the United States, AFMD 84-11.

General Accounting Office (1985), *Improving operating and staffing practices can increase productivity and reduce costs in SSA's Atlanta Region*, GAO/GGO-8-85.

Gibbs, R.J. (1985), 'Updating the performance package', *Health and Social Service Journal*, vol. 94, no. 4953, 20 June, p. 763.

Goldacre, M.J. and Griffin, K. (1983), *Performance indicators, a commentary on*, The Literature Unit of Clinical Epidemiology, University of Oxford, mimeo.

Gomulka, S. (1979), 'Britain's slow industrial growth', in Beckerman, W. (Ed.), *Slow Growth in Britain: Causes and Consequences*, Oxford, Clarendon Press.

Grosskopf, S. (1986), 'The role of the reference technology in measuring productive efficiency', *Economic Journal*, vol. 96, June, pp. 499-513.

Guillebaud, C.W. (1957), Committee of Enquiry into cost of National Health Service, *Report, Cmnd. 9663*.

HM Treasury (1983), *Financial Management in Government Departments*, Cmnd 9058.

HM Treasury (1984), *The Next Ten Years: Public Expenditure and Taxation into the 1990s*, Cmnd 9189.

Hagen, E.E. and Budd, E.C. (1958), 'The product side: some theoretical aspects', in *A Critique of the United States Income and Product Accounts*, Studies in Income and Wealth, vol. 22, National Bureau of Economic Research, Princeton University Press.

Hewer, A. (1980), 'Manufacturing industry in the seventies: an assessment of import penetration and export performance', *Economic Trends*, June.

Hill, T.P. (1971), *The Measurement of Real Product: a Theoretical and Empirical Analysis of the Growth Rates for Different Industries and Countries*, OECD.

Hill, T.P. (1979), *Manual on national accounts at constant prices*, United Nations, Statistical papers series M, no. 64.

Hirshhorn, R. and Geehan, R. (1977), 'Measuring the real output of the life insurance industry', *Review of Economics and Statistics*, vol. 49, May, pp. 211-9.

Home Office (1984), *Criminal Statistics, England and Wales 1983*, Cmnd 9349.

Inner London Education Authority (1986), *The ILEA Junior School Project*, London, ILEA Research and Statistics Branch.

Jarman, B. (1983), 'Identification of underprivileged areas', *British Medical Journal*, vol. 286, 28 May, pp. 1705-8.

Jaszi, G. (1958), 'The conceptual bases of the accounts', in *A Critique of the United States Income and Product Accounts*, Studies in Income and Wealth, vol. 22, National Bureau of Economic Research, Princeton University Press.

Jencks, C. *et al* (1973), *Inequality: a Reassessment of the Effect of Family and Schooling in America*, London, Allen Lane.

Johnston, J. and Murphy, G.W. (1957), 'The growth of life assurance in UK since 1880', *Manchester School*, vol. 25, no. 2, May, pp. 107-82.

Joyce, M.A.S. (1985), *Spending on law and order: the police service in England and Wales*, National Institute of Economic and Social Research Discussion Paper no. 104, September.

Joyce, M.A.S. (1987), *Measuring relative efficiency in the public sector: an application of data envelopment analysis using police authority data*, National Institute of Economic and Social Research Discussion Paper (forthcoming).

Kendrick, J.W. (1958), 'Measurement of real product' in *A Critique of the United States Income and Product Accounts*, in Income and Wealth, vol. 22, National Bureau of Economic Research, Princeton University Press.

Kendrick, J.W. and Vaccara, B.N. (Eds.) (1980), *New Developments in Productivity Measurement and Analysis*, London, Chicago University Press.

Kind, P., Rosser, R. and Williams, A. (1982), 'Valuation of quality of life: some psychometric evidence', in Jones-Lee, M. (Ed.), *Value of Life and Safety*, North-Holland.

Kinsey, R. (1985), *The survey of Merseyside police officers*, Centre for Criminology, University of Edinburgh.

Kinsey, R. (1984), *Merseyside Crime Survey 1984*, Centre for Criminology, University of Edinburgh.

Kirkpatrick, D.L. and Pugh, P.G. (1983), 'Towards the Starship Enterprise – are the current trends in defence unit costs inexorable?', *Aerospace*, May.

Kopp, R.J. (1981), 'The measurement of productive efficiency: a reconsideration', *Quarterly Journal of Economics*, vol. 96, pp. 477–503.

Lerner, B. (1982), 'American education: how are we doing?', *Public Interest*, 69, Fall.

Levitt, M.S. (1984), 'The growth of government expenditure', *National Institute Economic Review*, no. 108, May.

Levitt, M.S. (1985), *Productivity in central government*, Public Finance Foundation Discussion Paper no. 4.

Levitt, M.S. (Ed.) (1987), *New Priorities in Public Spending*, Aldershot, Gower Publishing Co Ltd.

Levitt, M.S. and Joyce, M.A.S. (1984), *Public expenditure, the next ten years*, National Institute of Economic and Social Research Discussion Paper no. 76.

Levitt, M.S. and Joyce, M.A.S. (1987), 'Public expenditure trends and prospects', in Levitt, M.S. (Ed.), *New Priorities in Public Spending, op. cit.*

Lindbeck, A. (1985), 'Redistribution policy and the nature of budget growth', in 'Nobel Symposium on the growth of government', *Journal of Public Economics*, vol. 28, no. 3, December.

McPherson, K., Strong, P.M., Epstein, A. and Jones, L. (1981), 'Regional variations in the use of common surgical procedures', *Social Science and Medicine*, Part A, vol. 15, pp. 273–88.

McPherson, K., Strong, P.M., Jones, L. and Britton, B.J. (1985), 'Do cholecystectomy rates correlate with geographic variations in the prevalence of gallstones?', *Journal of Epidemiology and Community Health*, vol. 39, no. 2, June, pp. 179–82.

Mark, J.A. (1980), 'Reply to Searle and Waite', in Kendrick, J.W. and Vaccara, B.N. (Eds.), *New Developments in Productivity Measurement and Analysis, op. cit.*

Mark, J.A. (1981), 'Measuring productivity in government', *Public Productivity Review*, March.

Marks, J. *et al* (1983), *Standards in English Schools: an analysis of the examination results of secondary schools in England for 1981*, London, National Council for Educational Standards.

Marris, R. (1983), *Problem services*, Special Conference of the International Association for Research in Income and Wealth, Luxembourg, mimeo.

Meara, J. and Gossman, P. (1986), *Performance indicators for the NHS*, Oxford District Health Authority, mimeo.

Meeusen, W. and van den Broeck, J. (1977), 'Efficiency estimation from Cobb-Douglas production functions with composed error', *International Economic Review*, vol. 18, no. 2, pp. 435–44.

Ministry of Defence (1986), *Statement on the Defence Estimates 1986, Cmnd* 9763–1 and 2, London, HMSO.

Musgrave, R.A. (1985), 'Excess bias and the nature of budget growth', in 'Nobel Symposium on the growth of government', *Journal of Public Economics*, vol. 28, no. 3, December.

National Audit Office/Ministry of Defence (1984), *Dockyard Efficiency*, London, HMSO.

National Audit Office (1985), *Ministry of Defence, Profit Formula for Non-competitive Government Contracts, report*, HC 243, London, HMSO.

National Audit Office (1986), *Ministry of Defence, Control and Management of the Development of Major Equipment*, HC 568, London, HMSO.

National Economic Development Office (1983), *Civil exploitation of defence technology*, NEDO Electronics EDC.

Niskanen, W. (1971), *Bureaucracy and Representative Government*, New York, Aldine Publishing Company.

Nove, A. (1961), *The Soviet Economy: an Introduction*, London, Allen and Unwin.

OECD (1978), *Public Expenditure Trends*, Paris, OECD.

O'Higgins, M. and Patterson, A. (1985), 'The prospects for public expenditure' in Klein, R. and O'Higgins, M. (Eds.), *The Future of Welfare*, Oxford, Basil Blackwell.

Pidot, G.B. (1969), 'A principal components analysis of the determinants of local government fiscal patterns', *Review of Economics and Statistics*, vol. 51, May, pp. 176–88.

Pite, C. (1980), 'Employment and defence', *Statistical News*, no. 51, November, HMSO.

Plowden Report (1967), *Children and their Primary Schools: a Report of the Central Advisory Council for Education*, London, HMSO.

Prais, S.J. and Wagner, K. (1985), 'Schooling standards in England and Germany: some summary comparisons bearing on economic efficiency, *National Institute Economic Review*, no. 112, May.

Public Finance Foundation (1985), *Financial management and public spending*, PFF Discussion Paper no. 3, April.

Pyle, D.J. (1983), *The Economics of Crime and Law Enforcement*, London, Macmillan.

Richmond, J. (1974), 'Estimating the efficiency of production', *International Economic Review*, vol. 15, no. 2, June, pp. 515–21.

Rosser, R. (1983), 'A history of the development of health indicators', in Teeling Smith, G. (Ed.), *Measuring the Social Benefits of Medicine*, London, Office of Health Economics.

Rosser, R. and King, P. (1978), 'A scale of valuations of states of illness: is there a social consensus?', *International Journal of Epidemiology*, vol. 7.

Rowley, C.K. and Peacock, A.T. (1975), *Welfare Economics: A Liberal Restatement*, London, Martin Robertson.

Royal Statistical Society (1984), 'Assessment of examination performance in different types of schools', reported in *Journal of the Royal Statistical Society*, Series A, vol. 147, part 4, pp. 569–81.

Rutter, M. *et al.* (1979), *Fifteen Thousand Hours: Secondary Schools and their Effects on Children*, Open Books.

Saunders, P. and Klau, F. (1985), *The role of the public sector*, OECD Economic Studies no. 4, Spring.

Savage, D. and Biswas, R. (1986), 'The British economy in the long term: the use of resources', *National Institute Economic Review*, no. 118, November.

Schmidt, P. (1976), 'On the statistical estimation of parametric frontier production functions', *Review of Economics and Statistics*, vol. 58, no. 2, May, pp. 238–9.

Schmidt, P. (1985–6), 'Frontier production functions', *Econometric Reviews*, vol. 4(2), pp. 289–328.

Searle, A.D. and Waite, C.A. (1980), 'Current efforts to measure productivity in the public sector: how adequate for the National Accounts', in Kendrick, J.W. and Vaccara, B.N. (Eds.), *New Developments in Productivity Measurement and Analysis, op. cit.*

Sizer, T.R. (1984), *Horace's Compromise: Dilemma of the American School*, New York, Houghton Mifflin.

Soete, L. (1985), *Technological Trends and Employment, vol. 3, Electronics and Communications*, Aldershot, Gower Publishing Co Ltd.

Taylor, T. (1985), 'A value added assessment model', *Economics of Education Review*, vol. 4, no. 4, Northeast Missouri State University.

Treasury and Civil Service Committee (1982), *Efficiency and Effectiveness in the Civil Service: Government Observations on the Third Report*, Cmnd 8616, London, HMSO.

Trinder, C.G. (1987), 'Public service pay', in Levitt, M.S. (Ed.), *New Priorities in Public Spending, op. cit.*

US Department of Commerce (1982), *Survey of Current Business*, November.

Wildavsky, A. (1985), 'A cultural theory of expenditure growth and (un)balanced budgets' in 'Nobel Symposium on the growth of government', *Journal of Public Economics*, vol. 28, no. 3, December.

Willis, K.G. (1983), 'Spatial variations in crime in England and Wales: testing an economic model', *Regional Studies*, vol. 17, no. 4, August, pp. 261–72.

Yates, J. (1985), 'In search of efficiency', *Health and Social Service Journal*, vol. 94, no. 4953, June.

INDEX

RECENT PUBLICATIONS OF THE
NATIONAL INSTITUTE OF ECONOMIC
AND SOCIAL RESEARCH

published by
THE CAMBRIDGE UNIVERSITY PRESS

ECONOMIC AND SOCIAL STUDIES

XXVII   *The Framework of Regional Economics in the United Kingdom*
By A.J. BROWN. 1972. pp. 372. £22.50 net.

XXVIII   *The Structure, Size and Costs of Urban Settlements*
By P.A. STONE. 1973. pp. 304. £18.50 net.

XXIX   *The Diffusion of New Industrial Processes: An International Study*
Edited by L. NABSETH and G.F. RAY. 1974. pp. 346. £42.50 net.

XXXI   *British Economic Policy 1960–74*
Edited by F.T. BLACKABY. 1978. pp. 710. £40.00 net.

XXXII   *Industrialisation and the Basis for Trade*
By R.A. BATCHELOR, R.L. MAJOR and A.D. MORGAN. 1980. pp. 380. £30.00 net.

XXXIII   *Productivity and Industrial Structure*
By S.J. PRAIS. 1982. pp. 401. £30.00 net.

XXXIV   *World Inflation since 1950. An International Comparative Study*
By A.J. BROWN assisted by JANE DARBY. 1985. pp. 414. £30.00 net.

OCCASIONAL PAPERS

XXXI   *Diversification and Competition*
By M.A. UTTON. 1979. pp. 124. £19.50 net.

XXXII   *Concentration in British Industry, 1935–75*
By P.E. HART and R. CLARKE. 1980. pp. 178. £19.50 net.

XXXIV   *International Industrial Productivity*
By A.D. SMITH, D.M.W.N. HITCHENS and S.W. DAVIES. 1982. pp. 184. £19.50 net.

XXXV   *Concentration and Foreign Trade*
By M.A. UTTON and A.D. MORGAN. 1983. pp. 150. £19.50 net.

XXXVI   *The Diffusion of Mature Technologies*
By GEORGE F. RAY. 1984. pp. 96. £17.50 net.

XXXVII   *Productivity in the Distributive Trades. A Comparison of Britain, America and Germany*
By A.D. SMITH and D.M.W.N. HITCHENS. 1985, pp. 160. £19.50 net.

XXXVIII   *Profits and Stability of Monopoly*
By M.A. UTTON. 1986. pp. 102. £12.95 net.

XXXIX   *The Trade Cycle in Britain, 1958–1982*
1986, pp. 108. £12.95 net.

XL   *Britain's Productivity Gap*
By STEPHEN DAVIES and RICHARD E. CAVES. 1987. pp. 145. £17.50 net.

NIESR STUDENTS' EDITION

2   *The Antitrust Laws of the U.S.A.* (3rd edition unabridged)
By A.D. NEALE and D.G. GOYDER. 1980. pp. 548. £15.00 net.

4   *British Economic Policy 1960–74: Demand Management* (an abridged version of *British Economic Policy 1960–74*)
Edited by F.T. BLACKABY. 1979. pp. 472. £11.95 net.

5   *The Evolution of Giant Firms in Britain* (2nd impression with a new preface)
By S.J. PRAIS. 1981. pp. 344. £10.95 net.

THE NATIONAL INSTITUTE OF ECONOMIC AND
SOCIAL RESEARCH

publishes regularly

THE NATIONAL INSTITUTE ECONOMIC REVIEW

A quarterly analysis of the general economic situation in the United Kingdom and the world overseas, with forecasts eighteen months ahead. The last issue each year contains an assessment of medium-term prospects. There are also in most issues special articles on subjects of interest to academic and business economists.

Annual subscriptions £45.00 (home), and £60.00 (abroad), also single issues for the current year. £12.50 (home) and £18.00 (abroad), are available directly from NIESR, 2 Dean Trench Street, Smith Square, London, SW1P 3HE.

Subscriptions at the special reduced price of £18.00 p.a. are available to students in the United Kingdom and Irish Republic on application to the Secretary of the Institute.

Back numbers and reprints of issues which have gone out of stock are distributed by Wm. Dawson and Sons Ltd., Cannon House, Park Farm Road, Folkestone. Microfiche copies for the years 1959–85 are available from EP Microform Ltd. Bradford Road, East Ardsley, Wakefield, Yorks.

Published by
HEINEMANN EDUCATIONAL BOOKS
GOWER PUBLISHING COMPANY

THE UNITED KINGDOM ECONOMY
by the NIESR. 5th edn. 1982. pp. 119. £2.95 net.
DEMAND MANAGEMENT
Edited by MICHAEL POSNER. 1978. pp. 256. £6.50 (paperback) net.
DE-INDUSTRIALISATION
Edited by FRANK BLACKABY. 1979. pp. 282. £12.95 (paperback) net.
BRITAIN IN EUROPE
Edited by WILLIAM WALLACE. 1980. pp. 224. £8.50 (paperback) net.
THE FUTURE OF PAY BARGAINING
Edited by FRANK BLACKABY. 1980. pp. 246. £16.00 (hardback), £7.50 (paperback) net.
INDUSTRIAL POLICY AND INNOVATION
Edited by CHARLES CARTER. 1981. pp. 241. £18.50 (hardback), £7.50 (paperback) net.
THE CONSTITUTION OF NORTHERN IRELAND
Edited by DAVID WATT. 1981. pp. 227. £19.50 (hardback), £9.50 (paperback) net.
RETIREMENT POLICY. THE NEXT FIFTY YEARS
Edited by MICHAEL FOGARTY. 1982. pp. 224. £17.50 (hardback), £7.50 (paperback) net.
SLOWER GROWTH IN THE WESTERN WORLD
Edited by R.C.O. MATTHEWS. 1982. pp. 182. £19.50 (hardback), £9.50 (paperback) net.
NATIONAL INTERESTS AND LOCAL GOVERNMENT
Edited by KEN YOUNG. 1983. pp. 180. £17.50 (hardback), £9.50 (paperback) net.
EMPLOYMENT, OUTPUT AND INFLATION
Edited by A.J.C. BRITTON. 1983. pp. 208. £25.00 net.
THE TROUBLED ALLIANCE, ATLANTIC RELATIONS IN THE 1980s
Edited by LAWRENCE FREEDMAN. 1983. pp. 176. £19.50 (hardback), £7.50 (paperback) net.
EDUCATION AND ECONOMIC PERFORMANCE
Edited by G.D.N. WORSWICK. 1984. pp. 152. £18.50 net.
ENERGY SELF-SUFFICIENCY FOR THE UK
Edited by ROBERT BELGRAVE. 1985. pp. 224. £19.50 net.
THE FUTURE OF BRITISH DEFENCE POLICY
Edited by JOHN ROPER. 1985. pp. 205. £18.50 net.
ENERGY MANAGEMENT: CAN WE LEARN FROM OTHERS?
By G.F. RAY. 1985. pp. 120. £19.50 net.

UNEMPLOYMENT AND LABOUR MARKET POLICIES
Edited by P.E. HART. 1986. pp. 230. £19.50 net.
NEW PRIORITIES IN PUBLIC SPENDING
Edited by M.S. LEVITT. 1987. pp. 136. £17.50 net.